ANTHONY TROLLOPE

The
New Zealander

EDITED WITH AN INTRODUCTION
BY
N. JOHN HALL

CLARENDON PRESS · OXFORD
1972

Oxford University Press, Ely House, London W. 1

GLASGOW NEW YORK TORONTO MELBOURNE WELLINGTON
CAPE TOWN IBADAN NAIROBI DAR ES SALAAM LUSAKA ADDIS ABABA
DELHI BOMBAY CALCUTTA MADRAS KARACHI LAHORE DACCA
KUALA LUMPUR SINGAPORE HONG KONG TOKYO

C

PRINTED IN GREAT BRITAIN BY
NORTHUMBERLAND PRESS LIMITED
GATESHEAD

0198124422
6001649773

The New Zealander

PREFACE

W H E N in the fall of 1969 my interest in Anthony Trollope led me to make inquiries about the unpublished *New Zealander*, Robert H. Taylor, owner of the manuscript, graciously allowed me to examine it. The work proved to be of far more importance than perhaps anyone had expected, and he generously gave me permission to edit the manuscript. In addition to making this book possible, he has assisted with difficult readings and made invaluable suggestions.

To Gordon N. Ray, Professor of English at New York University, I am especially indebted. He has examined the text in detail, and he has patiently guided, encouraged, and assisted the project from its inception as a doctoral dissertation to the publication of this final version.

I have also had important assistance from the following: Professors Gerald B. Lahey, William E. Buckler, Warren Harendeen, and Evelyn B. Vitz of New York University; Professor E. D. H. Johnson, Princeton University; Professor Thomas Pinney, Claremont College; Professor Ellis K. Waterhouse, Barber Institute, Birmingham University; the staff of the Clarendon Press; Mr. P. Warwick, the British Museum; Miss Pamela Eyres, the National Gallery; Mrs. Sally Kington and Miss Joan Pollard, the London Museum; Mr. D. G. Banwell, Dulwich Gallery; Mrs. C. McNamara, Post Office Records Department; Mrs. Cecil Woodham-Smith, Mr. Christopher Hibbert, Mr. W. H. Watson, Mr. Robert S. Call, Mr. Maurice K. Spanbock. I wish to thank Mr. Alexander P. Clark and Mrs. Wanda M. Randall, Division of Manuscripts, Princeton University; Mr. Wilbur J. Smith, Department of Special Collections, UCLA Library; the New York Public Library and its staff; similarly, New York University Library, and in particular Dr. Theodore G. Grieder and his assistants at the Fales Collection.

I acknowledge gratefully a Faculty Research Fellowship from the State University of New York, and a grant from the City University of New York Research Program.

Finally, I express my gratitude to my wife Marianne, who, as first assistant, researcher, and proofreader, has assisted me throughout.

New York, 1971   N.J.H.

CONTENTS

The New Zealander

LIST OF PLATES

EDITOR'S INTRODUCTION

ANTHONY TROLLOPE, who in his busy lifetime wrote sixty-five books, including no less than forty-seven novels, wrote one full-length work which was never published. Perhaps simple over-abundance of material has contributed to its neglect, but, whatever the reason, virtually nothing is known of *The New Zealander*. Trollope himself did not mention it in his *Autobiography*, nor did his first biographer, T. H. S. Escott. Michael Sadleir, who had access to family papers and other pertinent documents (some of which have since been destroyed), devoted a few paragraphs to *The New Zealander*, but he apparently had not looked at it very closely. He limits himself to quoting letters in reference to the manuscript and finding in its failure to be published the happy turning point which killed the reformer in Trollope.[1] Bradford Booth, another leader in Trollopian studies, thought it was a novel.[2] Present interest in Trollope is such as to warrant the publication of anything as substantial as *The New Zealander*, even apart from its intrinsic merits, which are considerable. For Trollope has long since recovered not only from the critical neglect and indeed disparagement which for a time overtook nearly all Victorian writers, but also from that particular displeasure occasioned by his own ingenuous disclosures in the *Autobiography*. Thus, more than a century after he wrote it, Trollope's book length excursion into social criticism is made available through the courtesy of the present owner of the manuscript, Mr. Robert H. Taylor.

The circumstances surrounding the writing of *The New Zealander* make curious reading. *The Warden*, Trollope's fourth novel but first critical success, was published in January 1855. On 17 February he wrote to his publisher inquiring as to the book's sale: if it were satisfactory, Trollope would continue work on a sequel (*Barchester Towers*) which at this point was 'about one third' complete.[3] When he received a discouraging

---

[1] *Trollope: A Commentary*, 3rd ed. (O.U.P., London, 1961), pp. 168-9.

[2] *Anthony Trollope: Aspects of His Life and Art* (Indiana University Press, Bloomington, 1958), p. 76.

[3] *The Letters of Anthony Trollope*, ed. Bradford Allen Booth (O.U.P., London, 1951), p. 24.

reply from William Longman, Trollope embarked instead on a
general survey of English life. Less than two months later, on
27 March, he submitted to Longman a manuscript entitled
The New Zealander, adding that 'There are some reasons incident to the MS. itself which will make it desirable that it
should be published soon.'[4] But Longman's reader advised
against publication:

The object of the work is to show how England may be saved from
the ruin that now threatens her!! And how the realisation of
Macaulay's famous prophecy of the "New Zealander standing on
the ruins of London Bridge" may be indefinitely postponed.... All
the good points in the work have already been treated of by Mr.
Carlyle, of whose *Latter-Day Pamphlets* this work, *both in style and
matter*, is a most feeble imitation.[5]

Trollope resumed writing *Barchester Towers* and *The New
Zealander* was never published.

No doubt this stinging criticism helped to discourage both
Sadleir's interest in *The New Zealander* and that of readers of
his *Commentary*. But not least among the surprises the manuscript has provided is the fact that what has survived is not the
work sent to Longman in March of 1855 but an entirely new
version. Marginal notes and internal evidence indicate that
Trollope continued to rework the text until at least May 1856.
Indeed, of some sections, as many as four versions may have been
written. Hence it is pointless to take issue with the assessment of
the reader for Longman. We are not dealing with the same
manuscript. However, it would seem that his verdict even on
Trollope's early draft was remarkably imperceptive. Trollope
does not believe that England could ultimately be saved from
that decadence to which all great countries have been subject.
Furthermore, Trollope, who had so satirized Carlyle as Doctor
Pessimist Anticant in *The Warden*, cannot fairly be represented

---

[4] This letter, since destroyed, is quoted from Sadleir, p. 168.
[5] Ibid., pp. 168-9. Macaulay's 'prophecy' appeared in 'Ranke's *History of
the Popes*', *Edinburgh Review*, CXLV (Oct., 1840), 228. In context Macaulay
was referring to the apparently perennially long life of the Roman Catholic
Church. Trollope in *The New Zealander* does not address himself to this
aspect of Macaulay's remarks but only to the eventual decay of England.
Macaulay, incidentally, took the image from Walpole: see *The Letters of
Horace Walpole*, ed. Peter Cunningham (Bentley, London, 1857), VI, 153,
Letter to Horace Mann, 24 Nov. 1774.

as simply going over the same ground covered in the *Latter-Day Pamphlets*. Trollope's first reading of this book, which he specifically parodied in his novel,[6] led him to write to his mother in 1851:

I have read—nay, I have bought!—Carlyle's *'Latter Day Pamphlets,'* and look on my eight shillings as very much thrown away. To me it appears that the grain of sense is so smothered up in a sack of the sheerest trash, that the former is valueless.... He has one idea —a hatred of spoken and acted falsehood; and on that he harps through the whole eight pamphlets. I look on him as a man who was always in danger of going mad in literature and who has now done so.[7]

The revised *New Zealander* admittedly has affinities to the *Latter-Day Pamphlets*. Both are critical of the press, democracy, and what today is called the coddling of criminals. Trollope's chapter 'The People and Their Rulers', with its emphasis on well ordered work and its call for 'aristocrats', is the most Carlylean in the book, but even here there is considerable difference: Trollope's aristocrats are so numerous as to include anyone who has charge over the work of others, even the man who has two kitchen maids in his house. Other differences are more palpable: Trollope, for example, would not have suggested even in jest that British consulates in foreign cities should be replaced by resident *Times* reporters; Carlyle's hated red tape is for Trollope orderly and necessary routine; Trollope is incapable of anti-Catholic, even anti-Jesuit, invective. But perhaps the keynote of honesty versus dishonesty best demonstrates the relation of the two writers. Trollope is alarmed at the dishonesty he sees about him in England, but, ever the realist, he writes of nothing (except perhaps *The Times*) in hyperbolic fashion. Twenty years later, while discussing the 'exaggerated' satire of *The Way We Live Now*, he points to Carlyle as a mistaken prophet of doom who too loudly laments that the world daily becomes more dishonest. Trollope continues:

Nevertheless, a certain class of dishonesty, dishonesty magnificent in its proportions, and climbing into high places, has become at

---

[6] See *The Warden* (O.U.P., London, 1918), pp. 183-4 (Chap. xv). (Unless otherwise noted, all quotations from Trollope's novels are from Oxford's *World's Classics*.)

[7] *Letters*, pp. 14-15.

the same time so rampant and so splendid that there seems to be reason for fearing that men and women will be taught to feel that dishonesty, if it can become splendid, will cease to be abominable.[8]

Trollope will concern himself with this sort of dishonesty but he must always dissociate himself from what he considers fanaticism. In 1867 he discussed the question at length in an article, 'An Essay upon Carlylism', which is in many respects a small version of *The New Zealander*.[9] If 'Carlylism' means that 'we are all going to the—Mischief', Trollope replies that in regard to England's decay the ordinary citizen

can probably hardly stop the progress at all otherwise than in a small degree by honest work.... And, moreover, it is after all comparatively but of small moment to the ordinary man whether his country be going to the Mischief or not. This we say hesitatingly, fearing that we shall be charged with lack of patriotism.... Have not all countries gone to the Mischief,—fallen into the sear and yellow leaf...?

Nor does Carlyle tell the individual anything new about how to manage his life well: 'He has heard it before in the line of an old song—"It is good to be honest and true." '[10] The kinship of this article with *The New Zealander* is obvious, and although at the later writing Trollope may appear a bit more sanguine about his countrymen's honesty, a dozen years have not altered his position essentially. He has some of the same misgivings as had Carlyle, but his answers are his own.

What we have then in *The New Zealander* is a book in which Trollope, at the mature age of forty, but at the very beginning of his career as a popular novelist, looks around him at England and takes his stand on the morality and social institutions of his time. To say at the beginning of his popularity is not quite accurate. We today regard *The Warden* as a very good book, a tremendous advance over his first three attempts, and the novel

---

[8] *An Autobiography*, ed. Frederick Page (O.U.P., London, 1950), pp. 354-5.
[9] *St. Paul's Magazine*, I (Dec. 1867), 292-305. Sadleir, in *Trollope: A Bibliography* (Constable, London, 1928), pp. 229 and 233, attributes this article only provisionally to Trollope. When read in conjunction with *The New Zealander* there can be no doubt of the authorship; the same phrases, metaphors, and poetry reinforce the evidence from content.
[10] *St. Paul's Magazine*, pp. 295-6.

in which he found his métier as a writer. As true as this may be, Trollope himself could not of course have realized in 1855 what a significant point of departure *The Warden* was to prove. His own career still hung in the balance. A handful of generally favourable reviews had not managed to sell the book. In fact, as we have seen, its disappointing sale launched him into *The New Zealander*. Thus, in spite of Trollope's forty years and four published novels, this work must be read as the effort of an aspiring and as yet unsuccessful writer. Perhaps some of the disappointment shows. When twenty years later in the *Autobiography* he describes his early struggles as a writer, he speaks from a certain eminence. Not only had his novels made him financially affluent, they had given him a name and introduced him to many of the great men of his century. But in *The New Zealander*, written in 1855-6, before *Barchester Towers*, *The Three Clerks*, and *Doctor Thorne* had made him a popular novelist, before his association with *Cornhill Magazine* had in 1860 introduced him to the literary circle of men like Thackeray and G. H. Lewes, we catch the genuine flavour of the early Trollope. And what we find is inconsistent with those critical judgements of the man drawn chiefly from his early novels: the 'feeling of contentment with things that be' of which John Hazard Wildman speaks is decidedly absent,[11] and Lord David Cecil's dictum that Trollope never opposed his age is surely ruled out of court.[12] Although we need not agree with A. O. J. Cockshut's terms 'gloomy' and 'pessimistic' for the so-called 'later' Trollope, certainly the seriousness of a late novel like *The Way We Live Now* had its anticipation in the 1850s. But the theory that the later years of his life can be seen as a 'progress' in the 'steepening curve of the author's pessimism'[13] is very questionable. Trollope was not so much gloomy and pessimistic as serious and critical, and never more so than in 1855.

---

[11] *Anthony Trollope's England* (Brown University, Providence, 1940), p. 8.
[12] *Victorian Novelists: Essays in Revaluation* (University of Chicago Press, Chicago, 1958), pp. 227-8. (First published as *Early Victorian Novelists*, 1934.)
[13] *Anthony Trollope: A Critical Study* (Collins, London, 1955), p. 11. *A fortiori* one must reject the Stebbinses' verdict: 'In the early 1870's Anthony Trollope suffered a gradual disillusionment more painful than his adolescence.' Lucy Poate Stebbins and Richard Poate Stebbins, *The Trollopes: The Chronicle of a Writing Family* (Columbia University Press, New York, 1945), p. 282.

In these pages Trollope evinces a good deal of Victorian 'earnestness'. Although *The New Zealander* is not without considerable irony and humour, on balance it will strike readers as admonitory, and, in places, even somewhat sermonizing. It was that kind of age. Sermons, at least in written form, were immensely popular. For many the 'crisis of faith' would come only in the sixties (for Trollope it apparently never came at all). Like so many Victorian writers, Trollope is very opinionated. He holds forth on all manner of subjects with a kind of apodictic definitiveness. Professionalism and specialization had not yet denied to the average educated man the prerogative of having his say in print on any controverted issue. But Trollope is always willing to make a qualification; if he is attacking some abuse, he will narrow his focus, and try to be accurate and within reason. This is readily seen in the matter upon which much of the book turns, the future decadence of England. Surely, he says, Great Britain will not prove the glorious exception and escape the decay which has beset all formerly great nations. In fact an incipient decadence can already be seen in the apathetic acceptance of public dishonesty. On the other hand, by an increase in personal honesty and a new awareness of public dishonesty, Britons may delay the coming of Macaulay's New Zealander for many centuries. This, while not embracing both positions of a dispute at one time, is surely seeing both sides. Here again one sees the difference from Carlyle, both Trollope's inferiority as prophetic reformer and inflamatory pamphleteer, and his superiority as a fair and balanced commentator upon English society. Even in regard to *The Times*, where he is most loud, one might even say frantic, in his censure, we discover a grudging attempt at fairness. The fault, he writes (not very convincingly), is not with the staff of the newspaper but with the readers who show no discretion or independence of judgement.

The opinions Trollope embraces in *The New Zealander* are clearly indicative of the conservative liberalism he was to ascribe to himself in the *Autobiography*. He supports the police against the charge of brutality in their handling of a Hyde Park disturbance: the newspapers have given an unfair account of the incident. But he criticizes churchmen for intolerance of Roman Catholics—a very liberal view in mid-Victorian England. In reference to the Crimean War (which forms a kind of back-drop for the entire work) he defends the Duke of Newcastle and Lord Raglan as victims of the country's unrealistic expectations, but complains that young men who agree to serve their country in the armed services get a very poor bargain for themselves. He believes in beating Russia, but sees victory as ultimately of very little importance compared with the problem of educating England's sons. He thinks Britain the greatest nation in the world, but feels this glory is of little use to governesses paid £10 a year or ploughmen who exist almost at the level of brutes in England. The man who was to see one of his sons leave for Australia is already encouraging emigration. He can at times seem alarmingly John Bullish in his impatience with native criticism of things British from foreign policy to the architecture of the new Parliament buildings, yet he will lament that Britons are generally too proud and stiff-necked to take any needful lessons from foreigners.[14] He decries tender treatment of convicts and early parole ('tickets of leave') for transported criminals, but can flail away at the law's delay as well as any liberal reformer. He fears democracy as 'mob' rule, but can be merciless towards the thirteenth century attitudes of the House of Lords.

In those areas where the admittedly unsatisfactory labels of conservative and liberal have no real applicability, Trollope's position is dictated by his keynote of honesty. Religion is dishonest when it advocates Sabbatarian beliefs which even its preachers must see as abhorrent to reason; both high and low churchmen are dishonest when they exhort their people to despise the good things of this world. Tradesmen seem to think that they can live by standards different from the rest of mankind, passing off chicory for coffee, cotton for linen, imitations for the paintings of masters. Mesmerism and quackery are invading medicine. Advertisements are lies and puffery. Englishmen even dishonestly pretend that they are enjoying themselves at dinners and parties which bore them to death.

Trollope's chapter on literature is naturally of interest to the

---

[14] Clearly Trollope is more the cosmopolitan than the provincial in *The New Zealander*. This conclusion is inescapable when, to his complaints about the dishonesty of his countrymen and the absurdities of England's constitution, laws, and mores, one adds the favourable verdict he pronounces on European customs and life styles. See particularly his comparison of English and continental labourers (below, p. 27) and social life (below, pp. 166 and 168-9).

student of his novels. His list of eighteen 'giants' among English writers contains some surprises. Chaucer, still not widely read (although Trollope mentions him elsewhere in the work), is not included; perhaps the more remarkable omission is Wordsworth whom Trollope had quoted in an earlier chapter. The modern reader will quarrel with the inclusion of Thomson, Southey, and Taylor. Burns and Tennyson emerge as his favourites after Shakespeare. No novelists are named; Scott is present, but as a poet; Defoe and Johnson gain entrance to the select group as prose writers because of their influence on English literary history. One suspects that had his list been revised some fifteen years later, say at the time of his lecture 'On English Prose Fiction as a Rational Amusement', it would have included Jane Austen, Thackeray, and Scott as a novelist. All his life Trollope regarded poetry as essentially superior to prose.[15] But the successful novelist, both in this 1870 lecture and in the *Autobiography*, delivers a vigorous defence of his trade. Whereas in 1856 one detects a slight condescension towards his future profession: 'That travellers should read little else but novels was perhaps to be expected' (below, p. 183) may be the words of an unsuccessful novelist. His displeasure with the titles offered at railway bookstalls reflects the same bias. Contemporary evidence indicates that both the best and the worst novels were sold at these convenient outlets.[16] Trollope mentions only the latter. It is worth remarking that in an authoritative article, the information for which was supplied by W. H. Smith, who first introduced railway bookstalls in 1849, the *Saturday Review* in 1857 ranked Trollope's mother among the ten best selling novelists at railway stations.[17]

[15] See *Four Lectures*, ed. Morris L. Parrish (Constable, London, 1938), p. 99, and *Autobiography*, pp. 217-18. It is noteworthy that Trollope wrote to Kate Field: 'It is a mistake to suppose that prose is grander than poetry per se [as Booth notes, an obvious slip of the pen for "that poetry is grander than prose"]. It may be so; and has been so. But ... Scott will be known by his novels & not by his poetry.' 6 June 1861, *Letters*, p. 104.

[16] *The Times* (9 Aug. 1851) wrote that in London stations 'unmitigated rubbish encumbered the bookshelves of almost every bookstall', but that elsewhere conditions were much better. The *Athenaeum* ('Railway Reading', 20 Aug. 1853) believed that the 'trash' was being eliminated, and the *Saturday Review* (31 Jan. 1857) spoke of Scott as 'very popular' in cheap editions, and listed Bulwer Lytton, Marryat, Lever, Mrs. Gaskell, and Jane Austen among the novelists most popular at Railway bookstores.

[17] 'Railroad Bookselling', *Saturday Review*, III (31 Jan. 1857), 101.

Finally, in view of today's renaissance of interest in all things Victorian, special attention is deserving to this most typical Victorian's discussion of art. Trollope decries the breast-beating, self-depreciating attitude of many of his countrymen towards England and the arts. After admitting the unquestioned inferiority of English sculpture, and passing quickly over music, he takes up the cudgels on behalf of the architecture and painting of Great Britain. He defends St. Paul's and the new Houses of Parliament, and suggests with real insight that the many marvellous country houses of western England, of which Hatfield, Longleat, and Montacute are simply the best known, are neglected masterpieces.[18] His knowledge and love of Ireland no doubt contributed to his appeal for recognition of the excellence of the erstwhile Irish Parliament House, the Bank of Ireland. And if subsequent generations have not been overly enthusiastic about All Saints Church in Margaret Street, Trollope was indeed correct in singling out this work of William Butterfield, for it was undoubtedly one of the foremost inspirations for churches built throughout England in the following decade.[19] His defence of English painters is not all insular exaggeration: his comparison, for example, of Hogarth and Wilkie as equal to Teniers and Dou, respectively, would not, at least in the first instance, meet with much disagreement today. Art historians will welcome his account of what he calls the 'mania' for collecting paintings by both old masters and contemporary artists. His chief concern, however, is the National Gallery.[20] He takes his side in the current disputes: he would move the Gallery, crowded in those days and sharing the same building with the Royal Academy, to Kensington Gore; he is with those who defend the

---

[18] See *Barchester Towers* (O.U.P., London, 1925), pp. 199-200 (Chap. xxii) where Trollope managed to get this assessment into print. Cf. also *Doctor Thorne* (O.U.P., London, 1926), p. 10 (Chap. i), and *Letters*, p. 179 (8 March 1866).

[19] See John Summerson, 'William Butterfield; or, The Glory of Ugliness', *Heavenly Mansions* (Cresset, London, 1949), pp. 159-76; Henry-Russell Hitchcock, *Early Victorian Architecture in Britain* (Yale University Press, New Haven, 1954), II, 587 ff.; and Paul Thompson, 'All Saints Church, Margaret St., Reconsidered', *Architectural History*, VIII (1965), 73-94.

[20] Trollope's interest in the National Gallery continued. See his article, 'The National Gallery', *St. James Magazine*, II (Sept. 1861), 163-76, and also 'The Art Tourist', *Travelling Sketches* (Chapman & Hall, London, 1866), p. 68 (reprinted from the *Pall Mall Gazette*, 22 Aug. 1865).

'cleansing' of old paintings even though something be lost in the process. More central to his treatment is the desire to make the National Gallery one of the great collections in the world. His particular suggestion for removing works of art from Hampton Court and Dulwich Gallery to Trafalgar Square never materialized (although Raphael's cartoons were placed in the South Kensington Museum in 1865), but his general recommendation that considerable priority be given towards establishing a truly great gallery has certainly been vindicated.

The New Zealander thus tells us a good deal about Trollope. It is not extravagant to claim that in many respects it ranks with the *Autobiography* and *Letters* in the glimpses it gives us of his views on many facets of English life. As evidence of the mind of the early and not yet successful Anthony Trollope it probably has no rival.

As much as *The New Zealander* is revelatory of the man who wrote it, the work has greater importance in reference to his novels, forty-three of which were to follow the publication of *The Warden* in 1855. Trollope, like many writers, did not like to waste material, and when *The New Zealander* was refused publication he set about rewriting the book. We have no evidence that he submitted the revised version for publication. But one can safely speculate that he managed to see into print in one form or other the two chapters, 'Trade' and 'The Civil Service', which are missing from the extant manuscript. The most likely place for the material on the Civil Service is the entirely intrusive chapter of the same name in *The Three Clerks*.[21] Here one finds

---

[21] 3 vols. (Bentley, London, 1858), II, 251 ff. (Chap. xii). Trollope deleted this chapter for a one volume cheap edition issued by Bentley in 1859. Other possibilities for the whereabouts of the missing chapter include an article for the *Dublin University Magazine* of October 1855, also titled 'The Civil Service'. But evidence in the manuscript itself, namely the number (14) given to an additional chapter written in 1856, indicates that the entire work was intact at this date. Moreover, the focus of this article, a rebuttal of the report upon the Civil Service by Sir Charles Trevelyan and Sir Stafford Northcote, is somewhat too narrow for *The New Zealander*. It does, however, resemble this work in its dissatisfaction with 'the national propensity to grumbling' against all public officials and the thirst for 'Utopian purity' in the reformers. Another possibility, a lecture Trollope delivered in 1860, 'The Civil Service as a Profession', is not only further from *The New Zealander* in time, but is addressed specifically to his fellow civil servants and their families. It is noteworthy that Trollope wrote a rejected (and now lost) article in February 1856

echoes of the spirit of *The New Zealander* in Trollope's opposition to ignorant and irresponsible criticism of the Civil Service (especially as fostered by the newspapers and their correspondents), his quarrel with 'public opinion', and his praise of ambition. Trollope answers the charge of red tape and routine by saying that orderly procedure is the only way of really accomplishing anything, and in an aside alludes to the management of the Crimean War as a case where more, not less, routine had been needed. This is precisely the line of argument set forth in Chapter V of the present work, 'The Army and Navy'. Furthermore, as will be seen, Trollope inserted verbatim passages from *The New Zealander* into this novel. The missing chapter on trade presents a greater difficulty, but it seems reasonable to conjecture that Trollope used this material in the early portions of *The Struggles of Brown, Jones and Robinson*, which was begun in July 1857 while he was still writing *The Three Clerks* and presumably had the manuscript of *The New Zealander* to hand.[22] Here his summarizing and repetitious method is helpful, for elsewhere in *The New Zealander* Trollope gives a capsule version of his quarrel with trade: dishonest merchandising and advertising, precisely the practices satirized in *Brown, Jones and Robinson*.[23]

Opposite three passages in the manuscript Trollope has crossed the text through and written 'Three Clerks' in the margin. Most of the material so designated has been worked verbatim into the novel in the chapter entitled 'The Parliamentary Committee'.[24] Only small changes have been introduced: the Honourable Member from Limehouse of *The New Zealander* becomes the Honourable Member from Mile End, and the astute 'Gentleman

---

for the *Athenaeum* on the third number of *Little Dorrit*. The article undoubtedly challenged Dickens' picture of the Circumlocution Office. See Bradford A. Booth, 'Trollope and *Little Dorrit*', *Trollopian*, II (March, 1948), 237-40.

[22] The first person narrative of *Brown, Jones and Robinson* does not present an insurmountable objection to this hypothesis. Trollope need not have used either missing chapter precisely in its original form.

[23] No connection exists between the missing chapter and a series of eleven articles on London tradesmen which appeared in the *Pall Mall Gazette*, 10 July to 7 Sept. 1880, eventually published as *London Tradesmen*, ed. Michael Sadleir (Mathews & Marrot, London, 1928).

[24] *The Three Clerks*, III, p. 50 ff. (Chap. iii). See Appendix II, p. 216, on Trollope's marginal notes.

of the Treasury' becomes the indefatigable Mr. Whip Vigil. Trollope also transferred verbatim passages from the manuscript into his account of the election and unseating of Sir Roger Scatcherd in *Doctor Thorne*,[25] in connection with which a curious blend of fact and imaginative re-creation has been effected in both *The New Zealander* and the novel. In the former Trollope takes up the case of one Henry Stonor who had been convicted of bribery for his conduct on behalf of a friend's election in Sligo. Trollope dramatizes what he believes to be the extent of Stonor's 'bribery', namely a promise to see that a publican's bill for a past election would be attended to. In *Doctor Thorne* Stonor becomes Mr. Romer, a young barrister campaigning for Sir Roger Scatcherd, the publican Boniface is Mr. Reddypalm of the 'Brown Bear' in Barchester, and those 'very safe' men, Twistem and Twinum, are called Nearthewinde and Closerstil. The brief scene from *The New Zealander* is considerably elaborated, but its main lines are not altered. Like Stonor, Romer is later recalled from a governmental post abroad by purists in Parliament.[26]

These then are plain instances of Trollope's use of *The New Zealander* as a 'quarry' from which he lifted material bodily into his novels. Far more numerous are the instances in which this work presents an early treatment of themes to which Trollope constantly returned in his fiction. In view of the number of novels that were to follow the writing of *The New Zealander*, an exhaustive analysis is out of the question here, but instances will be cited for some half dozen leading themes.

Trollope's assault upon political purism, the (often feigned) demand for angelic private lives in public figures, did not end with *Doctor Thorne*. Newspapers and the politicians themselves are responsible for the kind of climate in which such purism can flourish. In *Framley Parsonage*, for example, the Prime Minister, Lord Brock, made an appointment which prompted *The Jupiter* to ask whether 'vice of every kind was to be considered, in these days of Queen Victoria, as a passport to the Cabinet. Adverse

---

[25] See below, paragraph beginning 'In nothing is this pretended horror ...' p. 111 ff., and *Doctor Thorne*, p. 263 *et passim* (Chap. xxii).

[26] An Irish member, G. H. Moore, had moved in Parliament (6 April 1854) that Stonor's appointment to a judgeship in Victoria be investigated. Here Trollope was in agreement with *The Times* which called Stonor the victim of 'virtuous and cheap indignation' (8 April 1854).

members of both Houses had arrayed themselves in a pure
panoply of morality, and thundered forth their sarcasms with the
indignant virtue and keen discontent of political Juvenals.'[27]
Undoubtedly Trollope feared and detested the mock indignation
of leading articles more than the carryings on in Parliament. The
former has more influence. Thus the *Jupiter*'s outcry contributed to Brock's decision to appoint Harold Smith to the office
of Lord Petty Bag simply because it was hoped that Smith would
not offend anyone: '[he] lived with his wife, and his circumstances were not more than ordinarily embarrassed.'[28] And when
some few weeks later the same newspaper had in effect turned
Lord Brock's government out of office, Smith voices Trollope's
earlier complaint: 'we are becoming the slaves of a mercenary
and irresponsible press—of one single newspaper.'[29] Even less
scrupulous than Tom Towers of the *Jupiter* is Quintus Slide
of the *People's Banner*, an abominable opportunist who writes
'slashing articles' about everyone in high office. Formerly a hot
liberal who tries to ingratiate himself with the hero of *Phineas
Finn*, he later flip-flops into the conservative camp. In *Phineas
Redux*, Slide, while intending to publish a scandalous letter
from the half-mad Robert Kennedy, again tries to approach
Phineas: 'We go in for morals and purity of life, and we mean
to do our duty by the public without fear or favour.'[30] There-
after begins the series of 'thunderbolts' with which he tries to
ruin Phineas politically and socially. In *The Prime Minister* Slide
learns that the Duke of Omnium has paid £500 in election expenses for Ferdinand Lopez: '...we maintain that we have discovered a blot in that nobleman's character which it is our duty
to expose.... He came forward telling us that he, at least, meant
to have clean hands,—that he would not do as his forefathers had
done.'[31] The Duke's friend, Lord Cantrip, refusing to bring the

---

[27] *Framley Parsonage* (O.U.P., London, 1926), p. 197 (Chap. xviii). Cf. below,
pp. 108-11, *et passim*.

[28] Ibid., p. 197. These are remarkably similar sentiments to those which
Trollope claims were a subject for raillery to Sydney Smith, below, p. 16.

[29] Ibid., p. 245 (Chap. xxiii). Trollope's attack upon newspapers, begun in
The Warden, was long lived. The press is almost invariably in the wrong in
his fiction.

[30] *Phineas Redux* (O.U.P., London, 1937), p. 242 (Chap. xxii 'Purity of
Morals, Finn'). It is significant that the *People's Banner* belongs plainly to
the sensational press, unlike the *Jupiter* which was unmistakably *The Times*.

[31] *The Prime Minister* (O.U.P., London, 1938), II, 109-10. (Chap. l).

matter before Parliament, voices Trollope's own thinking: 'I do not think that every action of a minister's life should be made matter of inquiry because a newspaper may choose to make allusions to it.'[32]

Although the demand for purity extended to all sides of a public figure's life, it was in elections particularly, so Trollope tells us in *The New Zealander*, that the mania most fiercely manifested itself. We have already seen Trollope's use in *Doctor Thorne* of his condemnation of pretended horror at ribbons for girls and beer for men, of anti-bribery election laws so strict that it became necessary to employ as agents those very 'safe' men; nearly everyone had to transgress the laws, the sin was to be caught; only naïve outsiders believed otherwise. The subject fascinated Trollope, and elections are prominent in his novels from beginning to end. A passage from the bribery trial of Mr. Browborough in *Phineas Redux* reads as though it had been written twenty years earlier:

> The House had been very hot against bribery,—and certain members of the existing Government, when the late Bill had been passed, had expressed themselves with almost burning indignation against the crime. But, through it all, there had been a slight undercurrent of ridicule attaching itself to the question of which only they who were behind the scenes were conscious. The House was bound to let the outside world know that all corrupt practices at elections were held to be abominable by the House; but Members of the House, as individuals, knew very well what had taken place at their own elections, and were aware of the cheques which they had drawn. Public-houses had been kept open as a matter of course ...[33]

But the most interesting and lengthy account of an election comes in *Ralph the Heir* (1871), where Trollope's own benighted attempt to be returned as a Liberal for Beverley in 1868 is recorded.[34] In the novel Trollope recounts election antics with a heightened effect which is as Dickensian as anything he ever wrote. But a new seriousness is also present, and his comments in the *Autobiography* reflect his altered perspective:

---

[32] *The Prime Minister*, II, 192-93 (Chap. lvii).
[33] *Phineas Redux*, II, 33-4 (Chap. xliv). Cf. below, p. 111 ff.
[34] 'Beverley and Perrycross were, of course, one and the same place.' *Autobiography*, p. 343.

It had seemed to me that nothing could be worse, nothing more unpatriotic, nothing more absolutely opposed to the system of representative government, than the time-honoured practices of the borough of Beverley. It had come to pass that political cleanliness was odious to the citizens. There was something grand in the scorn with which a leading Liberal there turned up his nose at me when I told him that there should be no bribery, no treating, not even a pot of beer on our side![35]

First hand experience had taught him to be less ready to dismiss a horror of election bribery as purism.

Partisan parliamentary wrath disturbed Trollope in *The New Zealander*: it was not only indecorous but dishonest for members to attack one another like Roman gladiators, combatants who in private life might be friends but who for the sake of appearance must give no quarter in the House. Trollope switches the metaphor in *Phineas Finn*:

The leaders of our two great parties are to each other exactly as are the two champions of the ring who knock each other about for the belt and for five hundred pounds a side once in every two years. How they fly at each other, striking as though each blow should carry death if it were but possible! And yet.... In private life Mr. Daubeny almost adulated his elder rival,—and Mr. Mildmay never omitted an opportunity of taking Mr. Daubeny warmly by the hand.[36]

In a later novel he reverts to the old metaphor and entitles a chapter on the Daubeny-Gresham struggle 'The Two Gladiators'.[37] Phineas himself, in a depressed state of mind after acquittal on murder charges, finds these less savoury aspects of British political life so discouraging that he hesitates to return to Parliament:

Men are flying at each other's throats, thrusting and parrying, making false accusations and defences equally false, lying and slandering,—sometimes picking and stealing,—till they themselves become unaware of the magnificence of their own position, and forget that they are expected to be great. Little tricks of sword-play engage all their skill.[38]

---

[35] *Autobiography*, p. 306.
[36] *Phineas Finn: The Irish Member* (O.U.P., London, 1937), p. 100 (Chap. ix).
[37] *Phineas Redux*, p. 351 ff. (Chap. xxxiii).
[38] Ibid., II, 334 (Chap. lxx).

And in the final Palliser novel, *The Duke's Children* (1880), it is largely the exceptionally fierce and partisan behaviour of the conservative Sir Timothy Beeswax which induces the Duke's son, Lord Silverbridge, to return to his father's liberal party.[39]

In *The New Zealander*, party loyalty, upon which most of this internecine parliamentary battling is founded, is seen as especially fraught with dishonesty:

> It is known that men will argue, debate, and vote, not according to the facts of a case, but according to the political view in which party requires that they should regard those facts. If it be necessary to decide whether Black be Black ... men will go into different lobbies on the matter; and according to the power of parties at the moment Black shall be declared to be Black, or to be the opposite of it.... If Mr. Smith out of the House states that Black is White he will lose his credit for veracity, and men will gradually know him for a liar. But if he merely votes Black to be White within the House, no one on that account accuses him of untruth (below, pp. 121-2).

Phineas Finn, who believes that 'A man who is ready to vote black white, because somebody tells him, is dishonest',[40] agonizes over the problem of party loyalty. He wishes to be first a liberal and only secondly a member of a party. This is madness to a staunch party politician like Barrington Erle, who believes that debates and discussions are only to create outside public opinion and should never influence a member: 'any such changing of votes would be dangerous, revolutionary, and almost unparliamentary'.[41] The novel turns upon Phineas' struggle with himself: 'Could a man be honest in Parliament, and yet abandon all idea of independence?'[42] In the end he resigns his seat and returns to Ireland rather than vote contrary to his convictions on Irish tenant rights.

[39] See *The Duke's Children* (O.U.P., London, 1938), pp. 243-7 (Chap. xxvi) and p. 196 ff. (Chap. xxi 'Sir Timothy Beeswax').

[40] *Phineas Finn*, II, 284 (Chap. lxiii).

[41] Ibid., 18-19 (Chap. ii). Party loyalty was of course the whole point of the chapter on the Limehouse Bridge Committee which Trollope transferred from *The New Zealander* to *The Three Clerks*. All the testimony is of no avail because the lines have already been drawn according to party. Trollope's attitude was based upon personal experience. From 16 to 27 July 1855, he had testified before a Select Committee of the House of Commons inquiring into postal arrangements in Ireland. *Parliamentary Papers*, 1854-55, XI, 431-532.

[42] Ibid., II, 222 (Chap. lviii).

Far more complex than Phineas Finn is Trollope's greatest political figure, Plantagenet Palliser, the Duke of Omnium, who becomes Prime Minister of a coalition government. His (not unmixed) failure is owing to many causes: his pride, his 'thin-skinned' sensitivity, and the very nature of the coalition which was at best a stopgap measure when neither liberals nor con-servatives could form a government. But for all his faults the Duke is an honest man, and clearly one of those 'few best' seen in *The New Zealander* as necessary to the proper ruling of England. Just before Sir Orlando Drought makes his parliamen-tary onslaught which will topple the Duke, Trollope muses that in 'these days' the chief talent required in a Prime Minister seems to be that of attracting and keeping influential friends. Other gifts, including intellect and patriotism, can be 'downright hindrances'. And worse, 'Honesty is unpractical. Truth is easily offended.'[43] Trollope seems to be saying that a country in which the Duke of Omnium cannot maintain a place of leadership is already showing signs of decadence, or at least of that widespread disregard of truth which presages decadence.

In spite of Trollope's assertion that 'my object has been to paint the social and not the professional lives of clergymen',[44] his novels convey many of his ideas on religion. And *The New Zealander*, written after the first of the Barsetshire series, pre-sents a straightforward account of his religious thinking. He wants the various churches to be tolerant and at peace with one another, and to preach sensible, down to earth, workable doc-trines, doctrines which are neither too lax nor too rigid. Although he castigates both extremes within the Church of England he has more fault to find with the low church. His Evangelical clergyman, Mr. Everscreech, preaches constantly on but three themes: hatred of Rome, strict observance of the Sabbath, and the evil of worldly wealth and pleasure. In Everscreech one finds the beginnings of Mrs. Proudie and Obadiah Slope. These two cannot tolerate even mild manifestations of the Tractarian Move-ment, much less the Scarlet Woman herself. Mrs. Proudie, for example, once accused the wife of a clergyman of idolatry simply

---

[43] *The Prime Minister*, II, 382-3 (Chap. lxxiii).
[44] *The Last Chronicle of Barset* (O.U.P., London, 1932), II, 451 (Chap. lxxxiv).

because 'the poor lady had dated a letter, St. John's Eve'.[45] And as to Slope, 'his soul trembles in agony at the iniquities of the Puseyites.... His gall rises at a new church with a high pitched roof; a full-breasted black silk ·waistcoat is with him a symbol of Satan ...'[46] He is the scourge of 'Sabbath travelling', as is Mrs. Proudie. She is unforgettable shouting out 'Christianity and Sabbath-day observance' in interruption of Harold Smith's lecture on civilizing South Sea Islanders.[47] And when she says '...what are the things of this world?—dust beneath our feet, ashes between our teeth, grass cut for the oven, vanity, vexation, and nothing more!'[48] we know that Trollope would not acquiesce in this kind of thinking even from someone sincere in it. Slope and Mrs. Proudie are but the first in a long list of Evangelicals who fare poorly in his novels. Most of them deny pleasure and despise wealth in name only. The Reverend O'Callaghan, the Littlebath curate in *The Bertrams*, though very fond himself of the fleshpots, rails away at card players and Sabbath breakers. Similarly, in *Miss Mackenzie*, the Reverend Stumfold and his virago wife do battle against cardplaying, dancing, and hunting. Jeremiah Maguire, Stumfold's repugnant curate (Trollope gives him a repulsive squint), frantic with greed for Margaret Mackenzie's supposed money, begins his series of slanderous articles in the *Christian Examiner* with a sermon against wealth. The despicable Mrs. Prime, who refuses to live in the same house with her sister, Rachel Ray, simply because the girl has manifested an interest in a young man, is so possessive of her small fortune that she eventually refuses the hand of her equally greedy suitor, the hypocritical and sanctimonious Reverend Samuel Prong, another Evangelical. That a hatred of pleasure may in some perverse way be 'sincere' in no way redeems the doctrine. Mrs. Mary Bolton, the mother of John Caldigate's wife Hestor, 'was so afraid of the world, the flesh, and the devil, that she would fain shut up her child so as to keep her from the reach of all evil ... all sensual beatifications were evil in her sight.'[49] Her religious fanaticism

---

[45] *Last Chronicle*, p. 172 (Chap. xvii). This is precisely one of the practices Trollope mentions in connection with the young lady of very high church persuasion in *The New Zealander*. See below, p. 94.

[46] *Barchester Towers*, p. 25 (Chap. iv). Cf. below, pp. 96 and 100.

[47] *Framley Parsonage*, p. 67 (Chap. vi).

[48] Ibid., p. 490 (Chap. xlv).

[49] *John Caldigate* (O.U.P., London, 1946), p. 172 (Chap. xviii).

turns her into a frightening and inhuman persecutor of her own daughter. For Trollope, as *The New Zealander* plainly reveals, a love of wealth and pleasure is no more than natural. The possession of at least a moderate amount of both is not only a desideratum but the *sine qua non* of the good life, Christian or otherwise. Like his memorable archdeacon, Trollope would have distrusted anyone who evinced scruples such as Mr. Crawley's about worldly gain. What Trollope writes of Grantly could have applied to himself: 'He ... enjoyed the good things of this world, and liked to let it be known that he did so.'[50] Of Grantly's ambition to become Bishop of Barchester Trollope says that he cannot agree that it was wrong: 'Our archdeacon was worldly. Who among us is not so? He was ambitious. Who among us is ashamed to own "that last infirmity of noble minds!" '[51]

Trollope's handling of Tractarians in *The New Zealander*, as personified by Dr. Middleage, is harsher than one might have expected either from a reading of the novels or *Clergymen of the Church of England*.[52] He does say that 'the best and sincerest' (below, p. 98) were attracted to the Oxford Movement. But they make accidentals and 'appendages', such as attractive churches, vestments, and ceremonies, too central and too significant for Trollope's brand of tolerant latitudinarian Protestantism. Whereas the Evangelicals of the novels are in no sense an improvement on Everscreech, Dr. Middleage's successors are usually saved. The Reverend Caleb Oriel is directly developed from Dr. Middleage. While the borrowing has not been precisely verbatim, the material is unmistakably taken from *The New Zealander*:

[Oriel's] original calling, as a young man, was rather to the outward and visible signs of religion than to its inward and spiritual graces.

He delighted in lecterns and credence-tables, in services at dark hours of winter mornings when no one would attend, in high waistcoats and narrow white neckties, in chanted services and intoned prayers.... He eschewed matrimony, imagining that it became him as a priest to do so; he fasted rigorously on Fridays ...[53]

[50] *Barchester Towers*, p. 27 (Chap. iv).
[51] Ibid., p. 9 (Chap. i). Similarly on ambition see below, pp. 18-19. Even the same quotation from 'Lycidas' is used.
[52] (Chapman & Hall, London, 1866), pp. 24-5.
[53] *Doctor Thorne*, p. 381 (Chap. xxxii).

The New Zealander's unnamed pretty young girl who 'trips across the frozen snow two hours before the sun has risen to hear her favourite pastor intone gracefully through the nose a certain portion of the liturgy' (below, p. 94) is metamorphosed into Miss Gushing, who, 'through all one long, tedious winter, tore herself from her warm bed, and was to be seen ... entering Mr. Oriel's church at six o'clock.'[54] But Oriel eventually is converted to more sensible ways through marriage to Beatrice Gresham.

Unlike Oriel, the Reverend Francis Arabin of *Barchester Towers* is a prominent and important figure, and a more subtle development of Dr. Middleage. Arabin is clearly one of the 'best and sincerest' who, early in life, had been in danger of the same errors which beset Middleage. At Oxford Arabin sat at the feet of Newman and found that his own tastes were towards ceremony, fasts, feasts, celibacy. Tempted to asceticism and Rome, he had to convince himself that he was not remaining a Protestant simply because the Church of England bolstered and supported all his worldly interests. A curate of a small Cornish parish—apparently Mr. Crawley—helps him with the satisfying argument that a Christian must act from within and not from externally imposed duties. But to become an ideal Trollopian clergyman he must enter upon a modicum of wealth, marry, and have a family. Grantly's persuading him to leave Oxford obviates the first difficulty. As to family ties, Arabin 'had often discussed with himself the necessity of such bonds for a man's happiness in this world, and had generally satisfied himself with the answer that happiness in this world is not a necessity.'[55] Eleanor Bold completes his salvation and he learns how wrong had been his attempt to despise the blessings and pleasures of life. Trollope begs his readers not to be too harsh in their judgements on this man who did not reach a safe harbour until he was forty. But for Trollope there is no gainsaying the conclusion that modern Christian 'stoicism' is as great an 'outrage' as any ancient variety. Both teach, and, albeit unwittingly, dishonestly teach, that 'wealth and worldly comfort and happiness on earth are not worth the search. Alas, for a doctrine which can find no

---

[54] *Doctor Thorne*, p. 383.
[55] *Barchester Towers*, p. 177 (Chap. xx).

believing pupils and no true teachers!'[56]

Trollope begins and ends his chapter on religion with a plea that Anglicans of all shades exercise tolerance towards Roman Catholics and Dissenters. His own enlightened attitude towards Roman Catholics (a comparative rarity in mid-Victorian England) had been amply demonstrated in his first three novels. Presumably his ideally tolerant cleric is the Reverend Frank Fenwick of Bulhampton, who, though sorely tried by the construction of an ugly 'Salem' directly opposite his own church, acts nevertheless decently towards his neighbouring Methodist clergyman. 'Of this he was quite sure, that Mr. Puddleham's religious teaching was better than none at all; and he was by no means convinced ... that, for some of his parishioners, Mr. Puddleham was not a better teacher than he himself.'[57] But the Dissenter himself has no such attitude. 'He was painfully conscious of the guile of this young man [Fenwick], who had, as it were, cheated him out of that appropriate acerbity of religion, without which a proselyting sect can hardly maintain its ground. ... War was necessary to Mr. Puddleham.'[58]

Lawyers were as interesting to Trollope as clergymen and members of Parliament. In *The New Zealander* he is concerned that lawyers and indeed the law itself seem to strive to protect criminals rather than to discover the truth. He dramatizes the case of an apprehended murderer whom the constable cannot question without warning that he answers at his peril; in like manner the magistrate must remind him of his rights, and, thus encouraged, the accused refuses to say anything. Lawyers would be aghast at any suggestion that this man should be 'lured' into telling the truth. If he attempts to plead guilty at his trial, his lawyers will persuade him not to do so. His defence counsel, Mr. Allwinde,[59] does all he can to pervert the course of justice: he uses delaying tactics; he tries to get the case thrown out on technicalities; he so browbeats the key witness that the confused man mistakes his right hand for his left. But justice seems nevertheless to prevail, and the jury, helped along by starvation and

[56] *Barchester Towers*, p. 178. Cf. below, pp. 93-4 and 101-3.

[57] *The Vicar of Bulhampton* (O.U.P., London, 1924), pp. 116-17 (Chap. xvii). Cf. below, p. 104.

[58] Ibid., p. 243 (Chap. xxxv). Cf. below, p. 90.

[59] A Mr. Allewinde (sic) appeared in Trollope's first novel, *The Macdermots of Ballycloran* (1847), as a prosecutor for the Crown.

cold, declare the man guilty. Allwinde's efforts succeed in having the sentence commuted to transportation, however, and the
convict will soon return with a ticket of leave.

Mr. Allwinde effloresces into one of Trollope's most delightful
characters and Victorian fiction's most memorable barrister,
Mr. Chaffanbrass. This champion of the criminal courts first
appears in *The Three Clerks*, where we have already seen *The
New Zealander*'s influence. His business is to 'bamboozle' the
jury, chiefly by confusing and abusing witnesses: anyone coming unprotected into court, intent simply on telling the truth,
'must be badgered this way and that till he is nearly mad; he
must be made a laughing-stock for the court... he must be con-
founded till he forget his right hand from his left.... To apply
the thumbscrew, the boots, and the rack to the victim before him
was the work of Mr. Chaffanbrass's life.'[60] Of course in this
instance Trollope has Chaffanbrass defending Alaric Tudor, or,
more precisely, attacking Undy Scott, and the reader delights in
seeing the swindler sweat and contradict himself to the derision
of the court.

In *Orley Farm* Chaffanbrass is even more prominent, along
with a whole battery of lawyers of every stamp. Again we are
faced with the problem of the defence of a guilty party. Lady
Mason's defence can only succeed by breaking down the testimony of two witnesses. John Kenneby is such an easy mark that
Chaffanbrass's powers must be reserved for trying to make the
stubborn Bridget Bolster appear a rogue. Indeed, not only the
trial scenes but the entire novel probes the problem of the
defence of the guilty. In fact, *Orley Farm* can be seen as a
lengthy examination of questions raised in *The New Zealander*.
Felix Graham, a young lawyer whom Trollope labels the 'English Von Bauhr',[61] seems to espouse many of the views propounded in the earlier work. He complains of English 'love of
precedent and ceremony and old usages ... a system which

---

[60] *The Three Clerks*, III, 196-7 (Chap. xi). Alaric had wanted to plead
guilty but his attorney would not hear of it, Ibid., p. 192. This novel also contains an episode of the 'starving' of a jury, III, 231 (Chap. xii).

[61] Because he thinks there is validity in the arguments of the German
lawyer Von Bauhr, who, at a congress of lawyers in Birmingham, advocated
the continental system of justice wherein 'the same man might be judge,
advocate, and jury', as opposed to the English adversary system of law. *Orley
Farm* (O.U.P., London, 1935), p. 166 (Chap. xvii).

contains many of the barbarities of the feudal times, and also
many of its lies.' He is dissatisfied with methods of obtaining
confessions of guilt which tend only to teach criminals to lie.
The suspect should have a 'defender of his possible innocence,
not the protector of his probable guilt.... Let every lawyer go
into court with a mind resolved to make conspicuous to the light
of day that which seems to him to be the truth.'[62] But Trollope
himself seems more detached, more objective than he was in
the mid-fifties. He sympathizes with Graham, but it is not altogether clear that he does not consider him somewhat quixotic.
Graham, for example, may have higher ideals than Mr. Furni-
val, but he is not necessarily a wiser man. Chaffanbrass, of course,
has no patience with Graham's scruples about involving himself
in Lady Mason's case. And although Trollope will liken Chaffanbrass to a hired Irish assassin who never fails his employer, he
somehow places us on the barrister's side. Lady Mason is, except
in this one fault, so good a person, and those arrayed against her
so unattractive, that we cannot help but applaud Chaffanbrass's
performance on her behalf. Of course we are entirely on his side
in his final appearance, the defence of Phineas Finn in *Phineas
Redux* where he charms us by undoing the testimony of the
inept Lord Fawn.[63]

The question of the defence of the accused and its concomitant
matter of the client-lawyer relationship is present in Trollope's
work from one end to the other. In *The Bertrams*, for example,
Trollope allows the villain of the piece, Harry Harcourt, to make
good sense in his argument with George Bertram, who insists
that a man with a weak case ought not to have a strenuous
defence: 'what you propose is Quixotic in every way. It will not
hold water for a moment.... Such a doctrine is a doctrine of
puritanism—or purism, which is worse.'[64] Stubborn Josiah Crawley complains to Mark Robarts: 'You say I am innocent, and yet
you tell me I am to be condemned as a guilty man ... because I
will not fee an attorney to fee another man to come and lie on

---

[62] *Orley Farm*, pp. 178-9 (Chap. xviii). Cf. below, pp. 54, 62-3 *et passim*.
[63] See *Phineas Redux*, Chapters lx through lxiii. Even the ploy of the
wrong name, mentioned in *The New Zealander*, is used: 'It seemed that somebody had called him Phinees instead of Phineas, and that took half an hour.'
Ibid., II, 226 (Chap. lxi). Cf. below, p. 57.
[64] *The Bertrams*, 3 vols. (Chapman & Hall, London, 1859), I, 263 (Chap. xii).

my behalf, to browbeat witnesses, to make false appeals ...'[65]
When Sir William Patterson, Solicitor General, and advocate
for the Lovels, states in court quite honestly the true disposition
of the case, thus clearing the way for an easy victory for the
Countess and Lady Anna, many people feel that he has done
poorly by his clients.[66] John Caldigate's attorney and barrister
are in agreement with what we recognize as Chaffanbrass's dictum that a barrister ought not to listen to his client's protestations of innocence: this is not his business. However, Sir John
Joram, Caldigate's barrister, unlike so many of his colleagues,
'never condescended to bully anybody' on the witness stand.[67]
But one suspects that had the likes of Chaffanbrass browbeaten
the lying conspirators, Caldigate would never have been found
guilty. And as late as the posthumously published *Mr. Scarborough's Family*, we discover the lawyer John Grey and his
daughter arguing the merits of the legal defence of 'rascals' and
murderers—'this special question had often been discussed between them.'[68]

Trollope's novels often revolve around some point of law, as,
for example, in *The Warden*, or *Mr. Scarborough's Family*;
they feature some eleven trial scenes, from his first novel, *The
Macdermots of Ballycloran*, to his last, *The Landleaguers*; they
contain well over 100 lawyers.[69] This concern with the law is
for many one of the attractions of Trollope's fiction. And for
these readers who delight in his legal complications, court room
scenes, and, most especially, Mr. Chaffanbrass, *The New Zealander*, with its straightforward recital of Trollope's thinking on
things legal, provides an early and unsophisticated account of
where he began.

Trollope's analysis of English amusements in the chapter he
labels 'Society' touches another prominent feature of his fiction.
Dinner parties and hunting scenes abound in the novels. But
The New Zealander presents a highly critical picture of middle
class Britons in their hours of ease. It may well be, he writes,

[65] *Last Chronicle*, p. 215 (Chap. xxi).
[66] See *Lady Anna* (O.U.P., London, 1936), p. 348 (Chap. xxxiii).
[67] *John Caldigate*, p. 393 (Chap. xli).
[68] *Mr. Scarborough's Family*, 3 vols. (Chatto & Windus, London, 1883), I,
235 (Chap. xvii).
[69] See Winifred Gregory Gerould and James Thayer Gerould, *A Guide to
Trollope* (Princeton University Press, Princeton, 1948), pp. 138-9 and 54-5.

that most Englishmen are constitutionally incapable of enjoying
themselves, that in truth they enjoy their work more than their
amusements. But if such is the case they ought to be honest and
admit the deficiency; they ought to be willing to take lessons
from foreigners in the matter of leisure and pleasure. A man
ought to find his bent and follow it, whether it be ballooning or
hunting, or even simply eating and drinking. Instead, Englishmen usually prefer to regard the few who truly relish doing
anything as 'mad' or 'cracked', while they themselves pretend
to enjoy dull dinners and parties in which society expects them
to delight. The hideously boring party at the Gingham Walkers
illustrates the Victorian middle classes affecting to entertain in
the manner of Lord Palmerston. Trollope has his laugh at the
entire production: the damask curtains, silk covered sofas, dress
coats, coffee and tea 'handed round'; the inane conversation,
pitiful snobbery, and steadfast unwillingness to mix with each
other which characterizes the participants. (See below, p. 160 ff.)

Parallel attitudes inform his fiction. Expectedly, one finds
criticism of British social mores in the novel written simultaneously with *The New Zealander*: Signora Neroni complains
to the Bishop that 'all is so dull and stately'[70] at English dinner
parties, and Mrs. Proudie's reception would indeed have been
stifling had it not been for the Italianized Signora and her
brother Bertie. In connection with Miss Thorne's *fête champêtre*
Trollope himself comments:

The trouble in civilized life of entertaining company, as it is called
too generally without much regard to strict veracity, is so great that
it cannot but be matter of wonder that people are so fond of attempting it. It is difficult to ascertain what is the *quid pro quo*. If they who
give such laborious parties, and who endure such toil and turmoil in
the vain hope of giving them successfully, really enjoyed the parties
given by others, the matter could be understood. A sense of justice
would induce men and women to undergo, in behalf of others,
those miseries which others had undergone in their behalf. But they
all profess that going out is as great a bore as receiving; and to look
at them when they are out, one cannot but believe them.[71]

Britons put too much faith in the accoutrements of entertaining: 'Ladies ... mainly trust to wax candles and upholstery.

[70] *Barchester Towers*, p. 89 (Chap. xi).
[71] Ibid., p. 341 (Chap. xxxvi).

Gentlemen seem to rely on their white waistcoats.'[72]

Trollope's suggestion that Englishmen ought to learn social graces from the French is developed in *The Three Clerks* through the character of Victoire Jaquêtenàpe, even to the detail of the need for gentlemen to talk with elderly ladies.[73] Also, the Gingham Walkers and their guests ought to have played cards in the manner of Miss Todd's Littlebath set rather than let propriety drive them to boredom.[74] But perhaps Mrs. Proudie's 'conversazione' at her London house in Gloucester Place is the closest in spirit to the Gingham Walkers' debacle: again there are not enough chairs and guests have to 'stand about upright, or "group themselves" ' as Mrs. Proudie described it; every half hour tea and cake are 'handed round on salvers'.[75] Trollope interjects:

And indeed this handing round has become a vulgar and an intolerable nuisance among us second-class gentry with our eight hundred a year—there or thereabouts;—doubly intolerable as being destructive of our natural comforts, and a wretchedly vulgar aping of men with large incomes. The Duke of Omnium and Lady Hartletop are undoubtedly wise to have everything handed round.[76]

Moreover, if the object of all this entertaining is 'to kill Mrs. Jones with envy at the sight of my silver trinkets, I am a very mean-spirited fellow.'[77] And to elaborate dinners with cold soup and 'four kinds of ices after dinner', Trollope much prefers Mr. Toogood's 'pot luck' hospitality.[78]

The pages of Trollope's novels are notoriously crowded with men enthusiastic for hunting. These blessed souls have discovered and pursue diligently that which truly delights them. Lord Chiltern, prominent figure in the Parliamentary novels, was a monomaniac on the subject. But of course the real devotee is Anthony Trollope, who was as given to following the hounds in his novels as in life.

---

[72] *Barchester Towers*, p. 342. Cf. below, pp. 159, 161, 169.
[73] *The Three Clerks*, II, 188-9 (Chap. ix). Cf. below, pp. 168-9.
[74] *The Bertrams*, II, 164-5 (Chap. vii). Cf. below, pp. 165, 167.
[75] *Framley Parsonage*, p. 184 (Chap. xvii).
[76] Ibid., pp. 184-5. Cf. below, pp. 166-7.
[77] Ibid., p. 186. Cf. below, p. 160.
[78] *Last Chronicle*, p. 412 ff. (Chap. xl, 'Mr. Toogood's Ideas about Society'). See also *Miss Mackenzie* (O.U.P., London, 1924), p. 95 ff. (Chap. viii, 'Mrs. Tom Mackenzie's Dinner Party').

Trollope subscribed to his title page the words 'It's gude to be honest and true.'[79] This, he tells us, is his simple prescription for delaying the arrival of the New Zealander in England. Trollope is alarmed at a general insensitivity to dishonesty in his native land. A lack of regard for the truth is at the basis of his quarrel with newspapers, parliamentary debates, elections, lawyers, churchmen, merchants, the advertising system, and even British amusements and social gatherings. In the novels, to play fast and loose with the truth is the mark of a villain: Undy Scott, George Hotspur, Ferdinand Lopez. Even to neglect to pay one's tradesman's bill is highly indicative of dubious character, as in the case of Nathaniel Sowerby or Ralph (the heir) Newton. That men cannot discriminate between honesty and dishonesty is still more alarming. John Caldigate's honest gift of £20,000 to his libellous accusers is what really condemned him before judge, jury, and public. Such honesty is simply beyond credibility.

[79] The line is from 'Here's a Health to them that's awa', James Johnson's *Scots Musical Museum*, vol. V (1796), no. 412. Burns, who had sent the song to Johnson, had published his own version under the same title in the *Edinburgh Gazeteer*, 1792; for an earlier version see *The Jacobite Relics of Scotland*, ed. James Hogg (Blackwood, Edinburgh, 1819), p. 50, no. XXXI. Trollope does not, of course, deal with love and romance in a book of social criticism, but it is noteworthy that this line is for him the touchstone for genuine love between the sexes. Signora Neroni, when she crushes Mr. Slope, sings the entire four line chorus of Johnson's version: 'It's gude to be merry and wise .../ It's gude to be honest and true;/ It's gude to be off with the old love .../ Before you are on with the new.' *Barchester Towers*, p. 454 (Chap. xlvi). And the narrator had earlier remarked Slope's ignorance of the wisdom of these verses in that he courted Eleanor Bold and the Signora simultaneously, Ibid., p. 244 (Chap. xxvii). In *Doctor Thorne* Trollope comments that he will not inquire how Frank Gresham 'had contrived to be off with the old love and so soon on with the new, or rather, to be off with the new love and again on with the old ...' in connection with Mary Thorne and Patience Oriel, p. 82 (Chap. vi). Again, the four verses are quoted in reference to Frank Greystock when the allurements of Lizzie Eustace temporarily turn him from Lucy Morris, *The Eustace Diamonds* (O.U.P., London, 1930), p. 314 (Chap. xxxv). When Hetta Carbury is astonished to learn of her brother's involvement with Ruby Ruggles while he was engaged to marry Marie Melmotte, Hetta's cousin Roger informs her: 'You're old-fashioned. ... It used to be the way,—to be off with the old love before you are on with the new; but that seems to be all changed now.' *The Way We Live Now* (O.U.P., London, 1941), II, 204 (Chap. lxxii). Furthermore, all Trollope's lovers, especially female, are characterized as being 'honest and true' to their sometimes vacillating future partners. Although one thinks especially of heroines like Mary Thorne and Florence Mountjoy (*Mr. Scarborough's Family*), this is true throughout the entire canon of Trollope's fiction; perhaps the loyalty of Anna Lovel to the tailor Daniel Thwaite is the most protracted study of this theme (*Lady Anna*).

But surely Trollope's most sustained presentation of a dishonest society is in *The Way We Live Now*. Here one finds unprincipled editors giving favourable reviews to Lady Carbury's feeble plagiarism, the Beargarden crowd of billiard-playing (often suspect in Trollope, see below, pp. 22-3) young wasters who don't pay bills and who cheat at cards, cynical suitors who regard nothing but the financial aspects of marriage, venal aristocrats of all stripes, enterprising money managers of a non-existent railroad. But paramount over all is the great figure of Augustus Melmotte. The conservatives of Westminster elect him to Parliament; he is selected to entertain the Emperor of China in the presence of English royalty: 'It seemed that there was but one virtue in the world, commercial enterprise,—and that Melmotte was its prophet.'[80] Trollope did not discuss swindling stock dealers in *The New Zealander* (unless there had been something on this subject in the missing chapter on trade), but it is noteworthy that on the final page of his book, when he comes to sum up what for him is the general dishonesty of the age, he makes an obvious reference to John Sadleir, the banker, member of Parliament, and renowned swindler who had recently committed suicide:

It is not of swindlers and liars that we need live in fear, but of the fact that swindling and lying are gradually becoming not abhorrent to our minds. These vile offences are allowed to assume pseudonyms under which their ugliness is hidden; and thus they show their faces to the world unabashed and are even proud of their position. Could the career of that wretched man who has lately perished have been possible, had falsehood, dishonesty, pretences, and subterfuges been odious in the eyes of those who came daily in contact with his doings? (below, p. 211.)

The affinity to Melmotte is clear. Roger Carbury says:

[Melmotte's] position is a sign of the degeneracy of the age. What are we coming to when such as he is an honoured guest at our tables? ... And yet these leaders of fashion know,—at any rate they believe,— that he is what he is because he has been a swindler greater than other swindlers. What follows as a natural consequence? Men reconcile themselves to swindling. Though they themselves mean to be honest, dishonesty of itself is no longer odious to them....

[80] *The Way We Live Now*, p. 411 (Chap. xliv).

It seems to me that the existence of a Melmotte is not compatible with a wholesome state of things in general.[81]

The Way We Live Now, which so many modern critics put in the forefront of his novels, is not the product of a disillusioned, lately turned cynical, newly pessimistic Trollope. It is a masterly expression of his persisting anxieties and fears. Indeed, 'The Way We Live Now' would have made an excellent subtitle to *The New Zealander*.

Thus the present work enables one to assess more fully Trollope's achievement as a novelist. An acquaintance with his early ideas about Englishmen and English institutions allows one a peculiar insight into what was to come. That the novels in their dramatic presentation of themes treated in *The New Zealander* show a marked increase in subtlety and detachment is of course to be expected. Chaffanbrass may practise the evil art of defending the guilty, but his powers can be employed in protecting the innocent Phineas. A caricature such as Dr. Middleage can develop into Arabin. Felix Graham espouses ideas similar to those expressed in *The New Zealander*, but Graham is not Trollope, nor is he necessarily his spokesman. Roger Carbury has incisive comments on England but he is not presented as a flawless or even entirely balanced judge. Trollope's concern with honesty, political purism, the legitimacy and desirability of worldly gain are constant; his interest in lawyers, politicians, clergymen, and newspapermen remains, but his presentation becomes increasingly complex and objective. One further generalization is perhaps justifiable: the 'early' novels—let us say for our purposes from *Barchester Towers* to *The Last Chronicle of Barset* —represent an effort at restraint on Trollope's part. It would seem that in *The New Zealander* he vented his need to be hortatory, once for all, at least until the seventies. At which time the seriousness and discontent of some of the later novels, of which *The Way We Live Now* is but the most prominent instance, can be viewed not so much in terms of departure but rather of return with growth. To be sure, the debate as to the relative excellence of the early and late novels will continue, but the comprehension of both should be enhanced by a knowledge of *The New Zealander*.

---

[81] *The Way We Live Now*, II, 44-5 (Chap. lv).

A final word about style. Trollope has never been known as a 'stylist'; one does not look to him for startling images or memorable lines. *The New Zealander* is written for the most part in clear, simple, unambiguous prose; and, as such, it illustrates Trollope's shortcomings along with his strengths. At times it exhibits a style too simple, too repetitious, too cliché prone. It shows signs of hasty composition which a more careful reworking could well have improved upon. But a laboured, constantly refined prose is not to be looked for in a man of Trollope's temperament—and output. He was a facile writer of very readable English. And when to the straightforward style is joined interesting subject matter the effect is quite forceful. Take, for example, the following from his chapter on literature:

National glory is a great matter; but national education, if it can be accomplished, is surely a greater matter. It is well to beat the Russians; but this beating of the Russians, be it ever so complete, will go but a small way towards accomplishing the happiness of Britons. A month's excitement will end that happiness. But the happiness of any man to whom has been imparted the power of reading and enjoying a song of Burns' is to a certain extent ensured for his lifetime.... An educated people, though they be in their decadence, may probably possess more happiness and higher virtues than their ancestors with all their rising martial glory; and may also do much more for the benefit of the world at large. The idea of national pride has been inculcated in our breasts with too much vehemence, and those who have preached the lesson have not always been actuated by the most disinterested motives. There is no source of true happiness to the multitude in the idea of their belonging to the biggest of nations. The happiness arising from this, if any happiness do arise from it, is to the few. The glory and sense of greatness are to those who are concerned in great things. It is necessary for such that the multitude should support them, and therefore a pæan as to the continued strength and immaculate power of England is so often sounded into the ears of Englishmen. (Below, pp. 176-7.)

These were remarkable sentiments in 1855, and Trollope's plain style fits perfectly.

In these pages, then, a very talented servant of the Queen mirrors forth mid-Victorian England and pronounces his judgements thereon. Trollope of course was not an original or deep thinker. His book lacks the generalizing power of the two great contemporary foreign studies of English life, Emerson's *English Traits* and Taine's *Notes Sur L'Angleterre*; nor has his style the epigrammatic quality one so admires in these works. On the other hand, while in *The New Zealander* Trollope's opinions are set forth with characteristic bluntness, his picture of England is intimate, knowledgeable, and accurate. Furthermore, the book is in a sense unique: no contemporary English author of Trollope's stature attempted a broad general survey of this kind. Students of Victorian history and social life will welcome this unexpected *trouvaille*. Students of Trollope will learn a good deal more about him and will be treated to a first-hand look at many of the themes he was to touch with greatness in his novels.

THE MANUSCRIPT

THE manuscript, the earliest extant by Trollope and entirely in his hand, contains nearly 90,000 words. The missing chapters, 'Trade' and 'The Civil Service' (originally numbered chapters two and six) would have added approximately 8,000 and 10,000 words, respectively. The chapter entitled 'Art', which is not included in Trollope's table of contents and which survives in a seemingly first draft state, was written, according to marginal notes, in March 1856.

Although one cannot date the other chapters with such precision, topical allusions throughout the manuscript establish a time *ante quo non*: for example, the Hyde Park disturbances referred to occurred 1 July 1855; the letter to *The Times* about governesses appeared 13 October 1855; Lord Lyndhurst's speech on life peerages was delivered 7 February 1856; John Sadleir's suicide took place the night of 16 February 1856. In addition, there are four outright references to the year 1856. Finally, a marginal note (at the beginning of the chapter on the House of Commons), which, whether it refers to the composition of this draft of the chapter or to certain revisions and deletions therein, shows Trollope still at work on the manuscript in May 1856. From this internal evidence one salient and important fact emerges: what has survived as *The New Zealander* is in no part the manuscript submitted to Longman in March 1855, but an entirely new version written sometime between April 1855 (when presumably the manuscript was returned to Trollope) and May 1856. Furthermore, on the basis of three distinctly different paginations in the present manuscript, there is evidence that Trollope engaged in what for him was an almost unheard of amount of rewriting.

EDITORIAL PROCEDURE

THROUGH the courtesy of Mr. Taylor I have in effect been placed in the enviable position of presenting a first edition of a book by Anthony Trollope. My intention has been to offer a readable, 'normalized' text which essentially represents the book that would have appeared in 1856 had Longman accepted it. In so doing I have been guided by the first editions of those works most closely connected in time with the manuscript, namely *The Warden* (1855), *Barchester Towers* (1857), *The Three Clerks* (1858), and *Doctor Thorne* (1858). Indeed, as has been seen, the latter two contain published versions of portions of *The New Zealander*. This decision not to present a 'diplomatic' text would have had Trollope's sanction, for all the evidence shows that he expected his publishers to correct his textual errors and inconsistencies.[1] Accordingly, I have made the following silent corrections. Where Trollope's spelling is inconsistent ('recognise' and 'recognize') the form most frequently followed in the published works has been used throughout. In keeping with the same norm, archaic spellings such as 'shew' and 'antient' have been eliminated. Similarly Trollope's use of what we today consider 'American' spellings ('color', 'labor', 'honor' and other such words) have been rendered by their British counterparts. Abbreviations ('tho'', 'thro'') and the ampersand have been written out. Inadvertent verbal duplications have been deleted.

While keeping the flavour of Trollope's capitalization ('to vote that Black is White'), an attempt has been made to render it more consistent. In the manuscript words such as 'nation', 'member of

---

[1] See Robert H. Taylor, 'The Manuscript of Trollope's *The American Senator*', *Papers of the Bibliographical Society of America*, XLI (Second Quarter, 1947), 123-39. Mr. Taylor collates the manuscript with the magazine serial and first edition of the novel. He estimates, for example, that Bentley, the editor of *The Temple Bar*, wherein the novel first appeared, was responsible for some 'forty-five hundred additional commas and other marks in proportion', p. 128. Similarly, Arthur Mizener, in a textual appendix to the Riverside Edition of *The Last Chronicle of Barset* (Houghton Mifflin, Boston, 1964), writes that Trollope apparently 'counted on the printer to regularize' inconsistent spelling and 'exceedingly light' punctuation, p. 692.

Parliament', 'session' are indiscriminately either lower case or capitals. Here again the published works provided guidance.

Trollope's punctuation in places is very sketchy; missing periods, quotation marks and apostrophes have been supplied. Numerous dashes (a kind of universal punctuation in the manuscript) have been converted into periods, and, less frequently, into commas. Trollope is particularly careless about commas, and many have been inserted. On the other hand, even after one grants that nineteenth century writers used the comma rather more freely and certainly more frequently than is usual today, some commas have had to be removed. Trollope sometimes sets off by commas what we would call restrictive clauses; more frequently he uses only the second comma to close a restrictive clause: 'Men whose minds soar high, are attempting ...'; '... he who gazes at them, is forced into the consideration ...' He frequently separates 'so ... that' and similar constructions with a comma: 'there is so much energy, that they do not fail'; 'that under no circumstances such a visitation, can be possible.' Finally, some commas are simply intrusive and warranted removal by any standard: 'To each has been given to rule, the work of others.' 'March and April, are heathen denominations.'

In sum, every silent correction of spelling, capitalization, and punctuation has an editorial precedent in some published work of Trollope's of the 1850s. Moreover, most of the changes are authorized by usage elsewhere in *The New Zealander* itself.

More substantive editorial emendations have been noted in Appendix III. These include words supplied or deleted, and grammatical changes of any kind. In one paragraph Trollope's carelessness about detail has necessitated some changes of 'fact' which must be commented upon here. In speaking of Jane Austen's novels Trollope mentions 'Lady Charlotte De Burgh', an obvious slip for Lady Catherine de Bourgh (below, p. 158). He continues: 'With the Mansfields and the Crofts we have our sympathies and antipathies.' By 'Mansfields' Trollope evidently had in mind the Bertrams as owners of Mansfield Park. Furthermore, I have replaced 'Crofts' by 'Crawfords': the former are decidedly minor characters for whom no one could possibly have any antipathy. Further corroboration for these editorial changes is supplied by the next sentence of the text which refers to incidents in *Mansfield Park* and *Pride and Prejudice*: as amended all characters mentioned in the paragraph are from these two novels.

Trollope's textual deletions and marginal notes have been recorded in Appendices I and II. Of the deletions, only such as have significance are included. Thus unimportant changes which in no way alter the sense, such as the elimination of plurals, the substitution of one synonym for another, and simple alterations in phrasing, have not been preserved.

The New Zealander

"It's gude to be honest and true"

CHAPTER I

Introduction

I s the time quickly coming when the New Zealander shall supplant the Englishman in the history of the civilization of the world? Have the glories of Great Britain reached their climax, culminated, and begun to pale? Is England in her decadence?

These questions may seem to be both unpatriotic and unnecessary on the part of an Englishman in the middle of the nineteenth century. England now surely shows but small symptoms of decay. Her navy rides not only triumphant but entirely dominant in every sea to which she has a mind to send it. Her army has held, and is still prepared to hold its own in a distant corner of Europe, uninjured by any superiority of numbers, unconquered by any adversity of circumstances. Her wealth has enabled her to bear the enormous cost of war without serious detriment to her commerce or any cruel burden on her people.[1] While her enemies have suffered all the pangs of exhausted means, and are still tossing in the death agonies of spasmodic energy, she carries on her course all but unruffled. Thriving tenants pay their punctual rents to thriving landlords. Merchants send out their countless travellers, almost more eager for orders than for payment. Luxury, no whit abated by the war, or straitened in its means by growing taxes, encourages by a liberal expenditure every new production that adds to its indulgence. Though pressed for soldiers, England has fought with voluntary swords. England has so fought, and she alone; and even she for the first time in any considerable European war. She has fought by the side of a gallant friend, her sure ally, the first nation in the world, if any nation but England can be first.

Such are her strong grounds of comfort. Such her present reasons for hoping that she may escape the usual doom of greatness, and give the lie to the experience of history. What though Nineveh and Babylon fell and Tyre and Carthage; though Greece kissed the dust, and Egypt's kings and lordly Rome;

[1] The Crimean War (1854-6) is the focal point of Chapter V, 'The Army and Navy', below, p. 77 ff.

though Byzantium is what it is; though Venice crumbles to the shore a pauper's slave; though golden Spain has become a byword among nations; and Germany, strong in arms as she is, knows not which way to turn her head; still England stands erect. England, and she alone, has felt no foreign sword deep within her vitals. English matrons and English maids have never crouched in fear at the grim beard of a foreign foe. English bills are still paid with English gold, while Austria tries in vain to palm off paper in lieu of copper. The English commoner feeds off silver, while the Italian count scarce feeds at all. The best that every country can supply, England still buys and uses. And better still than this, are not English morals, English habits, English industry, and English truth still held to be examples for the world? If this be so, why talk of the decadence of England?

It is with such soft self-flattery as this that we are all so apt to honey up our ears, so that we become deaf alike to the voice of others, and the warnings of experience. After all an Englishman is but a man, and often not an acute man. It is a wish natural enough on our part that he alone should continue to rise in the world's respect, and to remain fixed and immovable on the apex of Fortune, while others are turned round with her wheel, and sink as fast as they rose. Nay, more than that, it is clearly our bounden duty to rise so high and there to stay, if by the wariest use of all our energies we may be enabled to do so. Self-praise, however, and self-confidence if over strong, will hardly help us. It may be well, even for us, to look around us, and see whether our walls are all sound; whether our towers stand fast; if our watchman be always awake, and our powder always dry. If we wish still to rise, we should at any rate be careful not to begin to fall.

Some time since one of our greatest living authors drew a picture for us in which the colours were certainly true to history, and the design one in strict accordance with the course of mundane things.[2] He described the figure of a New Zealander, some ornate man of art, some future polished tourist, standing on the ruins of London Bridge, while he sketched the time-worn columns and shattered though standing dome of our St. Paul's. To this picture one of our great statesmen has taken strong objection. He tells us that his eyes refuse to look on such a scene, or

---

[2] On Macaulay's New Zealander, see Introduction, p. xii.

his mind to imagine it. The stones of which St. Paul's is built will not fall as other stones have fallen; nor will London Bridge become subject to decay. A polished Zealander may indeed come to London; but he will come, not to sketch ruins, but to visit the centre of civilization. There is inherent in our institutions such manly strength, such a sap of virtue, such an adamantine worth that no Zealander, no Californian, no man of Geelong shall see them in their fall. King, Lords, and Commons, with a sufficient number of bishops, and occasional reform of Parliament, will preserve us from decay. All great people have hitherto become little; all power has fallen; all mighty realms have dwindled; the seeds of human evil have hitherto avenged themselves in all human institutions; but from such seeds our soil is free, to such plants our earth lends no succulence!

If such a happy state can be believed in, it is certainly useless to talk of the decadence of England. If however it be not credible, if such a theory, glorious as it is, has neither past experience nor future probability to support it, let us use the picture that has been put before us, and do what we can at any rate to retard the coming of our artistic visitor. Come, alas, he will. As surely as we stand gazing at the Parthenon thinking now of the glory of Greece as it was, and then of the glory of England as it is; so surely will strangers from the broad shores of the Atlantic and Pacific wander through the half-peopled labyrinth of our desolate streets and tell to each other with self-satisfied pride how great were formerly these people, but now how fallen. "Here on this little river," they will say, "lay half the wealth of the world of old. Here on these horrid muddy banks lay the rich ships of which their writers speak with so much pride. Yes here." And from the half-ruined bridge Mr. Macauley's Zealander will point with his jewelled cane to the slime of old Father Thames, and some fair young bride, brought from her rich home to see the ways of men as they lived in the ancient days, will raise to her eye a crystal cut from a pure diamond, and shuddering shake the thousand golden beads which glitter through her auburn hair.

This must be so some day. It much depends on ourselves whether the evil day come soon or late. A kingdom or a people will always rise according to the virtue that is in them, and will fall quickly or slowly as they allow those virtues to change themselves to vices. That even virtues do so change is the inheritance

we have received from Adam. When we look back at all the old
fallen nations of the earth do we not find the same history? Has
not industry generated avarice, and energy selfish ambition? Has
not the power of making brought forth the love of having; the
power of ruling the love of rule; the power of enjoying the love of
enjoyment? Has not virtue produced energy, and energy knowledge, knowledge civilization, and civilization refinement, refinement luxury, and luxury sin?

If it be admitted that such has been the course of mighty
nations, let us ask ourselves whether there be anything in us or
in our institutions, in our morals or our manners to save us from
a fate which has been so general. Have we repelled the seductions
of luxury, or adhered with rigour to the stern virtue of self-negation? Have we exercised power solely for the good of those under
us; never for that of ourselves? Have we been true and just in
our dealings? Have we kept our hands from stealing, and our
tongues from lying? Have we refrained from desiring other
men's goods? Let us ask these questions not alone of our rulers
and our great men, but each of us of ourselves. Are we an honest
God-fearing people, anxious only in this world for the fair fruits
of labour, but above all anxious for our reward in the next world?

That we are not such a people is no just ground for despair.
God has not thought fit so to create mankind. Englishmen are as
other men—imperfect, and being so can only expect the common
lot of imperfect humanity. We are most of us anxious to acknowledge our individual infirmities, and to own in our closet that we
can earn by our own merits neither happiness here nor hereafter.
Nevertheless, as a people we foolishly regard ourselves as without reproach. A nation may be great by the acts of one or two of
the noblest of her sons; but she can only be good by the virtues
of the multitude. If the people of a kingdom be individually false,
the kingdom will be false, and by its falseness will fall.

So it is with us. We have not exempted ourselves from the lot
which has hitherto been common to humanity. We buy and sell
dishonestly. In power we talk dishonestly to those below us. We,
the people, murmur dishonestly at those above us. Dishonestly
we enjoy in sloth the wealth which our fathers made; or else dishonestly we heap up wealth that our sons may do so. We too
often preach God's word dishonestly and hear it dishonestly. We
teach our children dishonestly. We treat our servants dishonestly,

exacting the last drop of sweat for the smallest reward. Among ourselves we associate dishonestly, cheating each other and ourselves with a vain belief that dullness is delightful, and tedium a pleasure. But worst of all, we write dishonestly. Even those who take upon themselves the sacred duty of instructing their brother men, of teaching from day to day what the duty of the people is; they also do dishonest work, thinking more, much more, of the greatness of the teacher than the welfare of the taught.

Few, perhaps, will find themselves ready to assent to the truth of all this. Few Englishmen will read the above black catalogue, and not accuse some portion of it of being an unnecessary libel. But is there any one who will not acknowledge the justness of much of it? Is there any portion of it that will not be admitted by some? Ask the member of Parliament who has sedulously listened to the foul list of adulterated foods which has been detailed to the Committee lately sitting, whether as a nation we sell our foods honestly.[3] Ask the half bankrupt tailor groaning over his long list of irrecoverable debts whether we buy honestly. Ask that deputation of merchants which is now filing its way from the office of a Secretary of State whether the civil nothings which it has heard from the great man were honest words. And then ask that great man, when in his closet he lays his grieving head upon his arm, and finds that all his labour for the public service, all his anxiety to do good to his countrymen has brought forth only discontent and hatred; ask him whether the people are honest to him. What does the working curate with his £70 a year think of the honesty of his absent rector? What does the stiff-necked Dissenter think of the honesty of the church, which forces him to pay for the building which his conscience will not allow him to enter? What does the parson think of the honesty of his parishioners who weekly come to sleep beneath his eloquence? Reader, are you honest to yourself, when you hardly endure with slow patience the tedium of some dull party, because society requires it? Are you honest when after such endurance you talk of the amusements of life? Do not rampant newspapers from day to day accuse all our public men of gross dishonesty?

[3] The Committee heard, for example, the testimony of one Dr. A. H. Hassall, author of a work on adulterated food, who stated it as his opinion that 'adulteration prevailed in nearly all articles, whether food, drink, or drugs.' *The Times* observed that after the Committee had interrogated Hassall, 'There could be no question as to the accuracy of the statements,' (16 July 1855).

—and were it politic to do so, would not our public men loudly
return the accusation? What can be thought of the honesty of a
critic who proclaims himself to be infallible, and who is ready to
write down any cause or any man who is unsuccessful?

Success is necessary to excellence. Such is the motto of the
present age; and the very motto is proof of dishonesty.

If then we suffer under those same imperfections which have
heretofore reduced other nations from their greatness, it would
be surely worse than weakness in us to flatter ourselves that we
have found the secret of everlasting youth and vigour. As others
have been before us full of sin, and weakness and death, so are
we also full. And so will be succeeding nations, till the Creator in
the full cycle of his time think fit to free mankind from their
burden. Let it then be not thought an unpatriotic thing to speak
of the decadence of England. Alas, the time must come when
England shall fall; when the English will shall no longer be
dominant round half the globe; when a few words spoken in
England's capital shall no longer settle the fate of millions both
to the East and to the West! As is the history of vainglorious
Greece and of Rome, the mistress of the world; as are the
memories of the Eastern and Western Empires, so undoubtedly
shall be the history and the memories of England.

Such, as far as mortal eye can see, is a doom already spoken. It
is not for us to hope even to annul it. But the period of its accomplishment does depend on us; on us and our children and our
children's children. Being as we are imperfect, it is still allowed
to us to struggle after virtue. And as that struggle is made
honestly or dishonestly, with true valour, or only false semblance
of valour, so will be our destiny and that of our nation. Surely it
may be worth while to see to this; to look into it and ascertain
whether with our Exeter Halls,[4] our new churches, our promised
bishops, our Sunday beer bills,[5] our model lodging houses,[6] our

[4] Built near the Strand in 1831 and accommodating four thousand persons,
Exeter Hall was a kind of headquarters for dissenting Protestants, but it was
also used as a platform for social reformers, philanthropists, and educators.

[5] In 1854 Colonel Wilson-Patten introduced the controversial 'Sunday Beer
Act' which limited the sale of beer on Sunday to the hours of 1.00 to 2.30 and
6.00 to 10.00 p.m. Such legislation was aimed chiefly at controlling the drunken-
ness of the working classes.

[6] From the 1840s onward, various schemes for providing the labouring
classes with decent housing were attempted. Prince Albert's model lodgings,
erected near Hyde Park on the occasion of the Great Exhibition in 1851, were
merely the most publicized.

national and other schools, our fasts and prayers in times of war
and scarcity and disease,[7] our tickets of leave[8] and penetentiaries,
our Manchester School politics, our telegraph and steam engines,
we are really as much better than our forefathers as we undoubtedly ought to be. If not, if we be growing rather worse than
better; if we be increasing in wealth only, and not in worth; if we
be losing in heart and truth what we be gaining in intellect and
knowledge, then let us look to the Augustan Age of Rome, and
see how quick was the decadence of Roman power.

"But Romans were slaves to an Emperor," an Englishman will
say. "To an Emperor, or worse still to an Emperor's body guard.
Englishmen are free." Of all the beautiful creations of man's
fancy, freedom is the most lovely. True; if he were free, he might
all but live for ever. But of what nature is his freedom? Is the
prime minister free? The Queen cannot lock him up in a vile
dungeon, and feed him on bread and water, as King Bomba
would;[9] but can he be called free to speak or free to act, being
driven as he is to weigh every word and deed, not by its innate
propriety, but by its probable acceptation with the public press?
Is the member of Parliament free when he is driven in like a
sheep to the shambles to vote, not as he thinks, for the chances
are he has not thought at all, but according to the direction and
order of his leader? Is the elector free when he loses his farm or
his custom[10] if he votes for the candidate of his heart? Is the
barrister free, when he quibbles, and all but lies for his fee to
save some rascal from the gallows? Is the publican free when he
is forced to sell, either no beer at all, or else some compound
which he knows to be poison? Is the politician free to choose his
politics? 'Tis true he may read what newspaper he prefers; but
unless things mend, even that choice will soon be denied to him.

Free institutions are noble means for noble ends, but they will
hardly save us unless nobly carried out.

---

[7] On 18 March 1855, pulpits echoed the Queen's wish that a public day of
fast and prayer for peace be observed. *The Times* (23 May) editorialized that
although the fast had been 'rather against the grain ... we thought it right.'

[8] An 1853 law stipulated that transported convicts who had received terms
of seven or ten years might, after three or four years of good behaviour,
be given 'tickets of leave', i.e. paroled.

[9] *King Bomba*: King Ferdinand II of the Two Sicilies (1810-59), so nick-
named for his bombardment of Messina in 1849.

[10] *custom*: the obligation, in itself also a right, to pay dues or rent to a landlord.

Let us look to the palmy days of great Rome and see how
quick was the fall of its glory. Wealth and intellect, and all the
arts of war and peace were of no avail. Gilded statues, and
temples built as temples never were built before; foreign
dominion, and ships sailing free on every sea, did not save Rome
from its ruin. Nay, did they not hasten it? When we gaze now on
what is left of Rome, we have to acknowledge that its noblest
monuments were built during its decadence. Will the same have
to be said of us? Is our present wealth and present glory, our increasing luxury, our love of art, our polished intellect of which
we are so proud, are these things but signs of our decay? Is the
Zealander already coming to feed his pride with our fall?

We read in history of a French King, to whom the things of
this world had become so terribly dear and those of a future
existence so dimly tragic, that all the Court was forbidden to
speak of death before him.[11] It was treason to suggest an end to so
much power, or to whisper that so royal a life should ever close
in a cold earthy grave. But yet he died. Whether or no a nobler
course of thinking might have reconciled royalty to death, it is
not for us to inquire; but it would certainly have robbed the
grave of its terrors. Can we, however, believe that that feigned
silence on a subject so general to the mind of man deceived even
for an instant this wretched victim of unmanly fears? The
tongues of his creatures might be ruled, but not the unbidden
thoughts of his own breast. Death pale and horrid, death without
a hope, stood daily by his shoulder and told him from hour to
hour that he was dying, dying, dying.

We should, I conceive, be ashamed to think of ourselves as of
that French King; and yet we shall be guilty of the same folly
and with the same result, if we endeavour to persuade ourselves
that our national power can live forever. If it be that we must
die, let us look Death in the face, and see indeed if we cannot get
comfort even from him. Let us above all things not try to persuade ourselves that we are immortal. Every Englishman knows
in his heart that England will decay; though like the French
monarch, he may forbid those around him to wound his ears
with such a thought.

But though this nation may not exist forever, or continue

[11] Louis XV. See Carlyle's *The French Revolution*, I, iv.

through endless centuries to be respected as the greatest of the great, though she will decline as others have done before her, nevertheless to her has been vouchsafed a destiny higher than that of other nations. Of this fact history already speaks in words which cannot be misunderstood and cannot be altered. The blood and the language of Englishmen will be the blood and the language of the dominant race of mankind, whereas the lineal descendants of the mighty men who ruled in Nineveh are to be found in nomadic tribes all but unknown, and the children of the kings of Egypt are slaves. The tongues of Greece and Rome have become classic luxuries, languages without a people. Not only have the thrones of the Caesars fallen, but also the very blood and sinews and reality of the races over whom they ruled. It is not to be so with us. The New Zealander when he comes will speak in his native tongue to the English guide who will show him the wonders of London, and tell him half-true tales of her former history. Though the throne of our Kings and Queens may not prove itself to be less perishable than the seats of other monarchs, the language in which we speak and the mixed blood which is in our veins are destined to transfer themselves to other countries, which in their turn will become dominant, and will again in their turn fall away and decay.

And is not such a destiny as glorious as that of prolonged self-existence? Does not the father live again as happily, and with a purer happiness, in watching the growing virtues and comely manhood of his son? When his hair is grey, and his limbs are stiff with age, is not the strength of his child as pleasant to him as was his own?

Thus much the Author says, apologizing to Englishmen for speaking of the decadence of England. Our object should at any rate be to see that our country's decay be not hastened through fault of our own. Such should be the object of each of us, not collectively but individually. It is by the omission of individual duty that all nations have fallen. Could we each be perfect in our conduct to God and man, there would then be no fear that we should fall as a people. Such perfection is of course unattainable; but as each of us individually strives to attain it, in so far do we work successfully towards perpetuating the glory of our country.

These seem to be but trite truisms; but exactly as they are truisms, so is the necessity of our repeating them to ourselves.

If we are or can make ourselves an honest people, there may be hope that not in our time, nor that of our children or children's children, not in that of many coming ages, will the flag of which we are so proud have to lower itself before that of any nation which may float hither either from the East or from the West. But if this is not so, and cannot become so, why should we even wish that the power of England should endure? The hope of every man is that his children may be good and happy. If it be possible that they can be so here, here in our England, merry of old, and now so rich and prosperous, in God's name let us put our shoulders to the wheel, and see that goodness and happiness be prepared for them. But if that be not possible; if nothing but dishonesty, falsehood, and pretence be any longer possible, then indeed it will be better for us, not to talk only of the decadence of England, but to prepare for it boldly, and so to train our children that they may seek in other lands that excellence of content which they may be no longer allowed to find in their own.

CHAPTER II
The People and Their Rulers

W H E N the people of a country is spoken of, it may be said that the labour of that country is spoken of. So when the aristocracy is named, that power is named which is supposed to rule the labour of the country. This aristocracy, these foremen in the great workshop of the world, are chosen from among the people, from out of the ordinary labourers, and should be so chosen on account of their special worth and value in regulating the allotted tasks of those beneath them.

And this selection must be made by the people themselves. They must and do, sooner or later, choose their own rulers, their own aristocracy, let the choice be made in what way it will. The despot cannot rule but by sufferance, and sufferance itself is the apathetic choice of men not sufficiently alive to express their thoughts with articulate decision.

The aristocrat is chosen from the people and by the people; and profession is at any rate made that he is so chosen as being of all men the best able to rule and control their labours. It is for this purpose, and this purpose only, that an aristocracy is needed and supported. It is quite true that the choice once made, even though it be a bad choice, cannot at once be annulled. It is quite true that an aristocrat, when once elected as such, cannot be summarily ejected from his seat and sent back to hide his ignominy among the crowd, even though he be found vile and bad. The evil of such mistakes as these takes years, nay ages, for their cure. Therefore it is that of all human work to which a man's care and skill is summoned; in that work of choosing his ruler does it most behove him to use all the care and all the skill that he can compass.

One might almost say that were this choice in all cases rightly made, the evils of the world would cease. If labour were always duly ordered, labour would be duly done. If labour were duly done, there would then be an end to crime and poverty; soon also to that gross ignorance which is now the disgrace of the majority of us Englishmen.

How far this crime and poverty and ignorance are the necessary consequences of Adam's fall, it is not necessary here to inquire. This at least will be allowed by the most literal interpreter
of the sacred book, that it is enjoined on man to seek as best he
may the remedy for these evils. When the Lord said to Adam,
"In the sweat of thy face shalt thou eat bread till thou return
unto the ground," he so said it on expelling him from the bliss
of paradise. To Adam so expelled, to Adam who had tasted of
the joy of angels, to Adam who could not hope to taste of it
again, such a command was indeed a curse. To us who have as
yet known none other than mortal life, to us who hope, as Adam
could not hope, that the joy of angels shall yet be ours, to us such
an edict is a blessing rather than a curse, a subject for joy rather
than despair.

There is neither disgrace nor sorrow nor pain in labour well
ordered and well done. If men could but be brought to love their
labour, to do loving work, how nearly happy would they be even
here below! It is in order that men may so love their work that
they should be above all things careful to see that those set over
their work are fit for their high calling.

Labour having become the great necessity of our lives, the due
organization of labour became equally a necessity, and hence is
the origin of every aristocracy whatever. From the evil passions
of men wars arose; and the organization of the work of war, the
work which in olden times soon made itself of all the most
urgent, created a warrior aristocracy, aristocrats with iron fists
and bloodstained brows, men from whose eyes flashed rage
instead of love, men who learned how to repress, but hardly how
to govern; men most fitted indeed for the hard task which they
had in hand, but who knew nothing, and could know nothing of
the godlike work of a true governor of mankind. But these men
were all well chosen and did that which they had to do. We know
how Joshua was chosen to slaughter multitudes of kings and that
he did it. We know how Jehu drove furiously and would not hear
of peace, how he also slew princes by seventies—and the kinsfolk
and friends and priests of him against whom his wrath was
directed—and did not leave any of them alive. Such has been the
allotted work of warrior aristocracies.

On the whole, the proper men for this sort of work have been
well chosen. Joshua and Jehu were chosen by the Lord and

could not therefore fail. But the fitting disciples of Joshua and Jehu have mostly been forthcoming when wanted. By degrees, however, the work of the aristocracy has changed. Warrior lords are, alas, still needed; but their behests are not now, as of yore, all in all to us. Nay they are comparatively of small importance. May it not be argued of how small importance from the fact that here in England in the year 1856, no man can be discovered who has found it worth his while to make himself great in that line, to make himself really an aristocrat of war?

In days of yore, as we have said, the main duty of an aristocrat was to lead his people in war. No man indeed could be an aristocrat who had not the gift of doing so. Men were forced into wars defensive, who had even no desire for aggressive war; and there were few men who had no such desire but those who were too weak to attack their neighbours with hope of success. Might was respected but right was not.

> For why? Because the good old rule
>   Sufficed them, the simple plan,
> That they should take, who have the power,
>   And they should keep, who can.[1]

Such was the motto of the world at large, and the ruler of men then was required to be a leader or duke.

Things are changed now. Even in these immediately present lamentable days of battling, the chief warrior is by no means the chief man, nor is he considered to have the worthiest employment. As peace and plenty and good will among men are nobler than bloodshed, poverty, and hatred, so is the ruling of labour a nobler trade than the ruling of war. But one may safely say that either the one trade or the other is nobility itself compared with the mere pursuit of pleasure. Of all Kings, King Sardanapalus is the worst. Of all lords, the worst is he who seeks to rule only his own belly, and his own back, not even to rule them but to misrule them.

Of such ill-chosen aristocrats, of men who have thus utterly ignored their vocation and betrayed the trust reposed in them, the world has for many years had much cause to be sick. We Englishmen have had quite our own share of this nuisance.

---

[1] Wordsworth, 'Rob Roy's Grave', ll. 39-40; 'sufficeth' in Wordsworth.

Aristocrats of this class have had their full swing here, and thoroughly ashamed of them any Englishman should be who takes on himself to study the history of his country. The reaction in the feeling of the people caused by the downfall of the Puritans first gave popularity to a pleasure-seeking nobility. The bow had been bent too vigorously. Praisegod Barebones and his awfully stern code of morals had pressed too severely on mankind;[2] and thus when escape from him and it became possible, a code of a very different kind, a hero of a very different class, was chosen. To Praisegod Barebones we decidedly object; but on the whole we think him preferable to Lord Rochester and the Marquis of Hertford.[3]

One may say that an aristocracy of this nature was prevalent here from the blessed days of the return of Charles II to the close of those similarly blessed days of George IV. Periods there were during even this time when debauchery was somewhat less honoured than at others; but on the whole debauchery was the thing for English noblemen during the latter part of the seventeenth century, the whole of the eighteenth, and the earlier portion of the nineteenth. It is hardly necessary to refer to the writings of Pepys, Grammont, Walpole and Chesterfield and a host of others to prove that this was so. Could we summon any noble family from their noble vaults to bear witness to the fact, no noble family but would bear witness to its truth. The very idea that a prime minister should live with his wife a loving life and rigorously pay his tradesman's bills was, even to such a man as Sydney Smith, a subject of raillery.[4] What business could

---

[2] Praisegod Barebones, or Barebone or Barbon (1596?-1679), was a prominent member of Cromwell's assembly or 'little' Parliament of 1653. It was in fact referred to as 'Barebone's Parliament'; Macaulay called it 'the most intensely Puritanical of all our political assemblies', *History of England*, ed. C. H. Firth (Macmillan, London, 1913), I, 145 (Chap. ii).

[3] Trollope deleted but failed to replace these two names. Lord Rochester (1647-1680), the most famous courtier of Charles II's 'merry gang', was renowned for his escapades, seductions, wit, and obscene poetry. The Third Marquis of Hertford (1777-1842), influential associate of and vice chamberlain to the Regent, is best remembered as a symbol of corrupt luxurious living; he was the original for Lord Steyne in Thackeray's *Vanity Fair* and Lord Monmouth in Disraeli's *Coningsby*.

[4] The remarks which Trollope here attributes to Sydney Smith are not in Smith's published works; perhaps Trollope drew upon conversation or some other source which has not survived. As a young man Trollope met Smith; see T. H. S. Escott, *Anthony Trollope* (John Lane, London and New York, 1913), pp. 139-40.

an Englishman have in high places who owned domestic duties, and subjected himself to domestic shackles?

Of this evil however we are now mainly quit. The aristocracy of pleasure only is quickly becoming sufficiently unaristocratic. Lords there may be and Ladies too of this description, and commoners also, who consider themselves as appertaining to the highest aristocracy. But be their titles what they may, they are ceasing to be in any way the rulers of the people. For so much reform at any rate may God be thanked.

We are apt to attribute this reform to the example of the Court. It is, however, much more probable that the Court has followed the bias of the nation, as the Court has ever done and must ever do. This is said without any wish to derogate from the virtues of those in high places, who at any rate have in this respect fully met the wishes of the people. But no amount of sternest moral principle in the bosom of two or of two dozen princes could change the course of a great nation's aristocracy. Such change has been effected by the improved education and higher religious feeling of the times. Such change has carried with it all the upper classes from the Court downwards, and there is much in it for which God should be heartily thanked. It cannot be said that the evil is utterly cured. We cannot altogether change our chosen aristocrats, even though they steadily refuse to do their duty. A sporting marquis with an enormous rent roll still has very many of the duties of a ruler to perform, and may still, and occasionally does still, decline to perform them. But take any sporting marquis who is that and *nothing else*, and any great working Railway Contractor, and it will be found that of the two, the Railway Contractor has the most to say towards the ruling of the country. He is everywhere admitted to be the better aristocrat of the two.

The tendency of the age is to seek for true aristocrats, if only it can find them. That they are to be found no Englishman and no Christian should doubt. Only let us take the proper mode. Only let us honour the true aristocrat when we do find him; and not begrudge him the power we are fain to entrust to him, with a jealousy beyond that which ever urged the Athenians of old to ostracise the best of their citizens.

True aristocrats there are, and will be, forthcoming; but it is necessary that they be treated as such. What true man, oh

reader, will serve you or me, if from the first moment of his
service we doubt his truth, suspect his honour, decry his motives,
and gainsay his actions? What decent steward would on such
terms manage for us our farms, or what foreman take charge of
our tills? How then shall the best among us be forthcoming to
rule the state, if the best, when we have got him, is so treated by
us?

Young men gifted with large fortunes and bearing illustrious
names do not think it necessary to eschew thought and study,
and to live debauched lives. The heir to an Earldom does not, as
a matter of course, and merely because he is such, keep a harem
of opera dancers. Nevertheless such men are more distrusted
than they were when there was such ground for distrust. We
now hear much to the prejudice of the English aristocracy, and
are told daily of our danger because the rule of the country is
altogether in aristocratic hands. Would that it were! In what
other hands can the rule of any country be safely placed? For
what purpose have we an aristocracy here among us, if it be not
that they may rule and guide us rightly?

The main duty of all aristocrats, and we may say their only
duty, is to govern; and the highest duty of any aristocrat is to
govern the state. The greatest writers, when speaking of ambition,
have spoken of it as a vice. "That last infirmity of noble minds,"[5]
is Milton's thought of ambition, when he wished to think of it
at the best; and so says Shakespeare also, who tells us of "Vault-
ing ambition, that o'er-leaps itself,"[6] and declares of Caesar that
if he were ambitious "'twas a grievous fault."[7]

In the face of such heavy weight of argument how shall a poor
essayist dare to say that among human virtues ambition should
be held, if not first, at least in the first rank? Yet is it not so? Is
it not ambition that prompts the noblest of men "To scorn
delights and live laborious days"?[8] To all men unmitigated un-
relenting labour is in itself grievous; nay more, to all men such
labour is impossible, unless the inward spirit be sustained by
ambition. Yet it is by labour such as this, and by such labour
only, that the duties of a great statesman can be performed. Is it
no virtue in a man to devote days and nights to the service of the
state with no reward but that which ambition gives? To be

[5] 'Lycidas', l. 71.   [6] *Macbeth*, I. vii. 27.   [7] *Julius Caesar*, III. ii. 85.
[8] 'Lycidas', l. 72.

pointed at with the finger as the guardian of his country is the
great ambition of the English statesman; and can such ambition
be other than a virtue?

But ambition loves power, and power is dangerous—therefore
ambition is a vice. It is true that ambition loves power, but by
no means true that power is dangerous. Indeed we may say that
nothing can be so dangerous as the lack of a man capable of
being powerful. Nothing, but that envy which forbids us to use
such a man when we have found him. This is the rock on which
we are splitting; the same rock on which so many other state
crafts have been driven to their ruin. It is not the ambition of
our ruling men that is our bane, but the envy with which grati-
fied ambition is regarded.

A man among us who devotes himself to public matters no
sooner rises to high employment than he becomes the mark for
abuse of every description. He is found to be endowed with
Bœotian stupidity, or faithlessness worse than Carthaginian,[9] or
malignity that would not disgrace the Devil. He is as corrupt
as Verres,[10] fuller of pride than Wolsey, as unscrupulously crafty
as Machiavelli. Low threatenings of impeachment are murmured
round his ears, and the mildest terms in which his opponents
address him are those of a vote of want of confidence. His chief
duty is to be baited like a bull at the stake by any honourable
member who chooses to question either his truth, his integrity, or
his discretion. To questions put to him with all the venom which
spleen can dictate, he must answer not only rapidly and willingly, but with courtesy also and good humour. But woe to him
if his good humour approach to mirth, or if his courtesy be
accompanied by a smile. In such case he will commit the high
misdemeanor of joking over the wants of his country.

Rapidly, willingly, and with courtesy must he answer; but,
alas, not with truth. That were too much for a man so questioned.
The vessel of the state must be kept on its track. If every little
leak be owned and confessed to, all hands would be required at
the pump. The opponents of the minister oppose him on the
high principle that nothing imperfect should be admitted in the
state's governance. That much must be imperfect the minister

[9] Cf. Sallust, *Jugurtha*, 108. 3, *Punica fide*: 'With Carthaginian faith ...'
[10] Gaius Verres (115?-43 B.C.), notoriously corrupt governor of Sicily (73-71
B.C.), against whom Cicero spoke so effectively.

knows well, and his adversaries as well; the indignant writer of the thundering article in the morning newspaper knows it equally; the world all know it; but the minister is lost if he owns to the smallest peccadillo that human infallibility can commit. It is the trade of the opponent to attack, it is the trade of the newspaper to be indignant, it is the trade of the minister to defend; and the world looks on believing none of them.

Yes. Let a minister answer rapidly, willingly, courteously, nay jocosely if such be his role; but never truly. If truth appear to him necessary let him retire at once to his Sabine farm.

Yes—at once to his Sabine farm—

> Were it not better done as others use,
> To sport with Amaryllis in the shade,
> Or with the tangles of the Neæra's hair?[11]

Either that, or feed big oxen which will ask no venomous questions, or breed low backed, grateful pigs that will give due return for the care that is given to them.

There is very much in this to degrade the high profession to which the ambitious aristocrat has devoted himself, but we cannot on that account blame the ambition that has prompted him. Indeed we can only admire it, and hope that days may come when public virtue and public power may no longer be called on to wade so deep in mire. If it be otherwise, if it come to that, that public virtue and public power can no longer act together, then indeed the ambition of ruling will be a vice, and the ambition too of living under such rule will be equally vicious.

But the main work of aristocrats in this country must henceforth be to the due governance of labour; and it seems, one may say, plain enough that as this work is done or left undone, this country which we all love so well must sink or swim. Is our work well governed now? Is it so governed that, putting aside exceptional cases, a man may always earn what he is worth, and never earn more? Is it so well governed that the work of a man's body may coexist with the work of his soul? that the two shall not fight against each other? Is it so governed that a man's work shall always tend to ennoble him—never to debase him? Labour has surely a claim to be so governed; should surely be taught to look for such governance. It does look for it in this England of

[11] 'Lycidas', ll. 67-9.

ours, and failing to find it, grumbles forth low murmurs very inarticulate, and seeks relief in other lands. If a fitting aristocracy cannot organize itself here to rule the labour of the people, an Australian aristocracy for such purpose will not be wanting.

Look at a founder's yard. He does not turn his men into the furnaces each to work at his own portion of the trade without guidance. He has a manager; and under him foremen over every branch of his business, and under them every gang of labourers has its own head. Each foreman has been selected for his double skill: his skill in the management of metal, and his skill in the management of men. And each foreman has also a double interest: firstly, that the master should get his due profit, and then that the men should give only their due labour. It is for qualities such as these that a nation of labourers should select their foremen. A good foreman will make good workmen, and every good workman will be proud of his work. All labour that is hateful, all labour of which the labourer cannot be proud, will be debasing, but all labour that he loves will help to rouse his intellect and to wake whatever mind there may be within him. Look at the ploughman as he turns the furrow—speak to him, and see if he ever aspires to be much higher than the brute he drives. If indeed the farmer will treat him as a brute, if the greatest number of furrows at the lowest possible wages be the only object of the farmer, how can he be more? Has not this man been, as it were, given up to the farmer body and soul to use as it seemeth good to him, provided only that the serf and his little serflings be just fed so that the power of labour be maintained within them? On Sundays he is told that before God's throne the poor and the rich shall stand alike, and that he has a soul within him to be saved on condition that he be obedient, docile, contented, laborious, and that above all he believe rightly the incarnation of our Lord Jesus Christ. He sits gaping on his low stool, ever and anon smoothing his thin hairs with his horny hand, waiting with vacant mind but not impatient till the minister shall let him go, and then he lolls at ease upon the ground which during six days of every week he turns and rakes and turns again with so much torpid labour.

Can it be that we would laugh at this creature when we declare to him such conditions for his heavenly salvation, and require from him such a catalogue of earthly virtues, offering him so vile an earthly reward? He must rightly believe the incarnation of our Lord Jesus Christ! He can rightly believe nothing, but that bread and cheese will appease hunger, that beer will drown care, and that neither bread nor cheese nor beer will be forthcoming unless farmer Giles' furrows be duly turned.

But teach the ploughman once to rejoice in his furrows, and see how changed the man becomes. His mouth is opened and he speaks of his handicraft; the usual dullness of his eye is gone; he stretches himself to his full height, and begins to feel what it is to think. Ambition has already warmed his heart, and made a man of him. Heretofore he was in truth indeed hardly better than a brute.

Let us get a view of some man who really loves the work he is doing, and see how well that work is done. Our labour is generally so ill-governed that it is hard to find that man, but yet such may be discovered. Here—here is one who works night after night, with unceasing labour during the quiet hours when ordinary mortals delight to rest. For six, eight, ten hours at a stretch, he continues at his work indomitable. 'Tis one continued process of muscular labour, and that not of the lightest kind. It is labour not of the lightest but unfortunately most unprofitable, and yet he loves it. Yes, loves it with his innermost heart, with his very soul. If we could command such work as that, there would be no fear that the days of the Zealander's visit were coming nigh to us.

This man is playing at the game of billiards. Alas, alas, though thus indomitably zealous in his calling no good can be got from this young man. To many occupations besides that of billiard playing have his sad parents tried to inure him. They dreamt of the bar, but could not induce him to wade through the first chapter of Blackstone. They sent him to a merchant's counting house, but the merchant soon sent him back again. They desired him to walk the hospital, but he would walk nothing but the billiard room. They got him into a government office, but he was declared to be unfit even for that. Oh—if it could but be arranged that playing at billiards should be held to be a useful, reputable, decorous, money making occupation, with what an excellent son would these now disconsolate parents find themselves to be blessed!

See the industry, the patience, the skill, the forethought, the mechanical ingenuity of the man! How he labours against adversity! How he watches his opportunity! How he uses it when it comes! How he counts the chances of the table, calculates the strength of his own hand to the last quarter of an ounce, and is always prepared for every turn of the game! Had this man been in the Crimea and been appreciated, surely one should have taken the Redan![12] If other men could but love their work as he does!

But this fellow is at play. Of course he likes play. All the world is diligent enough when called upon to amuse itself. True. It is much to be lamented that this fellow is at play. That instead of earning bread honestly, he is doing whatever in him lies to waste the bread of other people most dishonestly. True: he is journeying by no means towards God, but straight towards the Devil. His zeal is worse than useless; every hour of labour helps to strip his back of his last coat and to bring him nearer to that anguish of soul which attends on self-earned merited poverty. This is quite true. Diligent, skilful, crafty as he is, his diligence, skill, and craft will never lead to good result.

But does not the question then arise whether such diligence, skill, and craft might not have led to good result, if well directed? Had that ponderous legal tome been pressed upon the youth with more discretion, had the hours of the work and the nature of the work in that merchant's counting house been less appalling; had our young friend been led in among the scalping knives and bandages of Guy's Hospital with a gentler hand, might not something have been made of him? Because amusement is seductive, is it necessary that work should be made as little seductive as possible?

It would appear that the world has consented to an arrangement by which work and amusement shall be considered as the opposites of each other; by which also the one shall be regarded as as undesirable in itself as the other is the reverse. It cannot be that such an arrangement is necessary. Work will of course produce fatigue, and cessation from work will thus become desirable; but the same thing may be said of any sport in which men

[12] *The Redan*: a seemingly unconquerable Russian fortification outside of Sebastopol. Raglan had ordered its bombardment on 17 June 1855, and on the following day many British troops were massacred in an unsuccessful assault upon it. Raglan died ten days later.

or women, boys or girls, engage. The very same pursuits are the work of one set of men, and the play of another. Look at a crew of Cambridge students training for a rowing match. Do they not work harder than any labouring waterman? Look at that young scion of a noble house, as he drives the "Last of the Visigoths" from Brighton up to town.[13] He does for amusement that which a trained coachman looks on as a good day's work. The truth is that these men have learnt to love such work.

It would be absurd to argue that this world's work, work which was Adam's doom, work which requires the sweat of our brows and the struggles of our brains, can be so managed as to become no harder task than a child's play; but it may be managed that all work can, and should become full of interest to the worker. The young Cambridge freshman who sticks to his oar till the skin peels from his unused hands, undergoes much of the hardship of labour, but he has an interest in the matter, and puts up with the pain. What are sore fingers and blistered palms to a youth who has an ambition to pull in the first Trinity? Or what pain do twelve hours of furrow turning give to a man who hopes that the country will look on him, and proclaim him the best furrow turner in the parish?

Thou sore stricken man, thou who realizeth so thoroughly the ancient doom of Adam, thou who workest wearily ten hours a day through thy sad tedious life, not doing things which thy heart can long to see done, not looking eagerly for the accomplishment of thy work, but only for the accomplishment of thy ten tedious hours, think well of this. Take it to thy breast and there consider it with all the thought that be in thee. It is for thee the one question of this world. There is but one other that is mainly important, and unless thou canst answer this to thy satisfaction, neither canst thou that.

Is it good for thee that thou shouldst be a labouring machine, cursed however as no iron machine is cursed, with the power of suffering, and the gift of weariness? And if it be not good, is it necessary? May it not be that no such dire necessity exists? That thou shouldst work with thy hands or brain and earn bread to fill thy maw, that clearly is necessary. If that be indeed a curse, the curse must be endured. But surely it is worth thy while to

---

[13] *Last of the Visigoths*: presumably a fictitious name. It was not unusual for noblemen to drive stage coaches for amusement.

question this as thou walkest along daily through the files of thy brethren. There are men to whom their work is interesting enough. Yes, thou answerest. There are such men. It is the money profit of their work that these men love. Give me work with money profit; profit over and above my weekly wages, and I also will love it.

Oh, man, if on no other terms than these thou canst be gotten to love thy work, thou must go on, and suffer. Creep on, thou base one, and let thy soul rot, steeped in the stagnant pool of thy unmanly apathy. Thou at any rate canst do nothing for thy country. Thou at any rate knowest not what it is to stretch thyself towards heaven, and feel that Adam's burden is dropping from thy back. If it be given thee but to guide a poor jade as she turns the windlass of a mill, thou may'st love even that work. Thou may'st love even that poor jade, and guide her to the very best of the power that be in thee.

It is not, however, possible that men should regard their work with interest unless those who set their tasks set them with proper care. It is for this mainly that we want and elect rulers, that they may set to each man his portion of work, reward those who duly do it, and punish those who neglect it. If this be not done, it must be that we have not chosen our masters rightly. That some right masters are chosen there seems to be evidence enough. Do we not hear of ships in which every man will work as though the honour of the British Empire depended solely on him? There is no hope of money profit here. We have heard also of a public office in which every clerk was an honour to the Crown. There is certainly no hope of money profit here. Do we not see houses in which each servant will labour as though all within was his own, and yet without thought of increased wages? In such cases the men have been well governed, and taught to love their work. It is well for them. The world's work to them has nothing in it to distress them.

To eat our bread in the sweat of our face is to us a necessity, but not to eat it in the blood of our hearts. It is not necessary that every uplifting of the muscular arm should be followed by groans and agony. Work screwed up to the point of agony, deprived of all interest in itself, reduced below the doings of the beast, does not vent itself in our days in shrieks and howls very appalling. Distressed needlewomen for a while make their sad

plaints heard, and genius energetic in their cause sends forth to
the world that terrible song of the shirt. Factory children are
protected by law against their parents and masters. Governesses
advertised for at £10 a head appeal to the compassion of Newspaper Editors.[14] And Dorsetshire and other labourers make
known their low estate by rude murmurs hardly articulate. Spasmodic eruptions are made by suffering humanity, and some
partial relief is attempted when mortal endurance can bear no
more.

Should not most trades in these days have their song of the
shirt?

> Work—work—work
> Till the brain begins to swim.
> Work—work—work
> Till the eyes are heavy and dim!
> Work! work! work!
> While the cock is crowing aloof,
> Work—work—work,
> Till the stars shine through the roof!
> Work—work—work!
> My labour never flags;
> And what are its wages? A bed of straw,
> A crust of bread—and rags.[15]

It is not needlewomen only who may with truth utter such
complaints as this. Their condition is bad, but so is that of such
multitudes of their sisters and brethren that no pre-eminence in
wretchedness can be allowed to any class.

Let him who would inquire into this go among miners, and
see what is their state. We are proud of the metals and great
smelting houses of Cornwall, Glamorganshire, and Monmouth-
shire. We are proud of the coalpits of Durham and Yorkshire.
But no Englishman can be proud of the state of the men labouring in these hives of industry. Let him who would see and know
penetrate into those strange and monstrous villages which in

---

[14] *The Times*, 13 Oct. 1855, printed a letter to the editor from 'A Poor
Governess' who called attention to the advertisement and suggested that *The
Times* call a meeting in the interest of the 'Abolition of Slavery in England'.
[15] Thomas Hood, 'The Song of the Shirt', first published in the Christmas
Number of *Punch*, 1843. Trollope's punctuation has been regularized, but his
order kept: he has quoted the first four lines of stanzas three, two, and six.

late years have sprung up on the hill-sides of Glamorganshire, and talk awhile to the dusky denizens who work beneath the soil, and he will hardly think that British energy is well cared for, and well rewarded. Sichem and Salem, Sion and Ebenezer are there. Among the Dissenters there is so much energy that they do not fail to build chapels and find preachers be they good or bad. But Sichem and Salem have done little towards civilization. Sion and Ebenezer have altogether failed to rival the attractions of gin, or to redeem the place from that look of hell which unrestrained immorality and uninspired labour have produced.

Or go into the quiet cornfields of heavy Wiltshire, and talk awhile with the clod pulling rustic. He is more simple than his brother of the Welsh foundry, but hardly nearer to a state of true manly existence. You can almost doubt within yourself whether or not this man has really a living soul within him. In what does this man differ from the brute, except that he will drink more than his thirst requires, and eat, if he can get it, more than his hunger needs? Nothing hitherto has been done towards civilizing him. No effort has yet been made towards teaching him to love his work and respect himself. It may be a hard task for an Englishman to bring home to himself and realize the fact; but it is the fact that in most of those countries which we delight to look on as lagging behind ourselves in the march of intellect, the state of the labourer of the soil is less debased than it is with us.

Who can see the German peasant dancing with his sweetheart or wife, with his sister or even with his fellow labourer, and not feel that he has a lighter heart and easier task than his brother in England? Who can see the gay Italian laughing in all his Sunday pride, or the stout Tyrolese with his rifle to his shoulder, or the gay Frenchman with his easy chatter, and not feel the same.

No Government, no Cabinet, no Minister can produce the change that is needful in this matter. No Houses of Parliament can pass a law that shall be efficient to make labour respected and respectable. Laws they may pass by dozens with their assumed omnipotence, but they will be wholly inoperative. People cannot suddenly be made great and good by the wisdom of a Jew.[16] Every aristocrat may do much in his own sphere;

---

[16] An obvious reference to Disraeli. Cf. below, p. 134.

be he an aristocrat over thousands of acres, or an aristocrat over hundreds of factory children, or simply the humblest of aristocrats guiding some score of men in a founder's yard.

The task of each is the same. To each it has been given to rule the work of others. From each will be demanded not only that he has well done his own duty in his own state, but also that those under him have been encouraged so to do. No farmer that employs a ploughman and a carter can divest himself of this responsibility; no small grocer to whom is entrusted the care of a single shopboy can be exempt from the necessity of answering as to his amount of governance. No father of a household under whose roof two red armed maidens earn their humble bread, but has on his shoulders so much of the burden of an aristocrat. It is by individual efforts, and by such only, that the evil complained of can be remedied.

Money profit from labour that is paid for is very necessary. Rent for lands let out to tenants is necessary. Due amount of useful work, usefully done in compensation for bread and meat, is necessary. But woe to him who looks on money profit from labour as the one only care that his labourers should give him. Woe to him who owns houses and lands and troubles himself only for the rent. Such men are the drones in the hive who make no honey for the public use. Such are they who will be most angry to hear of the decadence of England, and yet do all that in them lies to hasten that decay. Such men have never learnt the true value of labour, either for themselves or for others. They know not that every blow of the hammer well struck may give, not only bread but also joy to the striker, not only profit but also honour and glory to the master.

No Cabinet or Minister can set these matters right. But every Cabinet and Minister may do something, be the Cabinet in Downing Street or in Glamorganshire; let the Minister have his ministration in politics or in iron founding. The country must foster in itself a spirit which shall pay more honour to labour, which shall give to labour a better chance of becoming in the first place human, and then godlike. Otherwise, labour which is now all but brutal will hasten downwards till it be devilish. Labour such as that will maintain no nation in prosperity.

When the gold diggings of Melbourne first opened to the

British eyes so dazzling a picture of sudden wealth,[17] strange tidings reached us of the fortunes of those who crowded to those dazzling shores. Men with soft hands and unused muscles, who could quote a line or two of Virgil, and had solved equations, found themselves the menial servants of rough labourers of the soil. Girls who had been tenderly nurtured, and who fondly hoped that their accomplishments might earn for them comfort in this region of wealth, were forced to serve, and hardly would be allowed to serve, the daughters of their fathers' herdsmen. All seemed to have been rough, and much seems to have been unpleasant in this new land of promise; but labour nevertheless was and is honoured there. Labour there will not allow itself to be compensated only by bread sufficient to maintain life and beer sufficient to drown care. Labour there will have itself decently housed and decently fed and clad; soon also decently instructed. Is it not a fact that even already labourers' children there are better schooled than are those of our labourers here?

If these things be so, labour will not remain here to have the character and rewards of a brute, when it need only travel thither to find itself honoured by usage fit for a man. Let us look to Ireland and see how it is there. Seven short years ago how were the workmen of the soil treated? They were called the scum of the earth, the dregs of humanity, the "crablice" of creation. They were surplus population; burdensome paupers; the curse of the country. The work of their hands was not worth the bread that could keep them alive. Bread! no it was not worth the four pound of Indian corn meal, valued at one penny the pound which, according to strict economical calculation, would suffice to keep together the skeleton bodies and their souls of a father, mother, and their offspring.[18]

Irishmen could not realize to themselves then that not only the wealth of a country, but all its honour also, all its dignity among nations, must depend on its labour. They are beginning

[17] Although small finds had been made since 1839, Trollope is undoubtedly referring to the great discovery at Ballarat, 9 August 1851.

[18] Sir Robert Peel had first purchased Indian corn from the United States for Ireland in 1845. See *The Times*, 2 April 1846, for an account of the Relief Committee at Cork which sold corn meal at cost, viz. a penny a pound. Cecil Woodham-Smith quotes Sir Lucius O'Brien as reporting in April of 1847 that the poor were 'only just kept alive' on a pound of corn meal a day. *The Great Hunger: Ireland 1845-1849* (Harper & Row, New York, 1962), p. 295.

to learn the lesson, now that their labourers have gone from them.

. Every day the work of the workman, as compared with the work of his ruler, is becoming entitled to more honour than it has hitherto received. This is fully understood among some people; and it would be well for us that we could also understand it. The days are gone when a man could put his head into an iron pot, and his breast into an iron case, and go off to the wars, followed by his henchmen, there to meet peril and death in which the henchmen fully shared, or else honour and glory which the warrior kept all to himself. Now-a-days the henchmen will have a fairer share of what good things are doing. Who will deny this right? It will be well for those who seek to be the rulers of the people if they see that this right be respected. Otherwise, the people left to them will soon become little worth the ruling.

CHAPTER III
The Press

T H E most interesting question of the present day in England may perhaps be said to be this. Is public opinion to guide the Press or be guided by it? In other words, do men as a rule look to a newspaper for a mere reflex of their own opinions; or do they prefer to save themselves the trouble of forming any, and thus adopt without the labour of thought such as certain writers of the day may think fit to promulgate? This certainly is now a question of great import. From a true answer to this question, and from that only, shall we learn what is henceforward to be the ruling power in England.

It will be said, and said truly, that neither is wholly the case; that the two things act in a circle; that public opinion first forms the newspapers, and that the newspaper then reacts on public opinion; that no definite answer can be given to such a question; and that it must be left to every individual to settle for himself how far he will look into matters with his own eyes, or how far he will use the sharper sight of a newspaper editor.

This will be said, and said truly; and yet a thinking man will in these days hardly be satisfied with such an answer to such a question. It is true that no newspaper could live for a day which commenced its operations without supporting a code of thought endeared to some section of the community; but it is equally true that no successful newspaper will ever be content with so limited a sphere of action. Success is always ambitious.

When we hear of the fourth estate, of the omnipotence of the Press, nay, not infrequently of its infallibility, more is meant than that this Press is or should be the mere reflex of public opinion. It is sufficiently notorious that newspaper writers now assume to themselves a higher destiny than this; that they are by no means content to follow whither their readers lead them; that it is not sufficient for them even to be mere guides. Once they guided; then they would lead; now they drive.

Of course it is conceded that no newspaper can flourish unless supported by public opinion. Men will not buy that which they do not in some way value. Neither can any tyrant reign, or any demogogue disturb a state unless so supported also. A people's favourite is the worst tyrant whom a people can fear, and of all such favourites none can be so tyrannical, so irresponsible, so unapproachable, so far beyond punishment as a newspaper of the present day.

A false monarch has but one head, which, if such dire necessity exist, may fall by one blow. A newspaper may have 60,000 throats, and each throat require a dozen blows to silence it.

Of most of our existing institutions experience has shown us what should be the use, what may be the abuse. We live mostly according to customs and rules which have slowly grown up among us, and we know with tolerable accuracy what should be the condition and extent of jurisdiction of all those who bear authority among us. This, however, is essentially not so with the newspaper Press. Newspapers, such as they have become in this year of our Lord 1856, are a new institution. They form a power foreign to the constitution of which Englishmen perhaps boast a little too often; and have become so dominant that the method of rule in the country is becoming far different from what it was and would be but for this interference.

It does not therefore follow that such interference must be an evil. It may be that it is an unmixed good. But it does follow that a power of which the constitution has hitherto known nothing has newly and rapidly grown up among us; and that it behoves us at any rate to see whether such power be for good or evil.

No one in fact knows what is the duty of the daily Press. That we have to arrange and fix among ourselves. The duty of the Crown is sufficiently fixed. That of the ministers, of the judges, and great officers of the state is fixed. The duties of the aristocracy are sufficiently plain and marked. Those of the Parliament are either confined within certain rule, or, if left unconfined, are so left by rule also. The duty of the people, that namely of earning their bread honestly by the sweat of their brow, that too is closely fixed, and, if not done, is left undone at the heavy peril of the delinquent. The duties of most active men, one may say, are fixed. But not so the duties of a newspaper or of a newspaper writer.

Reader, canst thou suppose now that thou art called upon to

write suddenly a leading article for some powerful daily news-paper, and that the subject given thee is the last act of some minister of the day? Suddenly now write—*currente calamo.*[1] See, it is near midnight, and at 5 A.M. this hitherto unwritten article of thine must fly forth on the wings of the Press to the furthermost corners of the globe.

How wilt thou write it now? It is given to thee that thou canst write it, and write it well. All manner of proficiency in the art is allowed thee. Sarcasm and burning indignation are at thy dis-posal; or eulogy that shall not be insipid; or deep mystery able to write and write for ever without committing itself. The trick of the following paragraph is thine own, or of the curt, sententious statement. Write, but write quickly.

But what wilt thou write? Or whose opinion wilt thou thus make so public? What is thy duty in this matter, of thee who art to be paid so high for this skill of thine? Wilt thou express public opinion in this matter? The people have much clamoured against this minister; his doings have cost much and brought no glory; wilt thou therefore write him down with bitterest obloquy?

Or stay, that Editor and Manager who is over thee has an opinion in this matter, a well known opinion, or perhaps rather a well known purpose. Is he not thy Editor and Manager? What he would have thee express, is it not clearly thy duty to write that?

But stay again. This newspaper has surely had some line of conduct of its own; some fixed course with reference to this great man. It has perhaps admitted the failure of his counsels, but attributed the fault to his underlings. So have preceding articles been written. Write, as I bid thee, says the Editor, and write quickly.

The truth, sayst thou. Thou wilt write the truth! How is the truth known to thee in these matters? In these matters there is no truth. There is but opinion which for certain purposes is to be made public. The truth! Let us see this truth of thine.

"Touching the conduct of this minister in this matter nothing yet seems clearly to be known. Till the counsel which he has given be proved by subsequent events no opinion can with safety be expressed. It may be that he has been deficient in energy, but caution was doubtless—"

[1] *currente calamo*: with a running pen.

Out with thee. Out from that desk, thou lily-livered newsman. Out with thee and thy scruples, and thy truth. Out with thee and for ever. What is it to the world what thou thinkest, to the world looking out so eagerly this morning for opinion that may be called public? Thy opinion indeed! Was it for that thou wast brought hither? Who knows aught of thy opinion? That thou canst write sentences in glib language was indeed known. To write sentences was thy duty. Hadst thou for a while done that, hadst thou been trained to think in the school of this great newspaper, then indeed and by degrees might public opinion to some extent have been modelled also by thee. But now—out with thee at once, with thee and with thy scruples.

These questions are certainly difficult to answer. What should be the duty of a newspaper writer, and what the duty of a newspaper? The result, however, as regards ourselves at the present moment is very evident, and not very consolatory. We are bolstering up among ourselves a power that already shows us with sufficient absence of reserve that it knows how to use a despot's hand and a despot's voice. This despot claims to rule by the suffrages of the educated and the voice of public opinion. Such claim also makes the Czar of Russia. If the Russians choose to be serfs, whose affair is that? If we also so choose, who shall gainsay us? Alas no, none can gainsay us. No one can gainsay a prodigal who squanders his rich patrimony, or a luckless people that throws away its dignity.

A newspaper is in its origin a mere article of trade. The owner embarks his capital in it, and his first desire is profit. If he be an honest man, his main object will be profit with a conscientious performance of duty on his part.

As soon, however, as the success of a newspaper has become considerable, and the profits large, the property in it is generally divided among many, but not so the management. At any rate the property and the management go into separate hands, and whereas profit is the object of the owners, success, notoriety, and power are naturally the ambition of the manager.

And the two objects are so blended that the employer and the employed may well agree in the matter. The greater is the power of the writer's pen, the larger will be the profit in the owner's pocket; the larger also the profit of the owner, the more extensive will be the power and influence of the writer.

Had we been considering this subject some fifty years ago, we should probably have thought that any alarm on the subject was quite unnecessary. We should have declared that the field of the newspaper influence was so open to all, and that the certainty of antagonistic influence was so complete that any fear of a too dominant newspaper was preposterous. Even since those days any one remembering the tough battles of the Eatanswill Gazette and its rival contemporary[2] would have been inclined to say that one journal would always keep another in order. Now, however, we have among us a journal which none other can keep in order. One, which if not kept in order by itself, must go on out of order. One which is the sole judge of what sort of order is good for itself. One that no man may attempt to moderate with impunity. One without a competitor, without a rival, that has distanced all competition, silenced all rivalry, put down all enemies, made itself above all reproach; one that has at any rate given proof of its own power sufficiently clear to all men in England. One newspaper is "the Press." All others together fail to make up, not only an even balance, but any sort of counterpoise whatsoever. The Times with us is the Press.

Such a consummation cannot but be gratifying to those whose genius and industry have brought about so singular a result, but it may well be doubted whether it should be gratifying to an Englishman. Such success is not only gratifying but honourable to those who have achieved it, but it need not therefore be less injurious to the country.

We are not among those who regard ambition as a crime; no, nor even as an infirmity. The ambition of ruling is a noble feeling, and no country devoid of men thus ambitious can hope to be great in the world's annals. A Cincinnatus at his plough,[3] or an Oliver among his oxen,[4] is not usually to be found, fit to come out from such work and rule mankind. Men must train themselves for such high calling, and may perhaps go through such training on the staff of a newspaper as effectually as elsewhere.

---

[2] *Eatanswill Gazette*: See *Pickwick Papers*, Chap. xiii.

[3] Legend pictures Cincinnatus as leaving his small farm to become dictator of Rome in the sixth century B.C.

[4] Oliver Cromwell farmed at Huntingdon, St. Ives, and Ely before assuming his leading military and political roles. See Carlyle, *Oliver Cromwell's Letters and Speeches, with Elucidations*, ed. H. D. Traill (Chapman & Hall, London, 1897), I, 69-70 *et passim*.

But not the less on that account should we guard against such ambition, and check such power if it become too dominant.

Many men may aspire to rule most beneficently; and such aspirations are respectable. But we are not on that account to admit all such men as our rulers.

No man who uses a pen can do other than desire power. When a man sends a written article on his broad sheet forth to the world, it is but natural that he should wish to endow his words with eloquence, and to engraft his thoughts on the minds of others. The doing so is power.

Of such nature has always been the power of the Press, since a free Press existed. But never till now has that power been monopolized as it is now, and never till now has it become a strong political power in this country. Now, one may say, such power is not only politically strong but seeks to be politically supreme. If this be so, it is surely time for Englishmen to see whether such a state of things be honourable or beneficial.

But if such power be fairly gained may it not be fairly used? Alas, no power not under control is fairly used by men. It is the nature of man that he cannot see what is right for himself to do. He must be guided by other eyes than his own. The best of us, and those too who are fitly instructed with the highest duties, must walk according to the counsel of others.

Any power that is uncontrolled becomes despotic, tyrannic, overbearing, and at last unendurable.

Who is to guarantee that such power as that now exercised by the Times newspaper shall be safely used, safely, that is, as regards the best interests of the country? The public, we shall be told; the public who purchase and support it. True. There is no other guarantee. As long as this journal can sell itself with success so far exceeding that of all others no further guarantee can be exacted. The Press is responsible only to its purchasers. If the article be not good, people will not buy it.

It is so easy to beg a question. True, if an article be bad, people will not buy it; but this article is not bad. It is rather very good, the best of its kind ever produced—excellent, inimitable, and cheap withal. But yet so dangerous. It is in its excellence that its danger lies.

Were some uncommonly clever fellow to produce here in England brandy of the very best description, brandy quite equal to

Cognac, and sell it at half the present cost of gin; one could not say that the brandy was bad because one found the bad effect of such sale in a double quantity of drunken tiplers. The brandy would be good; but it would be well for us if this fellow had hid his light under a bushel.

So is the newspaper good, if it be good in a newspaper to be readable. One pays for it, reads it, and condemns; but still pays, and reads again. And thus with still increasing power the great Leviathan rears his head and roars; and other powers stand by and shake and shiver, and strive in vain to guess what the next roar may signify.

Vain hope! Why should an increasing Leviathan, now grown audacious and past all fear, give to an obsequious crowd of listeners any hint as to his future bellowings? That he will roar loudly and not unmellifluously all men may know, dangerously also to not a few. Further than that let no mere man predicate of this Leviathan.

Success when once obtained supports itself. So it has ever been with every monster power that has raised itself over mankind since ambition first warmed the breast of man. Political success if too successful is that danger against which all nations covetous of freedom have found it most necessary to guard themselves. A King too dominant, a minister too dominant, a party too dominant, have all been known, felt, dreaded, and finally overcome. Now we have a newspaper too dominant; that also is now known, and felt; will soon be dreaded, and must be overcome.

For a man who has ever loved the idea of liberty how sad it is to see that the very landmarks of freedom which have been longed for in one age, become, in the next, when acquired, the very strongest holds of tyranny! Look to the American States where every man is equal; from which all dominion of ascendant classes has been banished; where political power rests solely with the people, and there you will see such tyranny as is not compassed even at St. Petersburg. Who there can dare to advocate opinions contrary to those prevalent with the mob?

"Am I not free to think?" says the wretched disputant, "Am I not free to speak?" "Free, yes, perfectly free: free to think, to speak, to act," exclaim at once a score of hot freemen, jealous of their power, "free to do all you can do. So also are we. We too are free; free to squeeze out the eyes of any dastard such as thou art." And out go the eyes of the unfortunate whose ideas of American freedom have been so lamentably behind the times.

It is so also with the Press. How have we longed, and clamoured, and fought for freedom of the Press? How cherished has been the idea? How sure have Englishmen been that with freedom of the Press, unrestrained freedom to print all political opinions whatsoever, everything else must also be free? Freedom of the Press we now have certainly; freedom to print what opinion we like without fear of the law; but the freedom is still only to the strong.

What man can now dare to express any opinion on any subject of import differing from that held by the huge Leviathan of the Press? Let such a one have advocated a few months since a speedy peace with Russia, or speak with affection of the old Corn Laws, or defend the doings of Gog and Magog,[5] and we shall soon see how he is also gouged. Not with actual finger and thumb is his eye of flesh plucked out; but a keener torment even than this is inflicted. The tomahawk of the dread Editor is brandished over his head, the scalping knife of the ferocious warrior of the columns is drawn quick and sharp round his agonized brow. He is held up to men as the Pariah with whom none shall consort. He is to be pointed at by the finger. Such a man can love neither country, nor Christian friend, nor aught that good men love. He has dared to differ from the Times. Let him go out into outer darkness, and that at once. Suicide, Satan, and everlasting sorrows are all that remain for so miserable a wretch.

And is this the freedom of the Press then for which we have combated? this, that there should be among us one master Leviathan to whom all others must succumb? To this state, if we have not yet reached it, we are fast approaching. A man may read the Times, and thus put himself within the pale of public opinion; may thus become one of those on whose behoof opinion thus makes itself public. Or he may sever himself from his country and his countrymen, may thus throw himself backward among the ideas of past ages, or forward into the aspirations of some dreamy Utopia; he may bury himself in a living

---

[5] Although Gog and Magog are Biblical names (cf. Genesis 10.02, Ezechial 38.02, Revelation 20.07), in English legend these are the last two survivors of a race of giants destroyed by Brute. They have long been commemorated by giant statues in the Guildhall.

grave and read no paper whatsoever; or, more foolish still, may waste his money and his time on those witless sheets which still dribble themselves out, dying and nearly dead, from other presses than those of Printing House Square. He may thus neglect the Times and his duty as an Englishman; but he will exist only as a dead man among the living; only as a slave among the free; only as an idiot among those who carry brains. A man now to walk practically with the world in England must walk with public opinion as expressed in the Times newspaper. So; or let him look to his steps, he will soon stumble.

That bill which is to subject to a commission *de lunatico* any man of £200 a year who shall not read the Times, will, we are informed, most surely pass in the course of the coming session.

It is difficult to define the duty of a newspaper, but it is not difficult in this matter to define the duty of the man by whom the newspaper is read. It is with him that the fault rests, if fault there be; and by him must the fault be remedied.

In all cases of despotic rule, of power grown too powerful, the fault is with the subject, not with the ruler; with the men, not with the master. If power be within a man's compass he will always, sooner or later, take a hold of it. If the Times writes autocratically about the war or the Colonies; if it denounce *ex cathedra* the demerits of this man, or announces the merits of that other; such tone is taken because such tone has gradually become bearable, and is ultimately looked for. Is looked for, and waited for, and becomes indispensable. How is any opinion in any matter to become accepted as public, as the opinion agreed upon among Englishmen, unless by authority of this new God.

Having happily got a God with a printing press to say what opinion shall be public opinion, and what not, would it not be worse than profanity to abstain from using him? To some men such a God must be most useful. To others, however, it may appear that a God upon earth may do too much. That under the protection of such a godhead the power of thought might grow rusty by disuse, and the mind thus freed from the necessity of exertion might find itself disposed to sleep.

One would say that a thinking man would rather dispense with such a God, would perceive that after all it was no God; but a lying spirit; a spirit full of error, but admitting none, and therefore a lying spirit. Have not all pretences to infallibility here

on earth been false, and would not this Leviathan have us believe that he is infallible? Infallibility is the very breath of
his nostrils; it is on that that he trades to the incredible amount
of 60,000 fourpences a day; 60,000 or whatever greater number
may now have been achieved. It is by this that he rules; by this
right that he prophesies; it is through this gift that opinion once
promulgated by him becomes public. Were he not infallible, he
would be nothing, or a mere newspaper. On the whole, if one
would think awhile, one would feel inclined to say that it is a
mere newspaper.

The divinity of such Gods is lent them by their worshippers.
One cannot but admire Mahomet, or fail to feel a certain sort of
respect for Joe Smith.[6] Joanna Southcott too,[7] and poor Mr.
Irving were not altogether despicable.[8] We will not, however,
say so much for their followers. It is not the staff of the Times
newspaper that we should condemn, but the spirit of an age that
suffers itself to be led by such leaders.

We are very apt in these civilized days to look back with complacent contempt on the dark ignorance of our ancestors. They,
however, in all the darkness of their ignorance, did look for some
excellence in a man before they would suffer him to take a place
among their leaders. We in our civilized days see no such necessity. We require no excellence but that of easy language, no
superiority but that of caustic diction. Let us have opinion put
daily before us in good readable articles, and it shall be public.

Let also public opinion be invincible. Is it not public, is it not
the opinion of the majority? Who then shall gainsay it or stay
it? Are not the ministers public servants, and shall they not
rule by public opinion? Are not the bishops paid by the public,
and shall not they pray as public opinion would have them?
Are not the judges public judges? They too shall give their
judgements as directed by this great exponent of public opinion;
shall so give them, or at any rate so reverse them. And the
Houses of Parliament too, are they not the public voice of the

[6] Joseph Smith (1805-44), American, founder of the Church of Jesus Christ
of Latter-Day Saints.

[7] Joanna Southcott (1750-1814), religious fanatic from Devon whose 'pro-
phecies' brought her an enthusiastic following.

[8] Edward Irving (1792-1834), popular preacher of the Church of Scotland;
excommunicated in 1833, he and his followers founded the 'Catholic Apostolic
Church'.

country? They also shall speak as public opinion may direct them.

Let gentlemen of the Lower House remember that a dissolution may be insisted on. To what obscure limbo then shall those betake themselves who have dared to rebel? Let noble peers bear in mind how frequently their august assembly has been made to take the guise of a synod of old women. Let public opinion so will it, and they shall be made to sit there in such guise continually till even so much privilege as that shall be denied to them.

God forbid that the freedom of the Press should ever be curtailed in this country. That matter may, however, be almost looked on as past the necessity of prayer; may be looked on rather as a subject for thanksgiving. Freedom of the Press is with us a thing accomplished. But not the less does it behove us to see that the longed for blessing be rightly used, now that it has been achieved. It may be said of all blessings that their blessedness depends on the power of those who are endowed with them to use them rightly. Of freedom this must especially be said. Alas, how often has freedom of action meant that one man should lead, and all others follow? Freedom of speech, that one man should speak, and all others hold their peace? Freedom of thought, that one man should declare an opinion, and all others coincide with it? Such also it appears is to be the freedom of the Press.

Men collectively have always fought for freedom; for freedom means collective power. Man individually has always fought against freedom, for freedom is the antidote to individual power. Those who have most truly loved the cause of freedom have seen the evil of every tyrant's rule but one; would have liberated the world from every thraldom but their own. No man can understand that he himself can be a tyrant.

Of none is this truer than of those who have faced death, and shed their blood; and strained their nerves; and cracked their voices in the people's cause, and who have done so sincerely. Men in such a cause are generally sincere. The fault to be found with them is that they are but men. He who begins life as a noisy democrat, and ends it with a sermon on the divine right of Kings has probably never been insincere. His inconsistency proves his honesty. Those who have so hated power when belonging to others, and have yet so tenaciously held it when within their own grasp, have all sincerely loved the theory of freedom. Look to the orators of Greece, look to the tribunes of Rome; look at the career of Cromwell, even of Robespierre, and a sincere tone of freedom will be found in all. Down even to that Citizen King Louis Philippe, down even as low as him one may look, and find some true gleam of sincerity. But where shall we look for the human heart that has disregarded power? for the man to whom rule, government, and authority have not been sweet?

The loudest claimants for freedom have carried the sword of power with the strongest hand; and as it has been so in other matters, so is it natural that it should be with the Press. If we have a tyrant ruling us from that throne of his in the close adjacency of St. Paul's Churchyard, we have none to blame for our thraldom but ourselves.

Any newspaper will domineer over us, if we allow it to do so. Any newspaper, or Editor, or Company, or institution whatsoever. It is easy enough to convince either newspaper or Editor, or even printer's devil that with him and with him alone remains for the present the only true power of governing mankind. It required but little to make the tinker Sly believe that he was a lord;[9] but little to induce Sancho to assume his government.

But what shall we say of those who would live under the lording of a Sly, or the governance of a Sancho?

Few Englishmen would wish to see the Press other than free. But few also, we imagine, would wish to see it dominant. The question to be asked is whether or not it be dominant or is it becoming so. That any or every newspaper will domineer, will become overbearing if allowed to do so, no man can doubt. Of the majority of such publications no immediate fear need perhaps at present be entertained. The Chronicle and the Herald and the Post are innocent.[10] The Press and the Leader do not aspire to a wide dominion or at least do not achieve it. The Spectator and the Examiner are eloquent within bounds. The Illustrated News does not trouble us, and Punch itself, though

[9] Christopher Sly, *The Taming of the Shrew*.

[10] Statistics for 1854 show the daily circulation of the *Chronicle* at 2,800, the *Herald*, 3,712, the *Post*, 2,667, and *The Times*, 51,200. W. T. Coggeshall, *The Newspaper Record: Containing a Complete List of Newspapers and Periodicals in the United States, Canada, and Great Britain* (Lay and Brother, Philadelphia, 1856), p. 89.

powerful, is so constrained to play a second fiddle, that he also is as yet endurable. But what shall we say of the Times?

Does freedom of the Press mean that the Press only shall be free? or does it mean that a portion only of the Press itself shall be free? Are freedom of the Press and the absolute dominion of a newspaper synonymous here, as freedom of the people and dominion of the mob are synonymous in parts of America? If this be not so, then the author of these pages, when he inveighs against the power of one newspaper, claims to be acquitted of any antagonism to the freedom of the Press.

Of any antagonism also to the writers for the Press would he hope to be acquitted. They use the bow as it is bent for them. So have all dictators used it. To them at any rate belongs the excellence of showing that in their hands such power is possible. But to that spirit which would allow a nation to look to a newspaper for its political guidance let all men, if possible, be antagonistic. Ministers may be bad, but we know when they are, and we can change them. A House of Commons may be corrupt, but that also is known and may be changed. A House of Peers even may be, how often has been, persuaded, coerced, cajoled, to go the way that the wisdom of the country would have it.

"And the Times newspaper, if you dislike that, cannot you change it for another? There is the Morning Herald." Our friend shudders as the suggestion is made to him. "The Morning Herald! how am I to eat my breakfast?" Nations have slipped into slavery in this way. How delightful, how alluring, nay, at last how necessary were the shows of Augustus. *Panem et Circenses* demanded the Roman. For the Englishman Tea, Toast, and Times are sufficient.

Is there then no hope? must we for ever be given over to the lording of Printing House Square? Is this Sancho in real truth to have the government of us? A Sancho indeed with much wit; but one on whose shoulders very little of the dignity, or truth, or equanimity of a true governor seems to have descended. If there be no hope, all wailing is amiss. In such case one would say that inquiries as to some vessel, A1 copper fastened, clipper built— 3000 tons burden, with unrivalled passenger accommodations, and engaged to sail on a very early day, had better be made as soon as possible. In such case let a man trouble himself little about the decadence of England, but think much of the rise of

New Zealand, or some other such strange shore.

That we are yet come to such a pass cannot be truly said. The orders issued are certainly absolute and authoritative enough; but the obedience sometimes fails. Occasionally the thunderbolt falls disregarded, and the God speaks in vain. It is beautiful to observe how the government and the newspaper watch each other, and how each in its own way takes advantage of the faults of the other. How skilful they both are! How warily the slightest mistake is noted and made much of. The newspaper with loud indignant voice pours forth whole columns of classical vituperation, appealing to the people, appealing to itself, eulogizing its own forethought, eulogizing public patriotism, and showing how unworthy of such a public is the base minister by whom the Crown is advised. Or else in one curt sentence it damns, or intends to damn the reputation of a dozen sessions.

But a government fights its battle with different weapons. A government must never be angry, at least never angry with the public Press. It is not etiquette for a government to abuse a newspaper. Occasionally some poor, maddened minister, driven beyond all human bearing by abuse unmerited, or perhaps even, still worse, by merited abuse, may incautiously speak of the ribald Press. But such is an exception, to be lamented. Any allusion to the Press, if made at all, should be made in that well pleased, half-jocular tone in which it is now the fashion for great people to speak on most subjects. The mere listener should gather from a minister's lips nothing to make him think that public opinion can ever express itself in a faulty manner. But not the less warily is public opinion watched. Let it be palpably wrong, let a leading article on a leading subject be written amiss, and the minister at once sees that he can have his own way.

Occasionally the God does thunder in vain. It has not as yet quite come to that, that the Times newspaper can say to the Prime Minister: Do thou so—or failing it, retire at once into obscurity, back benches, small type, and the third person. Nor has the Queen as yet been constrained to admit into her councils all writers of leading articles whom the newspaper may choose to put forward for such honour. It may be, however, that such power may yet be gained. The battle made for it is very great. The measures taken are well considered. The forethought shown is very excellent. The government is to the monster of the Press

as the dying gentleman in the East was to the Czar.[11] Bomarsund,[12] Sweaborg,[13] and Sebastopol[14] are as nothing to the for-
tresses of Printing House Square. It may be that Downing Street
will ultimately knock under, and that a man ambitious of the
name of a British statesman will have to seek it by commencing
with small newspaper effusions. Let us hope that such disgrace
is not prepared for us. As yet there is room for hope.

The Czar was too arrogant and too impatient, and so also is
the newspaper. It is hard to work calmly, patiently, zealously
for a reward which is to be enjoyed wholly by one's successors.
If greatness is to be won, one would wish to wear it oneself, before
one's death. So probably reasoned the Czar when he took such
memorable hold of a material guarantee and thereby disgusted
Europe.[15] There are signs of an equally wholesome disgust arising with regard to our tyrant at home.

It must be again repeated that if any Times, any Moniteur,
any New York Herald obtain to itself more influence than can
safely be left in the hands of a knot of anonymous writers, the
fault is not with the writers, but the readers. The writers do the
work of able zealous men, and reap what consequences such
work will bring to them. The readers do the work of brainless
idle men, to whom the trouble of thinking for themselves would
be a pain too great for endurance.

In olden times the Englishman killed and salted his own
beef, brewed his own beer, baked his own bread, and in some
sort or other created his own thoughts. They then had no shop
ready at which they could buy for 4d. a daily supply of skilfully
expressed opinions. The world we know has become beautifully

[11] In conversation with George Hamilton Seymour, British envoy to St.
Petersburg, the Czar referred to Turkey as the 'sick man' (9 Jan. 1853), Seymour to Russell, 11 Jan. 1853, *Foreign Office Papers*, 65 Russia, 424, 13.

[12] *Bomarsund*: Russian fortress in Finland's Aland Islands in the Baltic
Sea. French ground forces, assisted by British naval strength, captured Bomarsund in August 1854.

[13] *Sweaborg*: Russian held fortressed city on the Gulf of Finland. It proved
so formidable that Sir Charles Napier, British naval commander, cancelled the
attack upon it which had been planned for October 1854; the following August
the fortress was destroyed by a forty-five hour bombardment.

[14] *Sebastopol*: Russian stronghold and centre of military operations in the
Crimea; after eleven months of seige it fell in September 1855.

[15] Apparently a reference to Russia's invasion of the Danubian provinces of
Turkey in July 1853, ostensibly over the question of Orthodox vs. Latin control
of the Holy Places. Czar Nicholas I died 2 March 1855.

civilized, and very highly educated in these latter days; but still we doubt whether men think so much or so soundly as they did when ready made thought was not so easily attainable. Meat is now quickly carried and readily bought, and a man can hardly be required to kill his own sheep. Nor is he required to work his own brains. Has he not fresh every morning on his breakfast table, for 4*d*., much better thought than any that his own brains will produce for him?

We are apt to laugh at our ancestors. They did not write grammatically, nor always spell correctly. They drank a good deal of beer, and when they took up a prejudice, they stuck to it firmly. But nevertheless they did in a manner think for them-selves. They held opinions which were their own; and which, though perhaps not formed on the correctest grounds, were formed on grounds sufficiently intelligible to their possessors. The Cavalier of Charles I had a political belief, and a strong sense of national right and wrong deep seated in his heart of hearts. And so with a vengeance had his enemy the Roundhead. Squire Western had his satisfied convictions on the question of Church and State,[16] and was not to be blown this way or that way by the breath of public opinion. But now-a-days men can hardly be said to have any fixed political principles.

It has become so necessary not to be behind the world in one's ideas, not to entertain antiquated notions, that one has no resource but to adhere to an omniscient, omnipresent, infallible guide; and thus by thinking with the fashion one is saved the labour of really forming any thought at all. Men have a horror of protection, not because they have satisfied their own minds of the soundness of free trade, but because protection has been tabooed by the Press. It is the same with all matters of public interest. Men think, and speak, and act the Times newspaper. Prominent social orators talk leading articles, while humble individuals content themselves with paragraphs. Second hand indignation is quoted in words which have been read so often that they are customary to the ears; and at every political con-versation a man is tempted to remind the speaker that he has already seen the paper.

Children may and often do have too much done for them.

---

[16] Decidedly Tory and Church of England views; see *Tom Jones*, Bk. VI, ch. ii and xiv; VII, iii.

They are put into leading strings, and go-carts, and little car-
riages on three wheels, till legs appear to be an unnecessary
appendage to the coming generation. To the grown up English
world the Times newspaper is its carriage on three wheels, on
which men are wheeled about hither and thither with great ease
and comfort to themselves, but not without damage to their
mental legs. No legs will be of any use unless used. Little children in new fashioned go-carts are wheeled along by attendant
nurse-maids very pleasantly; but heaven only knows how they
are to walk hereafter. By the time that our children are sufficiently grown for such pastime, there will probably be go-carts
on the mountains from whence they will be able to shoot Scotch
grouse—also very pleasantly. Why should a man walk or think,
if such labour can be saved him by skilfully devised arrangements of civilization?

Skilfully devised arrangements of civilization have now pretty
well enabled us to dispense altogether with the trouble of forming any opinion whatsoever. Still, there is that awfully broad
sheet to be read, with its ever increasing number of columns—
really a day's work. Cannot civilization devise some means by
which it may be poured gracefully into our ears as we dress, so
that we may descend to our breakfast ready filled with such
matter as public opinion shall for that day have vouchsafed to
us?

For professional writers for the daily Press we cannot but
entertain respect. As a body they do their work with much skill;
and though we feel that all individuality of character in each
writer must be lost in the aggregation of motive, yet we are
forced to acknowledge the perfect harmony with which so many
minds are brought to work in unison together. It is a profession
which receives and is entitled to admiration. But we cannot say
so much for those who as amateurs lend their assistance to the
newspapers.

Can anything be more contemptible than the sycophant effusions of Common Sense, Veritas, Constant Reader, and Fairplay?
"It is only necessary, Mr. Editor, to secure the advocacy of your
inestimable columns to put a speedy termination to one of the
most glaring abominations with which the public of this metropolis are at present afflicted," and then Fairplay proceeds to
write down his neighbour, whose opposition he has been unable

to quell in any more open or honest manner. Or "Veritas" aspires perhaps to the honour of assisting in reforming the British Army; and, therefore, as the Widow Dash buys her tea of a rival grocer, he tells in indignant strains how Captain Dash, her son, has returned from the Crimea on urgent private affairs, which, as far as Veritas can see into them, consist in the slaughter of partridges.

"Sir," begins a constant reader ambitious of print, and proud of the manner in which as he flatters himself he can write up to the Times' mark, "The admirable article which appeared in your impression of the 8th Instant respecting Martha Scraggs and the Warwickshire magistrates is worthy of the highest praise. But for the energy of your columns where would England be? Perhaps you will permit me to make use of your invincible influence in holding up to deserved execration a case of equal iniquity which occurred last week in the parish of ——" And so Constant Reader gives his account of some transaction of which he has not been allowed to have the ordering.

Such and such like are the contributions of the public to the newspaper Press of the country, and from the multitude of such contributions is made up that public opinion of the possession of which newspaper Editors are so prone to boast. Who has not read hundreds of times the assertion that an Editor's table is covered with such documents? Let no man doubt it. There is in the country a sufficiency of the genus toady, and of the species scribbling toady, to cover hundreds of Editors' tables in this manner. Nothing now comes so natural to an offended little mind, as to write some anonymous letter to the Times in a true spirit of little vengeance.

The threat of doing so is now the common and immediate resource of impotent anger. An unreasonable lady makes some monstrous request to a railway official, and a refusal immediately brings down an assurance of a letter to the Times. An unfortunate custom house officer is unable to do all that some hot-tempered traveller requires in his haste, and the promise of a letter to the Times is the immediate result. That men should threaten in their anger is not surprising nor disgraceful. The Times newspaper affords us in this the discreeter way that we now have of uttering an oath in our anger. Of the two practices the Times newspaper is the better, if the matter be there allowed to drop. With the majority it does so drop. By the mean spirited, the malignant, and often by the vain, the matter is carried further, and the letter is written. Of such a judicious Editor culls the most fitting, and public opinion is so created.

With the rejected, as Editors so often tell us, their tables and waste-paper baskets are encumbered. We can easily believe it. Alas, for the man who has the reading of them!

It is human nature that the little should toady the big; and of course a Constant Reader, wishing to have his letter inserted, will say civil things to the Editor who is to sit in judgement on him. The cringing of such as these may disgust but cannot surprise us. But there are now other sycophants whose present state of bondage cannot be observed without sorrow. Many of that body of which the public Press is formed are willing to abandon their own idiosyncrasy and submit to an existence governed in a measure by their great rival. To be styled by the Times "Our very respectable correspondent" is, we should say, a poor compensation for the loss of independent principles. It must, however, be supposed that it pays, and that, with all vendors of news as of other articles, will be the one thing needful. Alas that it should pay! It is in that that our misfortune lies.

The practice of virtues, such virtues as we would wish to see grace our children and our friends, may probably be preached with much more efficacy in a newspaper than from a pulpit. Sermons as a rule are distasteful to all but the parson. Whereas leading articles are read with eagerness. Newspapers have therefore wisely taken upon themselves to inculcate morals. But it is with them as with the clergymen. Their code of morals is falsely high.

A man may be said to preach a false code,—not when he preaches above his own practice; that probably we would all wish to do—but when he advocates a code higher than that which he acknowledges to be necessary in his own immediate circle, when he asserts a doctrine not higher than that by which he lives, but higher than that by which he would wish to live. Is not this done now to a monstrous extent by all preachers in all places?

We have unfortunately among us two modes of argument, two modes of thought, two modes of speech, two modes of action, two modes of life, two modes of preaching: one esoteric, the other exoteric. They cannot both be true.

The Cabinet Minister when he rises in Parliament to answer some perplexing question from some indignant opponent never thinks of making a clean breast of it. But he thinks much of appearing to do so. In one strain does he talk over the mooted point with his friends and colleagues; in quite another does he give a confident answer to the outer world of the House at large. Such, he will say, are the political requirements of his position.

Your friend the parson, who is an excellent fellow in private life, inveighs against this world's pleasures, pleads how the pleasures of the next world should be all in all to us. Nevertheless he sees without dejection his pretty daughters in their pretty dresses tripping off to the county ball. "One is obliged," says he in the confidence of his heart, "to be strait-laced in one's sermons."

So it is with the newspapers. Faults which men among themselves would speak of hardly in terms of reproach become magnified into vile vices when unfortunately they are noticed in the Press. The guardians of the public morals must let the public know that they will guard those morals strictly. A.B., the Editor, may be himself a loose fish, given to bad language, and fond of wine and women, but when he writes he advocates the strictest decency. C.D., the contributor, is known among his friends as a terrible perpetrator of practical jokes, but yet with what indignant scorn does he pull to pieces that silly young lieutenant who threw his brother lieutenant's bed out of the barrack window.

Beds should not be thrown out of barrack windows. But such matters if written about at all, should be written of in the true spirit in which they are thought of by the writer. All other kind of writing is false, and must in the end be injurious.

A case occurs to us at the present moment in which a newspaper, animadverting on the rows in Hyde Park, fell heavily upon a certain superintendent of police because he swore at his men.[17] The officer had had a hard and anxious time of it; had gone through much, and been tormented by a perplexing duty; his men also had been worried; and on leaving the park it seems

[17] The Hyde Park disturbance, occasioned by popular dissatisfaction over Lord Robert Grosvenor's proposed Sunday Trading Bill, occurred 1 July 1855. The violence with which the police quelled the mob was the subject of much newspaper comment and an official inquiry by the Home Secretary. Police Superintendent Hughes was censured for, among more serious charges, 'using improper language'. *The Times*, 2 July, 22 and 24 Nov. 1855.

that they fell from the tight array in which they should have moved. "Damn it men," said the superintendent, "feel your left." We do not quite understand the meaning of the order, but the oath is intelligible enough. It is with the oath alone that we have present concern.

The superintendent should not have "damned his men." Speaking with strictest truth we cannot say that such figure of speech was worthy of eulogy. But we can say that, if worthy of reproach, the reproach should be of the mildest kind that ever fell from the lips of charity. The recording angel will hardly have found it worth his while to trouble himself with such an offence.

The newspaper writer, however, did find it worth his while to remark upon the poor superintendent with the utmost bitterness. At that time the doings of the police in Hyde Park had fallen under the heavy displeasure of the Times, and it was thought proper to visit their offences with a strong hand. The superintendent in question was particularly unpopular, and therefore his little slip of the tongue was published to the world as a great offence.

It may be that the writer of that article never swears; that his conversation is always yea, yea, or nay, nay; but it must be probable that in this sinful world his ears are often outraged by language at least as bad as that of the policeman. We wonder whether he would rebuke a friend who in his presence might let fall the same wicked expression.

Oh! Mr. Editor, was not such indignation mock indignation? was it not got up for the outer circle of the public? Was it the true expression of your own inner thoughts on such a matter? Ah, we fear not. With your inner thoughts on such matters the public have no concern. It is your outer thoughts only that are to be had for 4*d*. a number. The other are not for sale.

One thinking on such matters is half inclined to be as rude to such writers as the policeman was, and to say "D—— it men, feel the truth!" Your calling is certainly a high one. It is one in which no man without mind can for a moment get his bread. But it can only become a noble calling by strict adherence to truth, not only in fact, but in feeling. Let no man preach any doctrine as sound and good to his fellow men which is not sound and good for himself. If he does so he is but a false prophet, and sooner or later will reap the reward of his falsehood.

On the whole, the newspaper Press of this country is not in a state with which the country should be satisfied. It should not be well if one Leviathan in our seas were to swallow all the useful little fishes. The honour of possessing the biggest monster of the deep would not atone for the loss of red herrings, shrimps, and lobster salad. The Times will argue that its flavour is better than that of any fishes that ever swam, and that none were ever more easily put on the table. This may be true, but we would prefer to have a choice among the many.

In speaking of the English Press, it is impossible to do other than speak of the Times alone. Such is its own language; and the boast, though arrogant and unbecoming, is not untrue. In foreign countries the English Press is regarded as being wholly represented by the Times. Here at home its sale proves that such is the fact; and the influence which it has would be additional proof, if such were wanting. This is surely a misfortune. The Press now calls itself, and we are all apt to call it, the fourth power of the realm. It may be very well that it should be so, if divided; but it cannot be well that all the power of such a body should be concentrated on one set of hands.

The paper itself, if called on to plead to such an indictment, would appeal triumphantly to its sale, and declare that the fault, if fault there be, is not with itself, but with its customers.

Triumphantly, and truly also. What then must be the remedy? It were useless to suggest to any man to abandon the paper that he daily reads, as long as he reads it with pleasure. A crusade with such an object would be but a useless effort of patriotism. The time however will surely come when arrogance, grown overbearing, will not be pleasing; when pride, begotten by success, will work its own fall.

It is grievous to have to say that genius, skill, and industry, joined as they are to uprightness of purpose, are producing evil and not good. Such however we believe to be the case with the journal of which we have spoken. It is the infirmity of human nature that the desire even to do good can not safely be trusted with unlimited power to work its own will.

CHAPTER IV
Law and Physic

A s long as the mind of man continues to be unsound we shall
require laws; and as long as the body does, we shall require
physic. At present there appears to be no prospect of any
immediate change for the better on either of these heads, and it
may be taken for granted that for a considerable time to come
lawyers will be wanted to expound our laws and doctors to compound our doses. It is therefore a matter of moment to us that
our laws and lawyers should be good, and our physicians as well
as physic honest.

As regards our laws, the language in which they are set forth,
the manner in which they are propounded to us, and the singular
assemblage of words which is used when any of us are unfortunately brought into close contact with them, one may safely
say that so strange a gallimaufry of verbiage, so ill-arranged a
mass of unintelligible edicts, so preposterous a mixture of
obsolete and living tongues, was never elsewhere brought
together. This is the case as to our criminal laws and our civil
laws; both of which together constitute what we call our
Common Laws; and it is specially the case as to that fiction by
which we assume to arrive at a justice juster than legal justice,
namely the Courts of Equity and Chancery. Nor can those other
courts of law, yclept ecclesiastical, be at all exempt from the
censure. Indeed were we driven to a comparison we might
perhaps be forced to declare that of all English laws the laws
ecclesiastical are the most complex, the most unmeaning, and the
most barbarous.

If this be so, if we be in fact in a state of more utter confusion
as regards our laws than ever civilized people were before, we
would say that our condition in this respect alone must be full of
danger. It is full of danger; but would be much more so, were it
not that we have acknowledged the evil. We have as a nation
looked the matter in the face, and owned our shortcomings. We
confess the sin, and may therefore hope for improvement.

When we consider how high in the scale of civilization we class ourselves, and how high indeed we are classed by others, it is singular that we should not as yet have any entire code of our laws. The Visigoths made a code of their laws as early as the fifth century, which has been translated into Spanish, and is even now the parent of Spanish laws.[1] The laws of Charlemagne's empire were codified as early as the ninth century. The Pandects of Justinian were much earlier.[2] They had a perfect code of laws in the Kingdoms of Aragon and Navarre. We all know with how much success in latter days the French laws have been arranged, simplified, and published, in the Code Napoléon. Nevertheless as yet we have no such code. Nor is this the worst of the matter as regards our laws. Not only have we no code, but in their present state it can hardly be said that a code is practicable. We have clung so tenaciously to the language, usages, and manners of the past ages; we have, till very lately, so steadily set our faces against any improvement, that the matter has become one of now almost insurmountable difficulty. The legal Hercules of the time has even shrunk from the task as a whole,[3] and lawyers of lesser grasp of intellect or lesser audacity would look upon the attempt as evidence of insanity.

As we none of us, not the wisest, nor those most learned in the laws, really know what these laws are, it cannot be expected that they should be administered with expedition or certain justice. They are far from being so administered. They are so full of anomalies in themselves, that were those anomalies brought before us, not as a portion of a system to which we have always been accustomed, but as facts in themselves; if we were on a sudden brought to look on them, not as laws of our own, but as belonging to some other people, we who have lived daily under their guidance would be incredulous of their absurdity.

The criminal law is to all of us the most important, as under it our lives, our property, and reputations are, or are supposed to be secure. Let us see how we treat a great criminal when we get

---

[1] Trollope may be referring to King Recceswinth's *Liber judiciorum* (promulgated c. 654) which survived for many centuries as the basis for numerous later Spanish codes or *fueros*.

[2] In 533 Justinian promulgated his *Pandects* or digests of his earlier (529) *Codex constitutionum*.

[3] Almost certainly a reference to Lord Brougham, who, as Lord Chancellor 1830-4, effected some reform of the judicature, but abandoned his plan for an entirely new court system.

him. Great he too usually becomes, but were we to say a foul criminal it would be a better phrase. This man has committed a murder. He has with most atrocious cruelty, with long pre-meditated malice, with horrid cold blooded ingenuity, murdered his paramour. All his ingenuity, however, has availed him nothing. The police are good, if the laws be not; and the murder is out, as murder will. The murderer is suspected, nay known, and arrested. Now let us see how much the law will do for such a man as this; how little for the defence of those upon whom such men prey. How much to delay justice, how little to further it!

When arrested he is asked no questions as to his crime. In the first unguarded moment of his surprise, with the dread of death on him, in the first paralysis of his fear, it would be probable that the truth might escape from him. Something at any rate he might let fall at such a moment which would facilitate the dis-covery of the truth. But from this moment, as regards the murderer, the object of the law is to facilitate not the discovery of the truth, but the escape of the criminal. He has become from this moment in a peculiar manner under the protection of the laws. He is to be guarded at every avenue; protected from every onslaught; saved at any expense, if it be that the law can save him.

It is too probable that in the first agony of his fears the truth might unfortunately drop from him. The constable therefore is forbidden to ask him a question without slow and deliberate warning that if he answers, he will do so at his peril. The magis-trate repeats the caution, and repulses the effort at confession which remorse so often produces.

How, may we say, should a magistrate address himself at such a moment to such a man? "Oh man, if it be that thou art guilty, cleanse that foul breast of thine as far as truth can cleanse it. God knows thy sin. 'Twere better for thee that man should know it too. Man will know it and avenge it. I charge thee speak the truth, and thus begin, if it be yet possible, to make thy peace with God." Not so by any means does he speak. The charge having been made, and duly read to the prisoner, the magistrate thus addresses him. "Thou hearest what this man or these men witness against thee. I ask thee to say nothing. Thou mayest be silent if thou wilt, and perchance it will be better for thee. It is open to thee to speak if thou choosest. But remember, remember well, that if thou sayest aught against thyself, it will be used against thee."

"Under such circumstances, Mr. Magistrate, I decline to speak." Of course. Why wouldst thou not, thus encouraged? When all encourage thee to hide that dark deed of thine, how can it be expected that thou shouldst divulge it?

Let us address ourselves to a lawyer on this subject, to a lawyer conversant with the criminal courts of the country; let us express an opinion that these things should be altered, and let us hear what he will say. He will be struck with horror at the idea that any man in this English land of ours should wish to see a poor wretched prisoner lured into giving evidence against himself. He will talk of the honesty of fair play, and of the superior manliness of the English practice. Can there be manliness in encouraging falsehood? Can there be fair play in aiding foul play to escape unnoticed? Can it ever be wrong to lure any one into truth, be the consequences of that truth what they may? Does it not come home to the mind of every man as a first principle in morals that harm cannot come of the truth? There stands the accused with the dark knowledge of crime within him, with that within him or else with the blessed consciousness of innocence. Surely in such a case it should be the object of every one to get out from him that knowledge which he alone, probably, absolutely possesses—guilty or not guilty? Get from him his plea, but get from him by every available means a true plea; not by every available means a false plea, as is now the practice in our English courts.

But our lawyer will not admit this. It is not that he fails to look on the truth as excellent; it is not that he is less averse to murder than another; it is not that he would have crime escape unpunished; but the habits of his education, of his trade, and his life will not allow him to see clearly. He has long since learned that no man in England is required to criminate himself, and he cannot bring himself to question the value of the lesson. How many lessons of the same kind have we not all learnt?

Our prisoner, having thus declined to speak, is nevertheless committed to stand his trial. Murder, as we have said, will out, and cunning constables have been eager on his track. As his trial comes on he engages some able practitioner for his defence, and all the powers of the law are set in action. He is put to the bar, and solemnly called on to declare whether he be guilty or not of the deed which is laid to his charge.

Overcome perhaps with the weight of remorse, or conscious perhaps of the hopelessness of his case, or perhaps thinking that an avowal of the truth may operate favourably on his judge, he has prepared himself to declare that he is guilty. But his attorney will not by any means allow him so to throw away the many chances that remain to him. He is again fully impressed with the folly of telling the truth, and whispers with bated breath, and hang-dog look, that he is not guilty. "Not guilty, my Lord," says some loud denizen of the court standing by him, and so the trial proceeds.

But first of all an objection is taken that he cannot be tried at all. The whole thing is illegal. It does not matter a straw whether the prisoner at the bar did or did not commit this murder; he cannot at any rate be tried for it. He has been wrongly arraigned, and therefore the whole proceeding must be quashed, and the prisoner is entitled to his release. So at least says eloquent Mr. Allwinde. In the indictment he has been denominated John James ———, whereas Mr. Allwinde is in a position to prove from the baptismal register that he was christened John Jacob. Half a day is consumed in disputing the point. It is quite clear that in spite of his christening this murderer has always called himself John James; but the point is a very interesting one, and the judge reserves it. The trial therefore goes on, Mr. Allwinde being perfectly satisfied with the success of his first move.

Nothing can be clearer to the ordinary conception of man than the fact of this prisoner's guilt. The evidence is perfectly conclusive. He has been all but seen to commit the murder. The traces of the deed were strong upon his person. The blood of his victim still stained him when he was arrested. The implements of the murder are traced to his hands. The fall of his foot corresponds with the tell-tale marks which are found round the scene of the cruel struggle. He was seen as he went thither. He was seen as he returned. 'Twas he that lured the victim to that quiet wood. 'Twas he and he only could have desired her death. It is not too much to say that no shadow of doubt rests on the mind of any human creature in the court as to the reality of the prisoner's guilt. But yet Mr. Allwinde does not despair. He sits there jauntily and at ease, confident in the resources of his wit; little doubting but that he will earn his fee by saving this recreant's life. There is at any rate this honesty in Mr. Allwinde, that he is anxious to save the life of his client murderer.

How be browbeats that unfortunate witness who had the calamity to see the murderer as he emerged from the wood with staring eyes, and horror stricken face, and the mark of Cain upon his brow; the calamity to see him, and the audacity to declare that he had done so. The poor wretch, who has come there to tell, as best he may, what truth he knows on the matter, is exposed first to the ridicule, and then to the ignominy of the whole court. Nay, may it not be possible that he himself did the deed? It is clear, so says Mr. Allwinde, that this man is a liar, why not also a murderer? Mr. Allwinde will not accuse him, God forbid that he should accuse a man who may for aught he knows be innocent—but at any rate there is as strong ground for suspicion against him as against that prisoner at the bar. So argues Mr. Allwinde. And while so arguing he well knows, no one better, how innocent is the witness, how guilty the prisoner whom he defends.

One cannot but admire the felicity of ready wit with which this witness is first shaken out of his presence of mind, then bullied into error, then terrified into silence, then threatened into further speech, then lured into further error, and the indignant eloquence with which his want of presence of mind, his error, his silence, his speech, and his further error, are held up to the anger and contempt of the court. A spectator unaccustomed to such scenes cannot but think that the wretched man upon whose brow drops of agony are standing is the real criminal. The judge frowns at him from his bushy eyebrows, and with thick hoarse voice bids him beware of himself. Mr. Allwinde tosses him to and fro and turns him in and out, till he hardly knows himself whether or not he be the perjured villain that they are calling him. The jury look at him uncomfortably and whisper among themselves all but audibly. The younger bar watch the scene with laughing eyes and ears erect; it is to them a treat as rich as a battle of rats in which the famous dog Badger is backed to kill his twenty rats in the hour. Indeed Mr. Allwinde in his quickness, his tenacity, his courage, his fiery eye, and, we may add, his cruel mouth, is not altogether unlike that famous terrier. Sir Barnard Binly, the great Crown Counsel, sits on the other side complacent, and whispers to the junior barristers that Mr. All-winde is really very great.

And what is the damning fault which the wretched victim has committed? In the confusion of the cross examination he has mistaken his right hand for his left. Objects which were on his left when he was going to the wood, were of course on his right as he returned; and he has been teased into swearing that in both directions he found them on his left; then that in both directions he found them on his right; then he swore that they were on his right, when in truth they were on his left, and on his left when they were on his right; then that he didn't know his right hand from his left, and then that he did. Then, after the angry caution of the judge, and with much futile effort at thought, he positively swore that the footsteps which he saw were on the right of the road as he went to the wood—no, he meant on his left—that was on his left as he came back—or rather on his left as he went. And then he sat silent and agonized, while the court tittered, and Mr. Allwinde, gazing at him with angry eyes, said out loud, "You wretched miserable man, go down."

And yet this man came thither to do his duty by the state in telling with truth what he knows of the matter, and has faithfully so done his duty. Mr. Allwinde, moreover, knows that he has done it, and the judge knows it, and Sir Barnard Binly knows it. Nobody, however, has said a word to protect him. The judge with a nod of his head or a look of his eye could have quieted Mr. Allwinde and encouraged the witness; but the witness was a bad witness, and Mr. Allwinde is a great lawyer. A witness who can so easily be beaten out of his self-composure deserves no encouragement. A good witness should give his evidence well, and succinctly, and stick to his story; stick not only to the truth of his story, but to the manner of it; should remember not only the essentials of his evidence, but the non-essentials also; should at any rate remember accurately what he professes to remember at all. As to the essentials of his evidence there will be no difficulty. A learned counsel firmly convinced of the guilt of his client will not trouble a witness much about essentials. It will hardly be wise for him to touch on such at all. If a man has suddenly come upon a pool of blood, has found marks of a struggle, has picked up the bloody knife, he will hardly be brought to contradict himself on such matters as these. On matters of no moment he may do so, probably will if skilfully handled; and if he can be shown to be inaccurate in such, is not that a fair argument that he is inaccurate in all?

The witness was a bad witness, and deserved no encouragement. Therefore the judge, sternly looking, bade him beware of himself. Oh, Judge, if this witness had but been educated to a court of law, as thou hast, and these barristers have been, he would surely have done better in this matter. But say, would a witness educated for testifying bring ye all with those paraphernalia of yours nearer to the living truth? Nay do ye not all already know the truth in this matter? Do ye not know that the truth in no wise depends on that man's knowledge of his right hand or his left?

There is another point in favour of the murderer on which Mr. Allwinde rests with much confidence. The scene of the murder was exactly contiguous to the bounds of the county. That the little wood is in the county of B. no one doubts. The ditch which skirts the wood skirts the county also. The struggle was in the ditch. The blood was found in the ditch. Some of the blows at any rate were struck there. It was there that the woman died. The ditch, according to Mr. Allwinde, is in the county of D. He at least is prepared so to prove, and on that account claims that his client shall be acquitted.

It is found to be not so easy to prove in which county the ditch is situated. The ditch as now made was made by the owner of the wood, but the oldest inhabitant thinks that the owner encroached in so making it. A very pretty point is however raised, and the judge again consents to reserve it.

Many other attempts are made, some with no success, but others with some little, to mislead and bamboozle the jury. Nobody who has heard the case has the smallest doubt on the matter. The guilt of the prisoner has been proved over and over again, yet to a certain extent the jury are bamboozled. They know that the man is guilty, but they are not sure whether he be guilty according to law. It is no light thing to be a consenting party to the death of any one. Supposing the murder was committed in the county of D., not of B.? supposing it was not committed by John James, but by John Jacob? supposing that they are really in law to disbelieve all that that witness said because he mistook his right hand for his left? It is true that they cannot in truth do other than believe him, but then Mr. Allwinde has told them so often that they are entitled, nay, bound, to disbelieve him in law. With all these considerations the jury are bamboozled, and retire to an inner room.

For enlightening the minds of a British jury, there is nothing equal to cold, hunger, and darkness. What meditation and research are to the philosopher, starvation and misery are to the jurymen. These suasive powers will bring twelve men surely to the truth. Though here indeed there is another opportunity of exercising that spirit of fiction which is so dear to the law. Too much starvation could bring twelve men positively to their death; and to prevent so dire a tragedy a doctor is allowed who shall give certificate of approaching collapse. If therefore jurymen be obstinate, a doctor does certify, with what truth he himself must judge, that further starvation will endanger life. That starvation if persisted in will endanger life, one would say might be certified even without a doctor.

In our case, however, cold and hunger suffice, though life be not endangered, to produce unanimity; and the murderer is declared to be a murderer. Had twelve men declared otherwise, one would say that they had forfeited for themselves all right to the protection of the laws. The murderer, however, is declared to be a murderer, and the judge, with black cap and solemnity no longer fictitious but now real enough, awards to him his deserved fate. Such fate as this, that he be hung by his neck till he be dead.

But this is not the end; nor is this really to be the lot of the sinner. One might see by a glance at Mr. Allwinde that he has not yet given up the game. He suggests to his Lordship that certain points have been reserved, and his Lordship announces that no day shall be appointed for the execution till due consideration shall have been given to them. Finally the doom is commuted to transportation, and after a few years the man will reappear as a ticket of leave convict, free to murder another victim.

It will be said that this description of a trial in one of our criminal courts is grossly exaggerated. It would be exaggerated if we were to give it as an average picture of ordinary trials; if we were to say that trials in general were so crowded with absurdities as this one has been. But it is no exaggeration of the kind of anomalies which do disgrace our courts. In any trial all these absurdities might occur, and no special remark be made; all these and many more. In all our trials some of them do occur.

As to the conduct of Mr. Allwinde, which in the whole proceeding appears to be the most noticeable matter, is it not patent to everyone who ever enters a criminal court, or reads a newspaper report of what there takes place, that such is the mode in which he commonly defends his client? he, and others, his learned brethren? Did he alone do so, the evil were quickly remedied. Is it not also patent that this bar, of which Mr. Allwinde is a conspicuous member, claims for itself a very high position in the community? The highest officer of the Crown must be a member of it, and as such is ranked as the second subject in the land. All that the country has to offer to ambition, talent, and industry is offered to the bar. The great prizes of the bench are appropriated to it exclusively. The House of Commons is open to it, and if a man who lives by his work wishes to enter the House it is by the bar, and almost by the bar only, that he can do so. The House of Lords is recruited from its members with new blood and new ability. Two of its working members must be peers, and it not infrequently happens that a third is so. It forms for itself an aristocracy of learning and talent. It assumes to itself the privilege of advising mankind under all difficulties. The bar is never slow, and never slumbers. It always has its wits about it; it is always on the look out; is never to be imposed upon. It talks more eloquently than its neighbour professions; thinks more deeply and writes more fluently. It edits newspapers, thunders forth leading articles, and guides the world. The destiny of the bar is a great destiny, and conscious barristers feel it and are proud.

If such be the case, surely barristers should be more chary of their conduct even than other men, should be more careful that they do nothing to disgrace their high calling, or derogate from the nobility of the position which they have assumed. Yet one can hardly say that Mr. Allwinde did his duty nobly when he defended that murderer from the vengeance of the law. One would rather say that nothing could be less noble than his mode of doing so. What—can it under any circumstances or any arrangement of legal tactics be fitting work for a noble minded man to obscure the truth, to turn guilt into innocence, innocence into guilt, to perplex and punish the good man doing his duty, and save the bad man who has neglected his duty? Mr. Allwinde has won a high place in his high calling, and yet can find it consistent with his dignity to turn wrong into right, and right into wrong, to abet a lie, nay, to create, disseminate, and, with all the play of his wit, give strength to the basest of lies, on behalf of the basest of scoundrels! When Mr. Allwinde gave the jury to understand that the witness who was sweating in agony there before them might as probably have been guilty of the deed as the prisoner in the dock, did he not in effect tell the worst of lies for the worst of reasons?

And shall then a poor prisoner find no one to defend him? Shall the stern law execute her rigour against an ignorant man, and no power be given to him to urge on his behalf aught that legal knowledge might urge? The prisoner certainly has his right to be heard, and as he is in distress, let his right be doubly respected. Mercy requires it, and justice also. True, but will this justify Mr. Allwinde in what he has done? As well might it be argued that justice, and mercy too, mercy to those on whom murderers prey, require that the murderer should be hung, and that therefore Mr. Allwinde should take the hangman's fee and defile his hands with the hangman's rope. The argument in each case is the same.

If the necessary defence of a criminal require vile means, let it be given over to vile men. But it may safely be denied that anything vile is necessary. All the subterfuges to which recourse is now had to save crimes from punishment are evil in their immediate effect, doubly evil in their tendencies. May it not be asserted with positive certainty that the only object of such defence should be to save, not guilt, but innocence from punishment? to give every chance of escape, not to the man who has broken the laws, but to the man who has been wrongly charged with breaking them? Is this the view in which the matter is now looked at by lawyers? Is it not rather considered by them that the law is a system of meshes curiously constructed as an elaborate net, through which, if a man could but find it, there is always a loophole for escape? that it is their special duty, when duty fee'd, to assist men in finding such loophole?

Not that ye might maintain the laws and make them plain to

ordinary men, not that ye might see that they be rightly administered, not for such purpose, oh lawyers, were ye educated
with amazing skill, and patient industry; but that ye might
wittily assist mankind in evading them, that ye might show
how laws may be broken in the spirit, and kept to the letter,
that ye might make the laws an unintelligible, complex, in-
distinct, grandiose farrago of verbiage to become at last quite
unendurable by the British soul, for such purposes apparently
have ye, oh lawyers, been taught with so much care.

In what we have here said we have confined ourselves to the
criminal law, as being that in which the practices of our courts
most clearly lead to evil. But the courts in which questions as to
property are decided are at any rate equally open to censure. It
would not be worth while in pages like these to point out the
peculiar difference between the courts of common law, the
Chancery courts, and the ecclesiastical courts. It is no doubt
known to all that in the former cases are decided by a jury, and
in the two latter by the judge. In both is ample scope allowed to
the peculiarly ambiguous propensities of the lawyer.

Anything appears to be the object of the court, but that which
is clearly the object for which the court is there, namely the
speedy award of justice. My gentle reader, did you ever watch a
school boy eat a jam tart, one of those oblong tarts, which
pastry cooks of old sold for a penny—which they probably sell
now at much cheaper rate, with adulterated paste, fictitious jam,
and terribly diminished proportions?

Damnosa quid non imminuit dies?[4]

If so, have you not watched how he nibbles at the thin crust?
how he spares to touch the coveted fruit? how with slow, small,
circular bitings he goes round and round? how at last he undermines the rich centre of his luscious treat, and yet delays to eat
it? Surely when he made outlay of his penny, his object was to
eat that tart, and yet he eats it not. Eat it! what at once, and
thus rob himself of so long a pleasure of expectation? No, he
again goes round and round it, again undermines it with tender
nibbling, till at last the unsupported centre collapses. He sucks
from his fingers the scattered sweetmeat, and the tart, though
uneaten, is gone.

---

[4] Horace, *Odes*, III. vi. 45: 'What is there which damaging time does not
diminish?'

And reader, did you ever behold, in one of those dingy Lincoln's Inn courts, how the case of two litigants is handled? Does not the court, do not the learned barristers go round and round it, nibbling and still nibbling, as the boy did round his tart? Do they ever dream of dashing at the middle of it, making one wholesome mouthful, and so finishing the matter? Oh no: not so do boys eat their penny tarts, or lawyers dispose of the cases entrusted to them. Long custom, the usage of their brethren, and fathers and grandfathers, and their veneration for the secrets of law have made holy in their eyes the long delays and tortuous windings through which their clients will have to come, if they do at all so come, at their own.

Richard Roe and John Doe want to discover to which of them belongs a certain small field. They are cousins, and that the small field belonged to their grandfather is certain. Their fathers between them managed to get out of the field what was to be gotten, and to divide it without recourse to lawyers. But Richard Roe and John Doe, their descendants, are less fortunate. It becomes their fate to go to law about the small field.

Were it not well if they could go before a judge who should be able to tell them at once to whom the field belonged? who should hear from each what each had to say, looking into their documents, wills, and papers, and should then pronounce judgement briefly and finally? "Oh, Roe, this field is thine justly and of a certainty. Oh Doe, thou hast no earthly right to this field. It is not thine but thy cousin's." And so an end. Doe, certified that he could not properly get the field, would return quiescent if not contented, and struggle no further.

Surely if this could be so, it would be well for both of them. Lawyers will show many reasons why this cannot be so, reasons, the most of which have no truth in them, but are founded on adherence to time honoured prejudices; some of which, however, it might be difficult to gainsay. It may be that this curt way of deciding between Doe and Roe is not as yet practicable; but if so, let us at any rate approach to it as nearly as may be, not diverge from it as widely as possible.

That it would be best to have true justice thus quickly and cheaply dispensed, were it possible that true justice should be so dispensed, nobody will probably deny. But it seems to have been thought that as this is not possible, the other extreme should be adopted as the mode of treatment universally acknowledged to be second best.

Must it not have been on some such reasoning as this that so huge a mass of useless tautology has been introduced as a necessary component part of our legal proceedings? Go and look at that field of Richard Roe's. It is an innocent little field or paddock, lying contiguous to the village. A field and nothing but a field, unless you prefer to describe it as a paddock. Why then has it been so uselessly bedevilled by such a variety of ill-adapted denominations that Richard Roe himself, when reading of his own cause, hardly knows what it is all about? What is this farrago of messuages, tenements, premises, and hereditaments with lands, fields, paddocks, or crofts adjoining? and why are these eight appellations of one little field repeated nine times over in the same document?

Nine times over they occur, and will occur, till the legal world would have been taught that such verbiage of itself is an evil and not a good. Beseech your attorney to strike out but one of those nine repetitions, and he will declare that were he to do so, he would foully prejudice your cause. Other attorneys hostile to you would discover that the words had been repeated but eight times, and though the justice of your cause were as apparent as the sun at noonday, you would assuredly be overthrown. It is for that purpose that attorneys are required. If you, my reader, wish to frame a document that shall be binding both on you and on me, the terms to which the two of us would bind ourselves are known to both of us, and can be written down by you as clearly as by any attorney—how much more clearly we will not say. But you will not know—how should you?—whether that fiction of tenements, messuages, and hereditaments should be inserted nine times or only eight—nay, probably you might not insert it at all, and there were a pretty document with which to go into a court of law!

The English ear is beginning to be intolerably sick of whereas and aforesaid. The English stomach refuses longer to digest mountains of parchment. Reform in this matter has become not only necessary but probable, has moreover already begun to bestir itself. It will be well in these days for such lawyers as can bring themselves to assist the work, for the work will get itself done.

That a man who has grown grey in the practices of Chancery should see the absurdities of these practices and stigmatize them as absurd, can hardly be expected. It can hardly be hoped that Lords Justices and Chancellors, and Masters of the Roles should fully see the evil of that dilatory dignified dullness which has become one of the curses of the country. In such courses they have spent their lives. To them has accrued the dignity, to their clients the dullness and delay. Younger men will however do so, and by degrees we shall have Lords Justices and judges who will make it imperative that a field be called a field—and not even be so called more often than is necessary.

The trade of an English lawyer is a huge slough, but it is not the Slough of Despond. The drains are already being dug; the subsoiling has already commenced.

No profession probably owes so much to any one man wholly unconnected with it, as the profession of curing does to Molière. His raillery made the practice of the grosser absurdities of the art impossible in France;[5] and from France this impossibility has spread itself into other countries. Some college of physicians, some sanitary board, some great hospital should surely erect a statue to Molière. It is greatly to be wondered at that the schools of medicine in Paris have not already done so. To him we owe it in a great measure that at the present moment we have very little to say about English doctors.

In these latter days there may be reason to fear that trade is degenerating, that religion is becoming cold, oratory dull, and literature insipid. But science at any rate progresses. It is essentially an age of scientific research; and if science can suffice to make a people great and good, then it is probable that we may be in the right way to greatness and goodness.

The business of a doctor is in this respect unlike that of a tradesman, or a lawyer, or a clergyman, that it partakes of a scientific nature, and admits of and indeed requires scientific research.

The amelioration of medical practice has thus gone hand in hand with the requirements of the times, and to this it is

[5] See, for example: *L'Amour Médecin, Le Médecin malgré lui, Monsieur de Pourceaugnac, Le Malade imaginaire.* Cf. Trollope's comment about the wrath of Dr. Fillgrave: 'Had I the pen of Molière, I could fitly tell of such medical anger, but with no other pen can it be fitly told.' *Doctor Thorne* (O.U.P., London, 1926), p. 150 (Chap. xii).

probably owing that the daily work of a medical practitioner is at present less adulterated by pretence and falsehood than that of almost any other calling.

Science, however, can play pranks, and often delights to do so. When she speculates rather wildly on the infinite number of worlds which may, or, as she says, must coexist with our own, such speculation can at any rate do no material harm. When, however, she expresses her wish to speculate on our bodies, the matter becomes serious. Such speculations are now common enough. In former ages medicine had not sufficient aid from science. Now perhaps she may have, if anything, too much.

We are all of us fond of the marvellous. It is the frailty of human nature. We all feel that we could do some great thing, either in religion or medicine, if but a great thing could be vouchsafed to our faith. We all want to have Lazarus sent to us from Abraham's bosom. We are not contented to wash ourselves in the waters of Jordan. The waters of Jordan are too near to us, and too common. Thus we cannot bring ourselves to purge, leave sack, and live cleanly. We can drag ourselves and our diseases painfully to some German watering place, there to undergo ablutions in foul, fetid waters, to swallow loathsome drinks, and live idly and uncomfortably according to the stern behests of some quack medical autocrat.

Our own waters are as good as if we would but use them sufficiently (excepting always those of Father Thames),[6] our own drinks as wholesome, if we confine ourselves as strictly to those which be wholesome. Abstinence, cleanliness, and fresh air will here cure many evils, as they will do no doubt in Germany also. They will even do better than this; they will prevent them.

This taste for the marvellous has lately been indulged by the real or pretended begetting of spiritual results from medical agencies.

Men whose minds soar high are attempting to pluck what we fear we must call forbidden fruit, and to seek for the revelation of God's secrets from other sources than those which nature or religion affords.

It may probably be denied that medical science has in any way led to, or encouraged such inquiries. Medical science, as a

[6] The polluted Thames was a constant target for the comments of the press. See, for example, a cartoon in *Punch*, 21 July 1855, p. 27.

science, has not done so; but these studies and attempts have all arisen from medical phenomena, hitherto imperfectly understood; phenomena, which some men with more science than soundness, and others with more science than honesty, have pushed to extremities not warranted by experiment and not consistent with truth.

Mesmerism is by no means a recent innovation in medicine. The professor who has given his name to the practice lived about a century since,[7] and much attention was given to the matter in Paris and some parts of Germany many years ago. It is now about twenty or five and twenty years since the English public began to talk of mesmerism, and it then became the subject of much public inquiry.

That one man should exercise upon another a wonderful and indomitable influence without the aid of any medical appliances was at first sight startling enough, but it was by no means incredible. When we saw all the senses of a human creature brought as it were into a state of collapse, by the mere touchings or manipulations of another human creature; when we saw the movements and almost the instincts of one person placed under the control of another, at first we wondered, and disbelieved; and then we wondered and believed. The evidence adduced was too strong for disbelief, and none of the known laws of human nature were contravened. A wave of the hand from the healthy might have on the sick the effect of poppy juice or chloroform. The strong man might be able by his breath and touch to influence the weak. It might be that this was so, and as far as we could see into it, it appeared that it was so.

Medical men exhibited to us these phenomena, but they failed and have still failed to show us how to use them.[8] Science cannot always ascertain at once the use of its own discoveries. But phenomena such as these without a use soon become flat

[7] Friedrich Anton Mesmer (1734-1815), Austrian physician.

[8] In 1838 Dr. John Elliotson of London University College Hospital introduced into England the treatment of mental patients by mesmerism. He was the centre of much controversy; although at times given to somewhat theatrical methods of demonstration, he was a sincere and able physician. Trollope's mother and brother were friendly with Elliotson. See Thomas Adolphus Trollope, *What I Remember,* 2 vols. (Bentley, London, 1887), I, 366-74. Thackeray credited Elliotson's (non-mesmeric) ministrations with effecting his cure from a near fatal illness in 1849, and dedicated *Pendennis* to him.

and dull. Medical science could make nothing further of them; but medical charlatanry might do so. Then we heard of the wonders of clairvoyance. We were invited to see ladies with closed eyes read books from the pits of their stomachs; to be witnesses of ghost-like revelations of the doings of the absent; to hear wisdom and science fall from the lips of mesmerized babes. Electro-biology[9] followed, with a thousand changes rung on the same marvellous or supernatural instruments. We all went to see these wonders, but few of us were convinced that any lady did absolutely read any book with any portion of her body except her eyes. We think we remember that any lady who could do so might possess herself of a considerable bank note, if she would only so read the number of it; any lady or other person. Persons there were willing enough to turn an honest penny by their mesmeric powers, but we believe that the bank note so offered remained in the possession of the unbelieving offerer.

In fact such true discoveries as had been made were not sufficiently exciting to maintain their interest, and therefore falsehood was added to truth. Wonderful phenomena were produced if not by learned professors, at any rate by clever conjurors, and mesmerism and its train of absurdities for a while prevailed.

What of truth there may be in mesmerism, or animal magnetism as it may be better called, will no doubt again prevail; perhaps also the falsehood too for a while.

In the meantime the taste for the marvellous has progressed. The lady read so very little with that mesmeric stomach of hers that she gave but small satisfaction. Had she volubly and audibly given us were it even but the particulars of our own card cases it would have been much. What she read, however, was always submitted to her by strangers; and though nothing could be more respectable than her appearance, doubts somehow crept in, and we ceased to interest ourselves in clairvoyance.

But we were not left long in the dullness of every day human nature. Table rapping sprung into notice, and messages were brought to us direct from the other world by the recalled spirits

---

[9] Electro-biology was closely related to mesmerism except that it was performed upon persons who were (at least reportedly) fully awake. *Punch* saw it as the science or art 'by which it is possible to extract money ... from people's pockets.' (15 May 1852, p. 199.)

of our departed friends. Messages were so brought and are so brought. Now at this present time of writing any speculative Englishman may hold converse with his departed friends; such converse at least as this, that by due number of table rappings, sufficiently intelligent at any rate to an enterprising medium, the spirit will vouchsafe to say yes or no to any question that may not be perplexing. Your departed friend will also touch you, or rather not you, but your trousers or the skirt of your dress; perhaps even he may with covered fingers lay some flower upon your extended hand. But mark, only on one condition will he do this much, or indeed do anything for you—namely on this —that you sit duly obedient round a table sufficiently heavy, that you sit close to it, with head and body erect above it, so that no mortal eye shall watch how beneath the table he chooses to do his touchings and his flower liftings.

Music also shall not be wanting, but not music of the spheres. Music rather from an accordion, such as in toy shops are sold for 17/6. Is it not, nevertheless, sufficiently wonderful that your loved brother, oh reader, or that tender sister who with so much trust in heaven's mercy breathed out her last upon your shoulder, is it not sufficiently wonderful that she should return to earth, not to warn you to flee from the wrath to come, not to whisper to you of the joys of heaven when you shall be again together, but to play the accordion to you beneath the drawing-room loo table of a stranger?

It is sufficiently wonderful indeed. There is much to be said in favour of that theory of ghosts, which, in spite of the common sense protestations of most of us, finds so many ready believers. First, that the spirits of the dead have reappeared on earth we know from holy writ. That they shall again reappear we have never been instructed to disbelieve. That they will do so if such be God's pleasure we must all allow. That under no circumstances such a visitation can be possible, we think that no one, not the strictest utilitarian, in his innermost heart truly believes.

As children we used to dread that ghosts would appear to us among the dark branches of overhanging trees in the dead of night, or in the gloomy silence of long deserted rooms, or wandering among the graves of their departed brethren. Such a belief, though it were a childish creed, had in it at any rate something of the poetic. The philosopher might perceive that a

ghost would not in truth fly from the crowing of the cock, and
yet we have never had our sympathies or feelings hurt by the
general idea that he walks only at the dead of night. The table
rapping ghosts of modern days have, however, put children,
poets, and philosophers alike to the rout. Not wandering among
graves, not stalking like Hamlet's father upon castle ramparts,
nor creeping to the bed head with stealthy step at the silent
watches of the morn; nor rising with unwilling obedience at the
stern behest of the gifted bard, do the ghosts of our days appear
among us. 'Tis for past ages to be mazed by the ravings of a
crazed imagination. We are guided by facts and experience. To
us come spirits crouching beneath our drawing-room tables,
playing there upon little accordions which are handed to them
bodily, rapping our mahogany, and handing about with slow
action flowers from one to another. To this point has come the
ghost belief of the present age!

And this belief is a sound belief! There are hundreds of
educated people who do believe that in such a manner God
manifests himself to his creatures. For is not the return of a
spirit from the other world a direct and special manifestation
from God? What! that those we loved best shall return to give
us some word of comfort, some word of warning direct from
that other fearful world beyond the grave, and shall do so by
rapping thrice upon our tables! What! that our brothers and
our sisters shall come back to us but for a moment, the partners
of our bosoms, the children of our love, the lost darlings of our
inmost hearts, that they shall come back and satisfy their long-
ings and ours by twitching our lips, or playing a sorry tune upon
a child's toy! What! that such awful visitings shall be made not
in the deep solitude of our thoughts but in the presence of some
young American practitioner who chooses to tell us that he is
the medium for such phenomena![10]

Yes! such is the belief today of many educated men who tell
us that reason forbids them to believe anything without the

[10] Spiritualism and mediums were rightly considered an American importa-
tion; Trollope here may be alluding to the American medium Daniel Home
(the original for Browning's 'Mr. Sludge'). Trollope's mother and brother, both
interested in spiritualism, attended a seance conducted by Home at Ealing in
June 1855. See _What I Remember_, I, 374-7. Trollope's own scepticism about
spiritualism is again voiced in a letter to Kate Field, 3 June 1868, _Letters_,
p. 219.

practical evidence of experience! Men who cannot believe in the mystery of our Saviour's redemption can believe that spirits from the dead have visited them in a stranger's parlour, because they see a table shake and do not know how it is shaken; because they hear a rapping on a board, and cannot see the instrument that raps it; because they are touched in the dark, and do not know the hand that touches them! The Cocklane Ghost was as nothing to this.[11] The veriest scarecrow that ever schoolboy made out of a hollow pumpkin and a farthing candle has more in it worthy of belief than this. Oh—to what has that soul come that can believe in such visitings as these; that can put credit in spirits crouching among visitors' legs, and rapping tables with due assistance from some kind American medium?

It would be a gross misrepresentation to insinuate that the medical profession of England is in any way responsible for these vagaries. Such is by no means the case. It has, however, been by the agency of medical men, or of persons professing themselves to be such that these would-be spiritual manifestations have achieved notoriety.

It is greatly to be wished that the art of curing should be, among us, entirely free from that plague of the nineteenth century, the advertising system, that disease in which are combined the two most pernicious evils with which man can be afflicted, falsehood and self-praise. But it is, alas, becoming gradually infected. A man takes out a brazen trumpet sufficiently loud, and blows forth to the world a lying promise that he can cure all the ills that flesh is heir to. He, and he alone, he being the only true and duly skilful son of Galen! He! he can cure nothing! has no intention of trying to cure anything but the distressing emptiness of his breeches' pocket!

That a man should blow forth any lie, having well founded hope that money will thereby accrue, is, alas, not surprising. For money what lie, what abomination, will not be perpetrated among a people who profess to teach in their religion that a love of worldly things is incompatible with a hope of heavenly things? The odious self-laudation, odious at least till it has lost its odium by common use, and the falsehood are not surprising. But what shall we say of the belief in this egregious puffery?

[11] See Boswell's *Life of Johnson, aetat.* 54 (June 1763) and *aetat.* 69 (April 1778).

A.B. declares that for a sum of money he will cure any man of any affliction. C.D., afflicted, pays his money, tries the cure, and dies. Well, C.D. was an ass, and we think no more of him. But E. and F., and G. and H. do the same. We can no longer spare two letters to designate this mad crew. We want the whole alphabet, hosts of alphabets, to do so. A.B. publishes his name over doors sufficiently conspicuous and numerous, and sick crowds rush in depositing their coin, and looking for health.

We do not wonder at the lies, but the belief is surprising. In fact it is not belief. Were the falsehood repeated but twice or thrice, it would be scouted as a gross attempt at imposition. But when it has been repeated ten thousand times, men begin to think that the very repetition is proof of success. Dr. Curacoff, the celebrated Schlavonian practitioner, thanks the nobility and gentry of England for having been allowed to put them all upon their legs again, and refers to the sale of this ten millionth box of pills—also to certain letters from Lord A., Sir B. C., and the Viscount D. The base lie would not be believed, but the lie with all the circumstances is swallowed, and Dr. Curacoff makes his fortune.

We say that this system of puffing, this Barnum method of doing trade, is the bane of the nineteenth century, and is more operative than any one cause in sapping the strength of our empire. It is not only that each individual lie is in itself a mischief, but that men are taught to believe that lies and honest industry are compatible. Men are so taught who wish to live honestly but are not sufficiently awake to perceive the evil of the course prescribed for them. All wickedness is dangerous, but wickedness without disgrace is so with tenfold strength. Such is the wickedness of our British Barnums.

We have all laughed at the inimitable picture of the old quack mountebank. The man stands up with head erect, and flowing wig; with ruffles to his shirt and tawdry lace upon his coat. There he stands mounted above the common herd with his bottle of elixir between his fingers, ready to administer health to all—for a consideration. His boy between his legs spouts forth the long story of his skill, all his glory, all his success. He tells the long-eared and open-mouthed yokels how this thrice learned man has cured kings and princes and queens and princesses, and has nevertheless condescended to come to their low secluded village, actuated solely by the desire of administering to their ailments. And so he finishes his story. "What the boy says is true," says the quack. What can open-mouthed yokels do, but wonder and buy?

We speak now of scenes long past and gone. The old quack mountebank has become a subject for the comic muse. But do not open-mouthed, long-eared yokels wonder and buy in these days much more freely than ever they did in days of yore?

But, it will be said, the profession of medicine is as free from the plague spot as any calling in the country. Does any respectable doctor advertise for patients? Certainly none whom we should be inclined to look on as respectable. We should say that a man loses all claim to respect when once he commences so vile a practice. No—doctors in this country as a rule do not advertise. They do not yet do so—; but is there not a tendency that way? Alas, there is. Men striving to earn by hard work and competent skill bread for themselves and their children see that not bread only, but luxury, and coaches and splendour can be had by advertising, and the temptation is too strong for them.

A few years ago there was hardly such a thing as an English doctor, regularly graduated, advertising for patients and proclaiming his own merits in little paragraphs. Such doctors are common enough now.

A statement was made some little time since by a medical man to a Committee of the House of Commons that he abstained from sending his patients to the Apothecaries' Hall for their medicine because it was not expedient to create a monopoly in the sale of such articles.[12] Such a statement coming from a medical man does seem to be sufficiently perplexing. If one baker will sell good bread, and ten other bakers will obstinately persist in selling only bad bread, will you buy bad bread for fear of giving a monopoly to the good baker? Will you not rather draw off all customers to the last farthing from these bad bakers, so as to exterminate them utterly as bakers, unless they consent to bake on the same terms as that other one whose bread is good?

We would probably all do so as regards our bread—and if so, certainly we should the more anxiously do so as regards our medicine.

[12] *The Times*, 30 July 1855, reported one Doctor Thomson as so testifying.

Among other matters which have been proved to be grossly adulterated by the vendors or manufacturers, at any rate before they reach the consumers, it has been shown that drugs are so treated to a disgraceful extent. Would not any monopoly for the sale of good drugs be better than this?

Surely it should be the earnest wish of every honest medical man to save his patient from the effects of such roguery. Not only his wish, but surely it must be his duty to do so. The dealings of the chemist must depend upon the practice of the physician, and if physicians would boldly denounce all chemists whose drugs are adulterated, there would soon be an end of adulterated drugs, and an end also of the dreaded monopoly. Druggists will keep bad drugs only as long as they are vendible. When they are no longer so the shops will not be shut up, but will probably be supplied with articles such as people will buy.

With this small matter of advice, all that we venture to give, we take leave of our friends the doctors, thankfully acknowledging their merits.

CHAPTER V

The Army and Navy

J U D G E S and generals, soldiers and policemen are disagreeable necessities in this wicked world; but being necessary, should, one would say, be made as efficient as circumstances will allow.

The necessity for judges and police has never been disputed or doubted, never at least in sinful England. But keen as we have all been for war, now for these two last years, it is not long since the majority of Englishmen did entertain a hope that a state of European warfare was a barbarity never again to be repeated, as far as their country was concerned.

Elihu Burritt and theoretical peace principles never became popular.[1] We could not bring ourselves to declare that if as a nation we got a blow on the face, we would turn the other national cheek to the smiter. That pretty Christian idea of Lord Palmerston's correspondent met with but little encouragement, that which would have taught us meekly to receive the French as enemies and masters into London, and then shame them into behaviour by our meekness.[2] Practical Quakerism can hardly be said to be natural to an Englishman. One might as well attempt to persuade one's bull-dog to allow his favourite bone to be taken without resistance from between his jaws, by the semishorn parlour poodle. Nevertheless, bull-dogs as we are, we had begun to think that from henceforth and for evermore we should be allowed to mouth our own bone in this sea girt kennel of ours without being called on to show our teeth. The hope, however, was not long lived. We now find that if we wish to keep our home safely for ourselves, we must not allow other dogs to be too masterful.

[1] Elihu Burritt (1810-79), American linguist, reformer, and pacifist. He had very moderate success in England, founding the 'League of Universal Brotherhood' in 1846; the Crimean War routed his cause.

[2] In a speech to the House of Commons, 4 May 1852, Palmerston, successfully sponsoring legislation for establishing a strong national militia against a would-be invasion by the French, held up to ridicule an anonymous pamphlet, *The Rifle Club: being a Manual of Duty for Soldiers, whether Regular, Militia, or Volunteers* [John Tindall Harris] (London, 1852). See Hansard, *Parliamentary Debates*, 3rd Series, CXXI, 242-3.

Soldiers and policemen are, alas, still very necessary. But England, not being quite of this opinion a few years since, and imagining that policemen would do at home, and that soldiers would not be needed abroad, allowed her army to run rather into the yellow leaf. Other trades and professions doubled their own numbers in the course of a few years, whereas our army numbered only some 8 per cent more men in 1850 than it had done in 1820, at which latter time it had been reduced to a peace standard. Wages increased for every kind of work except fighting: but as fighting was much out of fashion, and looked on as a brainless sort of calling for which any man was good enough, soldiers' wages did not increase. Comforts and decencies of life found their way among most classes of labourers, much quicker than they did into barrack life. The barracks were filled with the dregs of the nation, with soldiers who could not appreciate comforts and decencies! Soldiers were to be treated like hounds; to be herded together, to be fed, to be spoken to, to be flogged, like hounds. Matters are now somewhat altered.

Fifteen years ago if a man listed he thereby owned himself to be a castaway. No statesman dared to speak of increasing the numbers or the cost of the army. On the reappearance of every year's estimates the necessity of a further reduction in the peace establishment of the country was dinned into the ears of unhappy ministers. The army was unpopular. Retrenchment and economy were the cry of the darlings of the people. Newspapers then preached quite other doctrine than that now held by them. No war with Russia was then feared; no, nor with Austria, nor Prussia, nor even France. The army was unpopular—nay almost unnecessary after 30 years of peace. Are the days of Joseph Hume so long since gone, that these things should be forgotten?[3]

Under such circumstance is it very strange that the army should have become inefficient? Would it not rather have been very strange if it had been found efficient for any great undertaking? Has the reader ever made one at a large dinner party given by a lady not accustomed to provide such extensive entertainments? If so, does he not remember how vile was the soup,

---

[3] Joseph Hume (1777-1855), a prominent radical member of Parliament for more than forty years, who was renowned as a campaigner against governmental waste of money.

how completely bedevilled by malcooking was the fish, how raw was the mutton, how cold were the plates, how disagreeably the potatoes and cauliflowers were handed to him after he had eaten, or completed his vain attempt at eating, the meat provided to him? how vain were his wishes to get some wine, his hostess clearly thinking any such distribution without the intervention of the greengrocer's assistant to be vulgar? Reader, have you not seen, and marked, and groaned under all this? And yet that lady worked as no lady will work in other cause than that of a grand dinner party. We will not speak of yesterday's labours, but early in the morn she began her toil; with tucked up sleeves she ate her morsel of breakfast, and for nine hours since she has striven among gravies and sauces, among glasses and napkins, among joints and trussed fowls, boiling pots and turning spits. With her own hands she made that pudding. It broke as it left its mould, and at the sight her own heart broke also.

If her cook got drunk under the novel exertions, was this lady to be blamed for that? Or if the greengrocer's man was proud, and would not be said by her; or if the hot plate, unused to the practice, would not become heated; or if the pastry cook would not send home the patties till the guests had arrived, causing the lady to sit on the sharpest thorns, were these things her fault? Poor lady! See how she has failed to reduce the redness of her o'erlaboured arms, or wash from her brow by special cosmetics the tell-tale traces of her toils. She descends to dinner, fights her great battle, and fighting, fails and falls. Bitter then is the pillow of that unsuccessful heroine.

Any man who can speak of such attempts with acrimony, any man whose charity is dormant on such an occasion as this, can have within his bosom very little of the true feeling of a Christian. Oh Lady, remember in thy grief that Rome was not built in a day. It is not given to human nature to conduct either a campaign or a dinner party to successful issue without much study and much practice. Thou art doubtless excellent as a mother, irreproachable as a wife, long suffering and kind as a mistress. But in evil hour that husband of thine exacted from thee suddenly gifts which thou hadst not, gifts which thou couldst not have. Thou didst thy very best, and now he scolds thee. Poor lady! Poor War Minister!

Some angry critic, scoffing, will declare that there is no analogy in the two cases. Had we not our wars with the Afghans, and the Sikhs, with the Caffres, and the Burmese? Did not these give us lessons which in the day of need should have been useful to us?

Yes—and that lady also—she had her Afghan and Burmese contests, she had also skirmished with the Caffres, and not without credit. Her husband's casual friend when brought in at the hour of dinner has never failed to find wherewithal to make his meal. The Curate on a Sunday has thought her parlour very comfortable. Nay, she in this modest way enjoyed much hospitable repute. It has been the sudden greatness of the undertaking that has upset her.

If one could have crept into Russia by degrees; if we could have had a year's preparatory campaign with small forces on each side; if we could have been satisfied with bombarding Odessa instead of investing Sebastopol, we might thus have learnt our work. Nothing, however, would satisfy the national honour, but that the nation should at once open all its doors and give its grand entertainment, unprepared as it was for doings on such a mighty scale. And now because the plates were cold the nation thinks that it has a right to scold and to be cross. The nation is surely most unreasonable.

The nation has been most unreasonable if the cry that was raised was really a national complaint. It is hard now-a-days to say what is the voice of the nation. If it be admitted that the Times newspaper is that national voice, the complaint has been very loud indeed. Such admission, however, let us be slow to make. If it be made, one would say that a rational man could not too quickly take himself and his family to Geelong or some such locality; could not with too much haste make himself the denizen of some nation using a voice, less audible indeed, but also less arrogant.

But let us see what we have done and what we have left undone as a fighting nation. There are two kinds of warfare prevalent among men, war by sea and war by land. To our insular habits sea warfare has been for many years the most appropriate. Although probably no nation in Europe has enjoyed so large a proportion of military success in comparison with her military reverses as England has done even on land, it is of her naval

prowess that she is the more specially proud. While we have ourselves ascribed to the large continental kingdoms the title of
great military monarchies, we have essentially circumscribed
our own claims to those of naval supremacy. Our boast has been
and is that on the whole wide ocean we cannot meet our superior.
Has anything in this war tended to show that such boast has
been vain?

Has it not rather been the fact that our own excellence has
been the cause of our own limited success? our own excellence,
let us say, and that of our allies. And as we do not scruple to give
to them the leading place of glory on shore, as little need we
hesitate to claim for ourselves the same lead upon the seas.

It is our own excellence that has impeded our own success. If we
cannot tell of such glories as those of Copenhagen and Trafalgar,
it has been because our adversary, with all his boasted maritime
preparation, has not dared to try the force of an English broad-
side. What we could do we have done; whatever can be done by
naval force we may safely hope to do, if this peace be not
ultimately confirmed.[4] We have succeeded in absolutely banish-
ing from the deep seas every trace of a Russian keel. We have
compelled our enemy to destroy with his usual self-immolating
tactics the whole of that fleet on the construction of which so
many years have been expended.[5] And now we are prepared to
follow him up through the intricate shoals of his own rivers.

What if Russia's fleet had been lying comfortably at the
Nore? What if Sheerness had been held by Russian gun boats,
and the entrances to Hamoaze and Portsmouth impeded
merely by the masts of our own sunken leviathans? We should
be apt to think in such case as that, that Russia had been
sufficiently successful. Such success we at any rate did obtain.

Latter day economists have been somewhat willing to allow us
our navy, on the implied permission that they should do what
they willed with the army; and the result has been a degree of
naval excellence unequalled not only in England but in any
other country, since navies first floated.

If this be so, and even that public opinion of which the Times

[4] Hostilities in the Crimea ended in January 1856. The Treaty of Paris was
signed 30 March.

[5] Early in the conflict and as part of the defence of Sebastopol, the Russian
Commander, Prince Mentschikoff, had ordered Russian ships to be sunk
across the mouth of the harbour.

assumes to be the voice will hardly deny it, then at any rate has the government of England no cause to be ashamed of the part the country has played.

It must be admitted that at the beginning of the war the army of England was not able to give a great military entertainment with *éclat*. Like the lady with her dinner party, she did not know how to set about it, and had not at her hand servants conversant with all that such occasions require. One thing she had; that indomitable pluck which no want of generalship would disgrace; that bull-dog propensity to fight which no amount of laceration could intimidate.

But if rightly looked at, it may be doubted if anything in the annals of England should give an Englishman more pride than the doings and sufferings of this Crimean army; or if history will tell aught of us which we may more honestly hope that our children may live to read. In this eulogy are included nearly all that have been concerned in the war; so nearly all, that no invidious exception need be made.

There is much honour to be paid to the Duke of Newcastle.[6] Honour ultimately will be paid to him, when the voice of the country as expressed by daily newspapers has floated by on the wind, and the voice of history begins to be audible. We can conceive nothing nobler than a man working as he worked, working night and day for the sake of his country, and so working in opposition to insuperable evils. Who has not felt in some minor matters the hopelessness of rushing into interminable toils from which circumstances have banished all method and all rule? Success is impossible unless some God would come and aid. But yet work, manly, heart given, true work, will lessen the evil and prepare for better days.

Such was the task to which the Duke of Newcastle was set. The country had for years past determined that it would not have an operative army. It then of a sudden determined that it would. To the Duke of Newcastle fell the impossible task of reconciling the discrepancy. Had he refused, as he might have done, our old friend, public opinion, would have called him a

---

[6] The Duke of Newcastle (1811-64) headed the War Office during the Crimean conflict until charges of mismanagement of the war brought down the Aberdeen ministry in late January 1855. Palmerston then became Prime Minister.

coward. He did accept it, and in the dread hour of his agony of failure, public opinion called him a fool. But when did public opinion, public opinion at least of this class, know either charity or honour, mercy or truth?

The Duke of Newcastle failed, as any mere mortal must have failed; and when clamour was strong against him, went out from his too arduous labour without a murmur; went out from it when the back of the great difficulty was already broken, when confusion had done its work, and chaos was on the eve of becoming order. He went out without a murmur to make way for a more lucky successor.

It is well for us, well also for Lord Palmerston, that he had not, as the people desired, been made our war minister from the first. Had such been his fate, he too would have undergone the ordeal of his colleague. He too would have been voted incompetent, and who then would have been our Premier?

Very probably the Duke of Newcastle.

The same amount of difficulty, and the same sort of embarrassment, fell to the lot of poor Lord Raglan,[7] and all others bearing onerous command in the expedition. Unalloyed success was made impossible by the want of preparation; but unalloyed success, and that also continuous and immediate, was imperatively required by public opinion. Public opinion also was somewhat unfortunate. She declared that such success had been won, and would never forget or forgive her own mistake.

And yet how hard we strove to be successful. Nothing would suffice for England's bull-dog spirit, but that she with her scanty regiments should take an equal share in the labour to be done. It was thus that we commenced; rashly probably, but at any rate with the concurrence of the country. Had we at that hour after the first glory of Alma,[8] the first regret of our mistaken ovations for fallacious success, spoken feebly of ourselves, and begged our multitudinous allies to give us only our fair share of work per man; what then would public opinion have said? Is there any man who watches the Press of this country who can doubt?

No. The whole army, from the highest man to the lowest

[7] Lord Raglan (1788-1855), British Commander-in-Chief in the Crimea. With Newcastle, he received most of the blame.

[8] Raglan had achieved an early victory at the Alma River, 20 Sept. 1854.

attempted the work—each man of two men. They attempted it, and did it. There can be no nobler sight to see than this. A noble sight, and yet a sorrowful. For though the heart to make such struggle may be given to man, not so is given the power to maintain it.

It would be well for England that she had no blush upon her brow but that which her Russian wars have brought there. Such blushes would become her.

We are told that English tactics and English generals have become bywords through the cities of Europe. Who can be surprised? When public opinion here is so ready to deprecate the doings of England, why should public opinion elsewhere be more chary of our honour?

Public opinion, so self-dubbed, is mainly anxious for her own supremacy, mainly desirous to prove her own infallibility. Her first object is to show how much more worthy of support she is at 4*d.* a day, than any other expression of opinion whatsoever. Public opinion, at 4*d.* a day, responsible only to its purchasers, may safely condemn ministers and cabinets, generals and admirals. She may safely call upon government to perform any amount of impossibility; to create an army in which no soldier shall be under 30, no officer over 40; to make in a day changes which must be the work of years; to take towns as fast as she herself can say that they have been taken; to alter the nature of men, and provide that every soldier at 1/6 a day shall be a Christian as well as a hero. Public opinion can demand that every servant of the Crown shall be faultless, and can yet find grievous fault with every act of every such servant. Public opinion can extol the energetic virtue of the people, and accuse the equally active vice of their rulers. This public opinion can do, and sell itself to an amazing extent at 4*d.* a day. By so doing she does maintain her own supremacy. That done, it is a small matter that the supremacy of the country should suffer!

If rightly looked at, the annals of this Russian war can take nothing from our national name, must indeed add much to it. To have suffered grievously is no disgrace; to have suffered manfully is great honour; to have suffered grievously, and through such suffering to have maintained our ground and achieved our object is most honourable. To how many minds last year had the idea presented itself of our army, the miserable relic of our army, escaping or trying to escape from that little harbour of Balaklava?[9] How often to Lord Raglan must have occurred the present pressing fear of so dread a necessity?

He held his ground, however, to the great glory of England. With his few men, with his scanty army, he and those under him skilfully, gallantly strove to do what skill and gallantry could do to support with small means a great part in a great contest.

Everything that the bitterest of our enemies could have said against our tactics, had our enemies had spies ever present in our camps, was said by—so called public opinion. Every evil, and the ills of the army were not small, was magnified and ascribed, not to the difficulty of the position, but to the culpability of men in command. If we did but borrow a ration of bread from our allies, public opinion in England complained of the loan with the bitterest sarcasm. No complaint, however, was made either here or in Paris, of the at any rate equal assistance which, from time to time, the English were happily able to afford to their friends. The poetic imagination of times long past accredited to the prowess of one hero seven wondrous labours, each far too heavy for the best efforts of merely mortal man. We know how Hercules achieved them all. Could, however, the adverse deity have conceived the idea of bidding him urge a war with "our own correspondent" in his camp,[10] Hercules would have been beaten, and never have taken his seat among the Gods.

Judging from the history of the past two years, one might almost say that fighting is that trade for which an Englishman is best adapted. That, at any rate, it seems manifest he will do when called on, in a manner very far from inefficient. Let us for a while speak now not of generals but of soldiers. In too many conditions of life we Englishmen will, if possible, shirk out of the task for which we are responsible. The day labourer if not

---

[9] Balaklava, British supply port in the Crimea and scene of much deprivation and suffering during the winter of 1854-5.

[10] William Howard Russell (1820-1907), war correspondent for *The Times*, whose relentless criticism of the British conduct of the war contributed greatly to the downfall of Aberdeen's government. Trollope, who later came to know and admire Russell, wrote of him as a 'marvellous' wit and a 'charming champion' both 'abroad as special correspondent, or at home amidst the flurry of his newspaper work,' *Autobiography*, ed. Frederick Page (O.U.P., London, 1950) p. 152.

watched will often do less than he should do. The tradesman will sell for the price named much less than he ought to do; the clergyman is seldom too fond of the houses of the poorer of his flock; we have heard even of judges who would take their pleasure when they should be on the bench. The soldier, however, does not shirk his responsibility of being shot at. Young gentlemen, who infinitely prefer billiards to Blackstone, or boating to Aristotle, have apparently no objection whatever to dying with the colours of the regiment in their hands.

It is perhaps somewhat startling that this should be so, considering all that has been said and thought of the progressive civilization of Europe, and the high position which we Englishmen hold in it. There is certainly no reason why courage should be lessened by civilization or why the powers of the body should not go hand in hand with those of the mind. Nevertheless, fighting will not often be the chosen profession of thoughtful men; and will be so the less frequently, the higher are the rewards offered for the works of peace.

Some centuries since there was hardly any profession open to one of gentle blood but that of fighting. Did such a man wish for active work, he necessarily became a soldier, and therefore in those days such men were always warriors. It was the natural result of the feudal system, and of the ignorance of the age. Had Cicero been born an English nobleman of the fourteenth century, he would have gone into the army.

Now, however, as we are accustomed to think, the way of our world is much changed. Gentility may engage itself in numerous pursuits, and in all may hope to attain higher reward, and as a rule more honour, than in the army. One would say that a barrister in high repute has more to gratify his ambition than a colonel of a regiment; or a bishop of a diocese, than a district general. A clerk in the Civil Service, low as may be his salary, will generally receive more than a captain in the line; and few doctors are so badly fee'd as regimental doctors. Nevertheless, the army is still our most popular profession; and, in spite of the actual slave's life to which the private devotes himself, the trade of a soldier is so well looked upon among the labouring classes that we are still able to fill our ranks without conscription.

At the present moment there is much to be thankful for in

this. It may well be doubted whether fighting is the noblest calling to which a man can apply his energies. It is in its very essence opposed to those theories which every good man hopes may become, in God's own time, the practice of the world. None think that war can in itself be a good. But the days of warfare are not yet over. Elihu Burritt and his friends are foolishly premature in their aspirations. It is well for us now that there is so much of the bull-dog breed left among us.

It is well; and we should be thankful that our soldiers are so true and good; that military order among us is still so dominant a feeling. For so much we may well be thankful, and express our thanks in far other voice than that now used by public opinion.

That changes both in our army and navy have become necessary, and will so become, no sane man will probably deny. It is, however, certain enough that the government is anxious to make such changes at any rate as fast, if not faster, than it can safely do so. How, however, can a poor government use its own discretion in such matter when under the all powerful pressure of public opinion?

CHAPTER VI
The Church

WHEN the Church is spoken either of four things may be intended. Allusion may be made to the material building of brick or stone in which we are wont to say our prayers. Or to the priesthood of the Episcopalian Church of England. Or to the members, lay as well as clerical, of that individual body. Or to the whole multitude of human beings who believe, or profess to believe, in the revealed religion of Christ.

It is in the latter sense that those who read these pages must be requested to understand the word for a short while. That such a reading of the word will be offensive to many whom the author would wish to propitiate is much to be deplored by him. It is in such sense, however, that the Church is here spoken of. Surely such is the only true sense in which one should venture to speak of the Church of Christ.

Who, here below, shall dare to say that among all the systems of Christ's worship now prevalent his and his alone is such as to conciliate the God whom he adores? Who again shall decide those who believe from those who do but profess to believe? Do we not all feel within ourselves that much of our belief is but a profession? That if we be even half sincere, our sincerity is more than ordinarily strong? That if there be a grain of truth within us to save our hearts from death and hypocrisy, it is well for us? Who then shall attempt to exclude from the Church of Christ those who are but professing believers?

By the word Church we would include all who believe, or think that they believe, or even say that they believe in our Saviour. All who rule the actions of their lives by his precepts; or who attempt to do so; or who would have it thought they make such attempt. It is of such that the Church of Christ is in truth composed. The gradations of belief are infinite, and fall by most minute points of descent from the rapt ecstasy of enthusiastic fire which warmed the martyrs of old down to the thin idea of angry omniscience which serves only to scare the hardened sinner in his moments of uneasy rest.

Such being the Church of which we are now speaking, it may be well to see whether, on the whole as regards this our own country, it be increasing in strength, vigour, and truth; whether it be growing in grace, and bringing men nearer to God than they have hitherto been. Or whether it be merely stationary, an inactive Church, satisfied with the amount of good it has done, satisfied to leave mankind as it finds them, if only it can so leave them. Or whether indeed it may be doing worse even than this; whether it be not going down from its high places, abandoning its struggle, and sinking from day to day lower and lower still in the scale of its faith.

This at any rate is a question of some importance. It may be presumed that if any nation adopt a religion it is desirous to live and die by the precepts which that religion teaches. It is not to be kept as many a museum is kept by many a town, for the honour and glory of the possession; into which no inhabitant ever dreams of entering unless for the purpose of exhibiting it to a stranger. One would not choose to fit up one's religion as the retired grocer's wife does her drawing-room; making it indeed the smartest of rooms, but one in which it would be very uncomfortable for her to live. One would not erect a religion as some nations do statues and arches, merely because it is the fashion to have them, indifferent as to the beauty and intrinsic worth of the ornaments. One would say that it is so essential a matter, this of religion, that a man or a people would at any rate make up their mind strongly whether they wanted it or not. That wanting it, they would know that they wanted it sorely, and would use it earnestly as a workman does his strong tools. That not wanting it, they would abandon it as the emptiest of idle mysteries, and walk along with assurance, showing manifestly by their course that man with his own reason is self-sufficient for all purposes of life.

Which do we do? Do we not dangle in the middle, vacillating like a pendulum? or rather not like a pendulum, for we vacillate without a rule.

That there is at present in England a considerably increased activity among persons professing religion is certainly true. We are building very many churches, and generally building them in good taste; we are increasing the number of our clergy, especially the bishops; we are increasing the number of our

services, though not infrequently, without any attendant servants. Church of England Protestants, of high church and of
low church; dissenting Protestants, Presbyterians, and Romanists, are all active, dragging in money and laying it out, building
and delving, and ditching and instituting, contriving with all
their cunningest wits each to uphold the standard under which
he has decided to do battle.

But with whom are they fighting, and what standard do they
uphold? Do they fight the Devil under the standard of Christ?
Is that their main stress of battle? No—they fight each other,
each under the small ragged banner of some petty revolt.

See that pious lady returning from her church, with thin
compressed lips, meditating deeply on the words she has
heard. Yes; she is meditating deeply. The seed that has been
sown in her heart is already germinating, and will not be
destroyed by birds or choked by thorns, but bring forth fruit,
such as is its nature.

And what is the lesson which she has so faithfully learnt?
The bitterness of religious rancour, the depth of religious contempt, the fascinating warmth of religious hatred. She is even
now thanking God in her heart that she is not as that wretched
publican, the Romanist, who, in the temple of idolatry opposite,
is gazing with ignorant adoring eyes on a vain picture of the
mother of God. Yes, the best lesson that her minister knew how
to teach her was the vileness of the errors of Rome. On that he
will preach with acrid eloquence from Sunday to Sunday; on
that he will harp on Thursday evenings and on Wednesday
mornings; at every hour that he can persuade an audience to
attend at his call. For the hearing of such anathemas against his
Christian brethren he thinks that all works should be postponed,
all amusements laid aside—amusements indeed, devices of the
Devil! amusements when Mr. Everscreech will vouchsafe to
hold forth against the harlotries of the scarlet woman!

And therefore that poor lady walks along filled with hatred
rather than with love; denouncing to herself within her little
heart doctrines of which she is incapable of understanding either
the truth or falsehood; endeavouring to prepare, not for herself
a place in heaven, but for her next door neighbour a place in
hell.

Oh, lady with thin lips and embittered little heart, tell me what is transubstantiation, or what consubstantiation? Tell me what is the doctrine of that Church in which thou trustest, thou and Mr. Everscreech. Tell me also thine own doctrine. No, that were too hard a task. Mr. Everscreech has as yet omitted to teach that. Mr. Everscreech has been contented to teach how vile is that Romish priest, that be-coped, be-stoled, be-caped rival of his, that fiend of Satan with his mysteries and his mummeries; to teach how that false shepherd is driving, leading, and alluring the souls of his sheep into the deep pits of hell. Such are the religious lessons on which that lady is meditating deeply.

Is the doctrine of the Church of Christ as taught by Mr. Everscreech one by which a Christian can contrive to live well in the world; to live in such a way as to entitle him to hope for a better world? Is it a doctrine by which his hearers do so live?

Let us listen to him with patience for some dozen Sundays and find out the points of conscience on which he most ardently insists. Are they not as follows: hatred of Rome; strict observance of the Sabbath; and abhorrence of worldly wealth, pleasure, and sensual appetites? It is on these subjects that Mr. Everscreech most delights to discourse.

Hatred of Rome, one would say, can of itself help no man on his path. Hatred of Rome cannot do so, or of Romans, or of any other Church or people. No hatred can do so, be the thing hated ever so vile. That the Church of Rome has grave errors Mr. Everscreech's hearers will all admit. How otherwise should they be there? But this repeated rabid denunciation of such errors will hardly of itself teach his disciples the secrets of Christianity. Christ rebuked the broad phylacteries of the Pharisees because they were the outward semblances of a religion which had failed to touch the hearts of those who wore them. But he abstained from repudiating the doctrines or laws of those whom he came to persuade.

Strict observance of the Sabbath! This is the sacred Shibboleth by which Mr. Everscreech and so many of his brethren endeavour to scare sinners into obedience. Let us inquire for a moment by whom and on whom it was enjoined, and what it means. The Jews were ordered by God to keep holy the Sabbath day, and to this was added an injunction that on that day they should do no manner of work; neither they nor their sons, nor their daughters, nor their manservants, nor maidservants. Such undoubtedly was the law given to the Jews, and it clearly enjoined an entire cessation of all the ordinary doings of life. As such it was taken by the Jews. On the Sabbath no bed was strewn by them, no food prepared, no board was laid. An utter abstinence from every worldly occupation testified that obedience which was for them the only evidence of faith.

That these commandments in their literal sense were not intended for us, any more than are other portions of the Jewish law, it would be easy to show. In them the practice of virtue is enforced by the promise of temporal reward. The stern justice which punished in the children of Ahab the sins of the father is inculcated; and strict literal obedience is commanded as the one thing needful to procure the love of the Creator. It were easy to show that Christ has repeated to us in his law those plain injunctions which God gave to the Jews not to steal, not to murder, not to commit adultery, not to covet; but that he has nowhere commanded his disciples to adhere to the ceremonial observance of the Sabbath which had been to their fathers so binding an obligation.

But assuming that this fourth commandment be clearly addressed to us, is Mr. Everscreech successful in securing obedience to it from any portion of his congregation? Is it not manifest to us, to them, and to him, that such an order as that which he endeavours to enforce is repulsive to our reason, negatived by our habits, and openly repudiated not only by all his hearers, but by himself also? He preaches with bitter anathemas a doctrine which he himself does not attempt to fulfil.

What shall we do on the Sabbath of the Lord? Sing praises unto him to whom it belongs, says Mr. Everscreech. "I will sing praises unto the Lord," says David, "because it is so comfortable." Oh yes, if it be comfortable. But are the psalms of Mr. Everscreech a comfort to his people? Is obligatory dullness comfortable, and an empty mind? are long unmeaning profitless hours comfortable, and constrained prayers, and an unsuccessful attempt at prolonged devotion? Comfort! Oh yes, whatever our Sundays be, let them be a comfort to us; a comfort to such as be rich; but a comfort especially to such as be poor. Unless our day of worship be a comfort, our worship will avail us but little. To Mr. Everscreech's people Sunday, one would say, is not comfortable.

The vanity of worldly things, of wealth, and sensual pleasures is insisted on by Mr. Everscreech in long discourses of which none of his hearers doubt the truth, but by which none of his hearers attempt to regulate their lives. If those hot eager words of his be true, how is it that they are thus ineffectual? In truth they are not true. Wealth and pleasure and worldly things are not vain; and it is utterly without effect for good, though with much effect for evil, that you, Mr. Everscreech, and so many others circulate so false a doctrine. If it be true, why cannot men live by it? By a true doctrine men can live. Why dost not thou live by it—thou thyself? Thou art as eager for thy tithes, thy well earned tithes, we will say, as is the doctor for his fee, the landlord for his rent. Thou art as anxious to provide some worldly sustenance for those hitherto unmarried daughters of thine, as either are for their offspring; as conscious that without the aid of some worldly wealth thou and the partner of thy bosom will hardly come at the joy of seeing them taken from thee, each by a loving husband. Hast thou ever preached so that men will fly from the seduction of a well cooked dinner, or women from the glib tongued gossip of the tea table? Hast thou succeeded in withdrawing the hunter from his hounds, or the eager whist player from his shilling points? And thou, thyself; thou dost not hunt, nor perchance play whist; but, say, in thine own heart are not the things of this world very dear to thee? the handsome cob on which thou ridest, the soft chair which receives thy weary limbs, ay, and the mellow wine which refreshes thee after those exertions of eloquence?

Wealth and the pleasures of the world are not vain. Who, but a few maddened enthusiasts, have proved by their lives that wealth to them was vain, or have succeeded in withdrawing themselves from the pursuit of worldly pleasure? The desire of wealth is planted in every bosom. Without it civilization could not have advanced; nor the scheme of God in the creation been carried out. The love, nay, the necessity of pleasure, is a part of our nature. Without it the life of man could not have been joyous and mirthful as our Creator has intended. They who preach against wealth and worldly pleasures preach a false doctrine; a doctrine by which men have never yet succeeded in living. Oh, Mr. Everscreech, if thou hadst but the power to teach how love of wealth may run riot, and become covetous-ness; but how also under due constraint it may be kept from doing so. If thou couldst teach how worldly pleasures may by over indulgence interfere with worldly labour, how they may thus become foul and wicked; but how by due enjoyment they will sweeten the tasks of life, and make even toil delightful; then indeed wouldest thou have earned thy tithes, and preached a doctrine by which men might learn to live.

Look again at that pretty girl, as she trips across the frozen snow two hours before the sun has risen to hear her favourite pastor intone gracefully through his nose a certain portion of the liturgy. How sweet and innocent she looks with her boa and her sable muff, and her little feet encased in fur, glancing on the shining ground. Surely there is no malice in that heart, no harshness in that teaching, no evil in such habits as those. Punctually she goes to primes and complines, to tierces and vespers. With pretty diligence she works coverings for altar tables, credence tables, and faldstools. With willing self-negation she fasts on Wednesdays and Fridays, on the eve of every feast, and through the long days of pitiless Lent. Well she knows (as well as any monk of old, and much more rigidly she keeps her rules) when to eat her jejune fish with melted butter and when to eat it dry; when to improve her tea with cream, when to deny herself the little luxury which she loves. See how her innocent letters are dated, those letters to the friend of her heart, in which she expatiates with enthusiasm on the new toy which she has found. The Eve of St. John, the Feast of St. James, Tuesday in Easter week. The common names of months to her are mere relics of pagan mythology. March and April are heathen denominations. Every word and thought with her must bear some impress of a Christian church.

And can there be evil in this? Yes, the huge evil of unreality. We would not use a harsh word for those whose efforts to do good are doubtless sincere; but would ask them on what authority they suppose that matins and vespers, complines and nones are a service acceptable to their maker? On what ground they presume that a few prayers intoned gracefully, or ungracefully, before daylight can be necessary to man's welfare here or hereafter?

That we have no heavenly command for such a proceeding is at any rate certain.

But how can such practices affect the ordinary life of man? If they be compatible with industry, honesty, and truth; if they be conducive to juster dealings among men, and a fuller appreciation of man's labour here on earth; if they be productive of sincere energy and faithful work, then let us all in heaven's name adopt them, even though we cannot plead God's word for their authority.

But how is this? Can thou, my labouring friend, who so honestly followest that plough of thine through miles of furrows, canst thou leave thy trusty Dobbin, and trusty Smiler, and go to nones and complines? would it be well for thee to give up, say, a third of thy wages, that thou mightest hear from day to day prayers be they never so gracefully intoned? Or for that wife of thine, with her five young bairns; would it be well for her?

But these are rustics who live far from churches; and customs may be fit for cities which are not fit for rural districts. Ask then that thin, emaciated, black-browed silent man who entered just now the foundry gates. Ask him to go to primes and vespers. He sounds his own matins with the hissing bellows and scorching furnace fire; he rings his own vespers with heavy hammer on the anvil. If he duly and carefully do the work of his master, it is so that he daily offers his sacrifice to his maker; and not unworthily. Will his wife go, who also has her five children? Will his sisters go, and leave the factory at which they earn their daily bread? Will he send his children? You have hardly yet taught them with patience to endure the tedium of one long Sunday service.

Will the merchant hear tierces, or his clerk? Will the lawyer or the doctor hear them, or the lawyer's or doctor's wife? Will the shopkeeper leave his counter for them, or the banker his till, or the artist his easel? Have all the bells that have yet been rung brought from their work men or women who have work to do, in order that nones and complines, matins and vespers, may be duly celebrated?

No one that has work to do can go through these ceremonies, and every one here in this world should see that he has work. And she too will have her work to do, that enthusiastic devotee, to whom intonations through the nose, and the preparation of credence tables are at present sufficient. She too shall have young children and watch their early cradles in the morning in lieu of matins, and comb their curling locks at eve, and hear from them, kneeling at her knees, the sweet prayers of childhood. These shall be her vespers. These, unless the disease have gone too far. Unless her young blood be fevered with the ambition of religious zeal; unless she be too sorely tempted, and so reject the woman's duties for which her Creator made her, and strive to be a saint before her time.

We cannot perceive that there is any valid objection to high breasted black silk waistcoats, be they called by whatsoever name. As an article of clothing indeed they are decorous, inexpensive, and suitable. But we can in no way accede to them as a part of our religious creed. We are also mainly indifferent to the vestment in which our clergyman preaches to us, so long as it be seemly, sober, and clerical. We think it well that the judge on the bench should be distinguished by purple and ermine. If it however seemed good to the Crown, or the Parliament, or the judges, or the proper powers whatsoever they may be, to replace the purple and ermine by sable and green, we should be no whit less willing than at present to accept justice from the bench.

It is well that churches should be built East and West. A certain regularity is at any rate secured. We can, however, understand that honest prayers may be truly said in a temple constructed without any reference to the points of the compass.

Forms and ceremonies are undoubtedly good, as long as they are made the vehicles and appendages of true doings. But alas, for a man, or a people, when he or they mistake forms for things, and ceremonies for deeds!

It is needful for the printer's sake that the author should produce a fair manuscript, written with decent order, in lines somewhat parallel, and with letters legibly formed. But how will it fare with the author if he give all his care to the writing and none to the thing written? His calligraphy will hardly carry him safely through the critics.

Nor will nones and complines, high silk waistcoats, credence tables, and intoning carry us safely through the world's cares. No, not though we add campaniles with bells regularly rung, marble arches of many hues, coloured glass, and every seemly ecclesiastical adjunct, each duly formed and in its proper place.

If such could be accepted as adjuncts, small graceful adjuncts, unnecessary indeed but very acceptable if added to higher things, it were well. But if they be taken as more than this, if they be looked on as symbols without which religion cannot show herself; if marble arches be necessary to our prayers, and coloured windows a portion of our very faith, then indeed it is not well with us. Then indeed shall we be caressing the shadow while the substance has passed from us.

There are many shades of religion among us, and, as far as we are able to look forward, it seems probable that there will be so. A Church that shall be in very truth a Church of England, that shall be persuasive to and sufficient for the Englishman in general, is a matter hardly to be hoped for; certainly not to be expected. But this would be matter of small moment, if men could be taught to look to their religion for that which it can give, and to look to it for nothing else.

Can we live well by the religion which we have chosen? If so, it matters little whether we follow Mr. Everscreech or his more artistic brother. It matters little whom we elect to follow, if we can get ourselves taught to follow the one teacher whom we all acknowledge to have taught aright.

Can we live well by that religion of primes and vespers as professed by our intoning friend Dr. Middleage? It would seem to us that Dr. Middleage has it all to himself; he at least and that pretty young lady and two or three old women living on the charity of the parish. For what purpose is he there intoning at 6 o'clock this cold winter morning? He will say that he is there to sing praises to the Lord. We do not doubt that he does so with sincerity of heart, but we do venture to doubt that that is his professed object in going there. He is there to lead the way that others, his flock, may sing the praises of the Lord. They wish he would sing them at home. But those others are not there, and will not be there, cannot be there.

David found comfort in singing praises to the Lord. What was good for David in that respect is no doubt good also for us, though we have far higher means of worship than were vouchsafed in David's time. But it cannot be good for us to pretend the comfort, if we do not feel it. If one and another do consent at the eager instigation of Dr. Middleage to tear themselves from their beds and face the rheumatic morn, they do not do so as David did. They do not rush to their high toned lyres with leaping hearts and ecstatic hopes, and sing forth like birds of heaven their untiring thanks for benefits already given. Their object should rather be to pray for strength that they may win those benefits which are to come. Let them at any rate do that, whether in the handsome church that Dr. Middleage has built, or in the silence of their own inner closets.

It is, alas, so easy to fall into pretences; so vitally necessary to avoid doing so. Do we not know how the monks of old fell into vast pits of dissimulation, how by degrees their religion became all a sham, all a pretence, because they were gradually taught to believe that obedience to rules of men, and strict adherence to formulas would suffice instead of heart worship of their God? Monasteries and convents, and those mighty piles of material churches which the zeal of former ages built, were not the productions of hypocrisy. There was true religion then; a true feeling, at any rate in some hearts, of the greatness of God. Men did not devote themselves to works of which they never could see the beauty, of which they never could reap the glory, without having within them the love of the Lord. But how quickly did this truth become untruth! How rapidly did this faith sink into hypocrisy!

With the frail ambition of human nature, the priesthood of those times taught the people that obedience to themselves and their rulers would do in lieu of obedience to God. God's rules were thus withdrawn, and so began the system of bellringing and matins, of candles and gold incense pots, of primes and nones and complines. Will it not be dreadful, if we have to see the best and sincerest of those among us again depending on such vain nonentities as these, again wallowing among such burnt out ashes, from which can come neither light nor heat?

And it is the best and sincerest who are now in this peril. And so it was in times of old. It was then the best and the sincerest, those who thought the most of the truths of religion and who were most anxious to make others think of them. It was they who produced the first germs of those deadly forms, which in the course of years became intolerable to thinking men. It was the anxious longing which dwelt in the heart of early Christians to enforce on others a habit of praying that first produced the order of the church that a certain form of prayer should be used at stated times—"Our father which art in heaven"—*Pater noster qui es in coelis.* Can there have been harm in the frequent repetition of such words as these? Oh, yes, the foulest harm, if nothing but the words be repeated. Fifteen paters, nine aves, and a dozen credos before breakfast; the like at noon, and the same repeated before going to bed, with the addition of the whole "Glory of Mary." Such is the harm which has arisen from the belief that a repetition of prayers can be a benefit. I will not calumniate a parrot by likening the religious observances of many Christians to its gabble. A parrot will repeat its lesson only as it pleases and will do so with what best power of articulation it possesses. I know no animal who abuses its vocal powers so vilely as do some Christians in the utterance of their prayers.

"And do not I perform my sacred services with what best power of articulation I possess?" will exclaim Dr. Middleage, indignant, thinking too with some pride of that intoning excellence for which he is much extolled. Oh, Dr. Middleage, with admirable power of articulation. And so also does that lady, whose rich tremendous voice, ringing out the praises of her God, is sweeter to me than the notes of the thrush. Had thine only object been that thou and she should warble there together in honour of thy maker, till ye were both taken to join the choir of angels above, thou hadst done excellently to attain to such articulation. But was such thine only object? is it so now? Is it not rather that of inclining towards their Saviour the souls of those two thousand labouring poor, for whose future well being thou art in some measure responsible? Will they by daily care sing "Oh be joyful" in suitable manner? Thou in thy short span will hardly teach them to sing or say anything aright. Thou mayest begin to teach them, either to utter from their hearts some word, some thought of prayer—or to say fifteen paters before breakfast with the dose repeated throughout the day.

It was men such as thou, and doing as thou now doest, who first produced this abominable babbling of thoughtless blasphemy. Good and true men, but who were still human, and fallible, as thou art. They said in those days to their people: Come to primes and nones. Come this way and that way. Stand still at this bell, kneel down at that other. When I bow do ye bow. When I look to the West do ye look there also. When I turn to the East turn also ye. And did it not follow of this, that these comings and goings, standings and kneelings, turnings and bowings became the religion of the people? These and these only?

The hearts and inner bosoms of men can never be wholly in the keeping of their brother men. Their bowings and turnings may be so. When such had become clearly the religion of the people, it was sufficiently easy for a priesthood to get dominion over them. God had not vouchsafed to prescribe for them an adequate number of paters and credos. They could therefore only look to man, to some authorized man to do it for them. And the authorized man was there, and the Christian would put his foolish neck beneath the foot of a priest.

You, Dr. Middleage, have no ambition to put your foot on the neck of man or woman. At any rate you are self-confident that no such desire lurks within your heart. But you have a desire, a strong ambition, to reproduce that state of religious feeling by which were generated ignorant flocks and wicked pastors. You are an earnest priest, but are your people an earnest people? Are your psalms so duly sung at 6 o'clock serviceable to make them so? Is not the fact of your being there alone (we may call it alone), of your saying those prayers without hearers, of your performing those services without a congregation, are not these things proof that the form of the worship is dear to you, above all things dear? Ah me! yes that, and a font made with the finest taste from mediæval patterns, and finials for every arch, and gargoyles beautifully hideous, and tower and roof, and storied window and covered porch, all after the fashion of olden times.

Finials and gargoyles are very good, and high pitched roofs and coloured glass. Churches such as we managed to build them some century ago are very bad—some of them, such as they had become, worse than bad; filthy, abominable, dangerous, disgraceful, everything that Dr. Middleage in his warmer moments delights to call them. Nevertheless, finials and gargoyles will not put a prayer into the heart of any man.

Can we live well by the religion that we have chosen? That is after all the question we should ask ourselves. That and one other. Do we live well by it? Is it a working religion, and do we make workman's use of it? Our religion may be of too low a standard for humanity, and often has been so. That religion of fifteen paters before breakfast was so. Or it may be of too high a standard, and religion has this fault as often as the other. It is likely just now to assume a standard much too high for general use.

If the worship of God be made a thing apart from our ordinary lives, an act to practise occasionally with short-lived ecstasy, or else to pretend to practise with veriest unecstatic sham; a thing to wonder at, to be talked of, to admire, to reverence, to look up at in a few devoted persons as martyrdom was looked up to heretofore, to believe in, but not to be guided by; then we may say that religion has assumed a standard too high for us to use. Of what practical service can such a religion be to us? Granted that it were well to eschew worldly pleasures, to despise worldly wealth, to ignore worldly motives; assuming that it be proper to stigmatise as the Devil's baits gifts which God has showered on us, allowing that an austere life of mortification be a blessing, allowing that Mr. Everscreech be right, how much nearer to heaven are we, if, after all his preaching and all our believing, we do not eschew pleasures or despise wealth; if we are still guided by worldly motives; and still gulp at these Devil's baits, knowing them to be of the Devil and from him?

Mr. Everscreech, and Dr. Middleage also, will call us materialists, and denounce our philosophy as Epicurean. Be it so. And what is their philosophy? If you, oh Reader, and I, do love wealth, and say so, and justify our love by reasons which seem to us to be drawn from our religion; if, on the other hand, they denounce all such love, declaring it to be a Devil born passion, and yet love it as well as we do; love it to the last gasp of their mortal breath, to the last struggle by which they rid themselves of their mortal coil; love it so that hardly can they endure to start without it on their long last dark journey; if this be so, whose then is the truer philosophy?

If we could but be true in our religion! True in it so that we might use it in the way in which we assume that it should be used! It is but human that man should hold a theory higher than his practice, that his conduct of life should fall short of his code of morals. But surely practice should in some degree assimilate to theory, and one's conduct in life should be at any rate influenced by one's moral code. What if a man dilated to us beautifully on the deference, the protection, the allegiance that is due to feminine innocence, and yet debauched every woman that would listen to his words! Should we not call him the basest of hypocrites, base in his crimes, but doubly base in his assumed hatred of such crime?

Is there not the same hypocrisy when a man rises in the pulpit on Sundays and howls forth his anathemas against worldly wealth and worldly cares, and on Monday steadily pursues the course of his life in one long care after worldly wealth? But the life of the pastor may be nothing to us, as long as his preaching be pure. True, his individual way of living may be nothing to us, but the way of living of himself and his congregation is much. By their fruits shall ye know them.

It is useless to assume a religion highly spiritual, if it be only assumed as a belief, and not as a practical guide. The beauty of its spirituality is nothing if it does not come home to the daily life of the believer. There is, alas, much vileness in man's nature, and man should use his religion for the purport of abating it, not look on the two as things apart, having no necessary connection with each other.

We would ask any hearer of the ordinary preaching of these days, whether he ever makes the faintest attempt to steer the course of his life in accordance with the sermons which he hears. Nay we would go further, if there were hope of a true reply, and ask any clergyman whether he expects or even intends that his hearers should so steer their courses. There can be no such expectation. We are told that our body is vile and worthless, and we sit tediously to hear the tidings, bedizened in our silks and satins. We are told that every thought of our mind and every aspiration of our heart is due to our Creator and Saviour, and our thoughts wander to other subjects even during the time of the telling, and our hearts are far away. We are cautioned not to allow the world to be too dear to us, while the world is all in all to us. Every action of our life gives the lie to our protestations. Our religion is becoming all pretence. In our orders to our servants, our admonitions to our friends, our loving cautions to our children, our secret counsels with ourselves in our journals, our books, our laws, our Parliaments, we do not profess the slightest regard for the religious precepts which are preached to us. It is worldly wisdom that we teach and practise.

And worldly wisdom has ever been taught and practised, and will be as long as the cycles of the heavens continue in their course. But worldly wisdom may work hand in hand with religion, if the teaching be true, and if above all the hearers be true.

"How wonderful has been the effect of Mr. ———'s ministrations here," says a lady walking through a populous district of London. "There is not a shopkeeper in this street who does not attend his church, nor whose family do not frequent his evening lectures."

"Mr. ——— is doubtless an eloquent man."

"Eloquent. Indeed he is. There is not a house in the street from which he has not got money towards his church, and the rich shopkeepers have given largely. He has only to ask again, and they will give again."

"That is certainly doing much. It is certainly much to have such dominion over the pockets of London shopkeepers. And they are all believers?"

"Believers. Indeed they are. Since Mr. ——— came here, the district has become truly Christian."

"How excellent! Who would not choose to deal in a Christian district? Where coffee will really be coffee, and linen free from cotton? I presume, Madam, the manner of trade in this district is very different from that of other parts of the metropolis?"

"Oh—Trade!—Mr. ——— says that he cannot meddle with their trade. Tradesmen you know will be tradesmen. Trade is a thing apart. You cannot touch that, as they live by it. But in their houses, among themselves, and in their church attendance they are a truly Christian people. There is not one house in this row in which there is not family worship twice a day. I wish, however, we could touch their trade."

It would certainly be desirable. If you cannot touch that with your religion, and cannot touch it because it is that by which they live, the inhabitants of this Christian district are, one might say, in a perilous state. It is in vain for the tradesman to get his religion into his house if he cannot take it into his shop. Or for the lawyer, if he cannot take it to the forum. Or for the labourer, if he cannot take it into the field. If our religion will not serve us for the present, it will hardly do so for the future.

Let every one at any rate choose for himself a religion by which he can live. The common sense of the commonest intellect teaches to its owner that such should be his endeavour, whatever any pastor of any denomination may say. To us Englishmen, it should be a matter of no small moment that our religions should be of this nature. Our religions, for we have many of them. Yes, Mr. Everscreech, to you and me, though we be not Romanists, it should be matter of heartfelt desire that this Church of Rome, be its errors what they may, should so far suffice to our poor Irish brethren. By us also, Dr. Middleage, though we love not that white washed Ebenezer from which such unwholesome howling is heard during the livelong hours of every Sunday, it should be deeply wished that there too our fellow countrymen might find a religion by which they might live. Unless they do so there, or elsewhere, our fellow countrymen must come to sorrow and destruction.

But not from the priest, or pastor, or clergyman, be he of what denomination he may, can any man rationally hope to obtain the comfort of religion, nor can the priest in any way help him to obtain it, unless he be true to himself. As long as he lies in his religion, his religion will fail him. Let every man ask himself whether or no he is guilty of such lies. Does he frequent his church for the sake of appearance? Does he kneel to pray without an effort at prayer? Does he profess what he does not even attempt, hardly even wishes, to practice? Does he utterly neglect to carry with him into the daily doing of his life the precepts which he affects to revere?

If so, he lies in his religion to himself, to the world, and to his God. If so, he has not chosen a religion by which he can live in comfort, nor one by which he can hope to die in peace. If so, the Church, be it called by what name it may, Church of Rome, free Church, or Church of England, is as far as he is concerned going quickly to decay. Nay, as far as he is concerned, is it not already utterly dead?

CHAPTER VII

The House of Commons

I T may be a dangerous thing to say anything about the House of Commons. We believe the law is still in force which empowers that body to call for, and admonish, and becastigate with words, and incarcerate, and probably also fine any who shall dare even to report beyond the limits of its own walls aught that shall have fallen from a member in his place therein.

That such a law is not very strictly carried out, the daily newspapers give us sufficient proof. But then the newspapers are too strong for the House of Commons. To incarcerate or admonish the Times for reporting or even for not reporting his speech would hardly appear expedient to the most Quixotic member. The newspapers indeed take liberties greater even than that of reporting, and not unfrequently speak in anything but eulogistic language of the doings of the House, and yet the indignity is borne with. But though this usage is borne with from the Press, it may not be put up with when coming from others. That which is permitted to the Times may be deep sin in the part of an individual.

The Press indeed has sufficiently proved that the law alluded to may be regarded as obsolete when those who break it are too powerful to be attacked. But the law is not the less in force. Such a subject as that of this Chapter must therefore be approached with caution, and treated with care. It may be no light thing for one who writes without the shelter of newspaper columns to speak with any mixture of censure of the practices of that body which we all regard as the great Palladium of our liberties. If so, the writer of these lines can only plead in his defence that few are more anxious than he is to respect and do honour to the great council of the nation. His only wish is that it may be respectable and honourable, in order that all men may respect and honour it.

Those who have written on the constitution of the House of Commons historically and philosophically have been used to represent its constitution as more than humanly perfect. And though we are accustomed to hear its doings criticised, abused, and ridiculed from day to day by the newspapers, nevertheless the nation yet feels a deep conviction that England sends thither the wisest and the best of her citizens, and that if she is to continue to hold the high place which she aspires to fill among nations, she must be enabled to do so by the vigilance, diligence, and prudence of the Lower House.

Such a confidence in their own national assembly is a great happiness for a people, and is qualified to give a stable comfort to the minds of men, which no true patriot would willingly lessen. Such a confidence still exists. But it may well be doubted whether it is now increasing. Such a comfort Englishmen still have. But the feeling is hardly so assured as it was some half century ago. The newspaper Press is now the rival of the House of Commons. These are the two great powers which are dominant in England, and there is not unnaturally a struggle between them for pre-eminence. They are both candidates for the suffrages of the people. and it is to be feared that in the contest the House may lose from its dignity, and yet add little to its popularity or its power.

For ourselves we must own that we would sooner submit to the old fashioned governance of a national assembly than the new fangled pretensions of a newspaper coterie. But the national assembly should be such in its manners, practices, and virtues as fully to warrant a nation's pride. All submission is painful which is made to a power of the true superiority of which the person so submitting is doubtful. But let such superiority be felt and acknowledged, and submission in thought as well as act follows as a matter of course. If the House of Commons have lost aught of its ancient prestige, it is because this confidence is not felt now as it once was.

Of all the writers on our parliamentary system of making and executing laws, none have excelled De Lolme[1] in admiration, eulogy, and expressed conviction in the wisdom of our constitution. He regarded our Parliament as perfect, and when he meant to prophesy in the strongest language the durability of its perfec-

---

[1] John Louis De Lolme (1740-1807), *The Constitution of England; or, an Account of the English Government; in which it is compared both with the republican form of government and other monarchies in Europe* (first published in French, 1771).

tion, he declared that the glory of the English House of Commons would never pale till the legislature had become more corrupt than the executive.

Let us take De Lolme's prophecy as true and inquire whether the time which he regarded as so distant be not near at hand: nay, whether it be not already here. When he wrote men regarded those to whom the task of carrying out the laws was assigned as necessarily corrupt. With the executive resided power, and the rewards and temptations of power. Men so entrusted would help themselves or their friends to more of the loaves and fishes than the nation had intended them to enjoy; and having the power, it was considered certain that they would use it. Such is the meaning of corruption. All political corruption resolves itself to this. Men may not desire loaves for themselves, but they desire the power of distributing them to others, and the distinction with which such power will invest themselves. To keep or to achieve this politicians have, alas, for many ages descended to falsehood, intrigue, and Machiavellian crookedness. Such is political corruption.

We all know what in such matters were the practices of Walpole, of the Pelhams, nay, even of those governments over which the Pitts presided. Happily it requires no argument to convince men at all conversant with public affairs that such practices do not, and cannot, now exist. It should not be attributed as praise to the leading statesmen of the present day that they have cleaner hands than their predecessors. Clean hands are now a political necessity to the aspirant for high place. Such has been the change effected in our habits of political business, that impure practices may be said to be banished from the haunts of our public men. No senior clerk can now order a dozen score of inkstands, and have them on their journey converted into a silver ornament for his own drawing-room. No contractor can now leave a £10 note in the palm of the gentleman who communicates to him the success of his proposal. No Chairman or Director can now receive a costly offering from the father anxious for an official income for his son. The days of sinecurists are done. Even from the highest of our civil servants work is exacted for wages paid. Men hesitate now to provide handsomely for an incompetent nephew out of the public purse. Such attempts are at once exposed, castigated, and annulled.

Nor is that other species of corruption permitted to an English statesman in these days, which, though perhaps less mean, is yet more hateful; that which in days of yore politicians were taught to look on as their special business; that which Machiavel dignified as an art and so many disciples of Machiavel have cultivated as a wondrous science. A statesman is now required to declare his views, expose his policy, and go straight to his mark. He is forced into a degree of honesty which would have been considered quite incompatible with statecraft a few years since, and is compelled to tell political truths in a manner that must be most astounding to the worn-out Nestors of the trade, who remember the sweetly devious paths in which they trod in those delightful days when Downing Street and Whitehall contained secrets, and First Lords and State Secretaries were not bound to make clean breasts.

In Downing Street and the Treasury Chambers our great men are now comparatively true. It is when they go down to the House and assume their guise of legislators that fallacy and intrigue are necessary or permitted. There they are both necessary and permitted. It is hardly going too far to say that no man can hold a high position in the government who finds himself unable to defend honest intentions by false excuses, or to repel undeserved accusations by disingenuous sophistry.

We may have gained more than we have lost; but why should we lose anything? In searching after truth in one place why should we be driven to sacrifice it in another? But it is this which we do. In our desire to achieve political purity we have become political purists. While repudiating the coquetries of our ancestors we have become prudes; and pretend to so exaggerated a tone of virtue that we are fain to hide our peccadilloes by falsehoods. It is now held as a political doctrine both in Parliament and by the newspapers that a statesman must do no wrong. He, if he be fit for his position, must be exempt from that law which binds all other children of Adam, and which denies to any of us the merit of perfection. To him, and him alone, is allowed no *locus penetentiae*. A discovered fault, be it ever so insignificant, ever so far removed in its commission from his own immediate sphere of duty, is sufficient to subject him to the wrath of the nation. And consequently no fault must be admitted. A minister, like a banker, can never own himself to have been wrong; can admit no error on his own part, or on that of his Secretary, Under Secretary, private secretary, or corps of clerks; must always protect as inviolate his character for infallibility.

Unluckily it is not given to mortal man to assume infallibility except at the expense of truth. And to no mortal man is such gift less likely to appertain than to a minister of the Crown of England. To no man is entrusted a deeper responsibility for the acts of other men; or an amount of work more utterly out of the power of one mind to compass by its own exertions. Such, however are the men who are expected to be able to repel any chance of the slightest error, or to yield at once to the clamour of an offended people if they find themselves unable to do so.

Is it not patent to every one who watches the debates of the Houses of Parliament that the result of such a requisition is very far removed from open honest truth? Is it not the fact that the minister who can tell a plausible story, in which the weak points of his case are so wrapped up in ambiguity as to be inapproachable by his adversary, has done that which his position requires, and carried on his battle with more credit to himself than he could have done had he been more candid and less crafty?

There is a sport prevalent among the downs of Hampshire to which, though not of high degree, much interest is attached.[2] Men and boys, with social glee and happy joyous shouts, congregate together on a hill side, at the mouth of a narrow hole, and proceed with the aid of a well trained bull-dog, to draw a badger. If the badger be at all commendable in his class this is by no means an easy thing to do. He is a sturdy animal, well fortified with sharp and practised teeth; his hide is of the toughest; his paws of the strongest, and his dead power of resistance so very great, as to give him more than an equal chance with the bull-dog. The delighted sportsmen stand around listening to the growls and snarls, the tearings, gnawings, and bloody struggles of the brave combatants within—"Well done badger! Well done, bull-dog!—Draw him, bull-dog! Bite him badger!" Each has his friends, and the interest of the moment is intense. The badger, it is true, has done no harm. He has been doing as it was appointed for him to do, poor badger, in that hole of his. But then, why were badgers created, but to be drawn? Why,

---

[2] Trollope used this and other paragraphs in *The Three Clerks*. See Appendix II, p. 216.

indeed; but to be drawn, or not to be drawn, as the case may be? See! the bull-dog returns minus an ear, with an eye hanging loose—, his nether lip torn off, and one paw bit through, and, though limping, dejected, beaten, glaring fearfully from his remaining eye, the dog comes out; and the badger within victorious, rolls himself up with affected ease, hiding his bloody wounds from the public eye.

So is it that the sport is played in Hampshire, and so also at Westminster—with a difference, however. In Hampshire the two brutes retain ever their appointed natures. The badger is always a badger, and the bull-dog never other than a bull-dog. In Westminster there is a juster reciprocity of position. The badger when drawn has to take his place outside the hole, and fight again for the home of his love; while the victorious bull-dog assumes a state of badgerdom, dons the skin of his enemy and in his turn submits to be baited.

The pursuit is certainly full of interest, but it is somewhat deficient in dignity.

There is no vice into which an age can fall so detrimental to the moral tone of the people as is the vice of purism. We all know in what estimation is held that scornful fair one who repudiates the innocent amusements of her sex, and affects to think that nothing short of the asceticism of an anchorite is compatible with true female virtue. Such a one has generally been frail, and may probably be tempted to be so again. Political purism is as suspicious, as frail, and as false.

Men now affect to think that any amount, however slight, of discovered impropriety unfits the delinquent for the public service, and renders him justly liable to contumely, scorn, and open disgrace. Such is the outward code of morals now assumed as the code of the age, and is so assumed especially in the House of Commons. There is an inward code far different.

It is that overwhelming curse of an esoteric and exoteric code of morals which now degrades our public life, and turns falsehood into truth even within the walls of Parliament. Things must be spoken of to the public ear as being too base even for human imperfection, which are looked on among the speakers as peccadilloes not worth a reproach. Faults which when patent to the public are held too heinous for pardon are matters only for easy joke when discussed in private circles. The offended virtue of the indignant legislator pours forth at Westminster fiery invectives against some discovered sin which is treated at the other side of St. James Park as merely so much political capital in the hands of him who denounces it. The sinner who is thus held up to the scorn of the nation is no whit damnified in the eyes of his own circle; no, nor in the circle of those who condemn him. He has committed himself in that he is discovered, and party politics require that he should be sacrificed. Retired men who live in country towns, and do not know the ways of the world, believe and admire the virtue of the age. The sentiments expressed in the newspapers are beautiful, and all to their eyes is as it should be. But the knowing fellows, the men of the world, those who live with their eyes open and see how things are done, they laugh in their sleeves and applaud the craft of the winner.

In nothing is this pretended horror of political delinquency so strongly evinced by members of Parliament as in cases of bribery.[3] The sin of bribery is damnable. It is the one sin for which in the House of Commons there can be no forgiveness. When discovered, it should render the culprit liable to political death without hope of pardon or chance of mercy. It is treason to a higher throne than that on which the Sovereign sits. It is a heresy which requires an *auto-de-fé*. It is pollution to the whole House, which can only be cleansed by a great sacrifice. Anathema, maranatha! Out with it from amongst us, even though half of our heart's blood be poured forth in the conflict! Out with it, and for ever! Such is the language of patriotic members with regard to bribery. And doubtless, if sincere, they are in the right. It is a bad thing, certainly, that a rich man should obtain votes by his riches; bad also that a poor man should so use a privilege allotted to him for a very different purpose. By all means let us have strong laws against bribery.

By all means also let us repudiate the system with heartfelt disgust. With heartfelt disgust if we can do so, but not with disgust pretended only, and not felt in the heart at all.

The laws against bribery at election are now so stringent in their different clauses that an unfortunate candidate may easily become guilty, even though actuated by the purest intentions. It

---

[3] Trollope incorporated much of this section into *Doctor Thorne*. See Introduction, p. xxii.

is difficult to say what is not bribery. A candidate must not only hermetically seal his own breeches' pockets during his election, but he must put a padlock, of which he himself must keep the key, on those of all of his friends. He must give neither ribbons to the girls, nor ale to the men. He must pay for no music, no refreshments, no band of followers. If a huzza be uttered in his favour, it is at his peril. It may be necessary to prove before a committee that it was the spontaneous result of British feeling in his favour, and not the purchased result of British beer. He cannot safely ask any one to share his hotel dinner. Bribery descends now to the most impalpable shapes, and may be effected by the offer of a glass of sherry.

We strain at gnats with a vengeance, but swallow the camels with ease. Is it not still considered necessary for any gentleman who prepares himself for a contested election to see that a considerable sum of money is also prepared for the purpose? Except in some few isolated cases such necessity undoubtedly exists. The money is necessary, is prepared, or at any rate is expended. The poor candidate of course knows nothing of the matter till the attorney's bill is laid before him when all danger of petition has passed away. He little dreamed till then, not he, that there had been banquetings and junkettings, deep drinkings and secret doings going on at his expense. Poor candidate! Poor member! Who was so ignorant as he? 'Tis true he has paid such bills before; but 'tis equally true that he specially desired his managing friends Twistem and Twinum to be very careful that all was according to law. He pays the bill, however, and on the next election will again employ Messrs. Twistem and Twinum.

Messrs. Twistem and Twinum are safe men, and may be thus employed with little danger. All these stringent bribery laws only enhance the value of such very safe men as Twistem and Twinum. To them stringent laws against bribery are the strongest assurances of valuable employment. Were these laws of a nature to be evaded with more ease, any indifferent attorney might manage a candidate's affairs, and enable him to take his seat with security.

Very valuable indeed are such services. Let us only see how fearful is the fall of the poor member who may be detected.

Let all the world know that his seat was purchased for him,

and he yet may hold his head at the Clubs as high as any one, if the fact have not been proved before a committee of the House. But let it once be declared by that august authority, by three men, that is, out of five, that he has so sinned, and he instantly becomes a byword and a reproach. It will generally be found that such a one has failed to employ those very safe men of business, Messrs. Twistem and Twinum of the Reform Club, or the equally valuable firm who may chance to be in the confidence of the Carlton.[4]

A most ridiculous instance of the affected horror with which detected bribery is treated occurred in the case of poor Mr. Bell.[5] He had contrived at some considerable outlay to get himself returned as member of St. Albans, and managed his matters so badly that the venality of the electors was clearly proved by a commission sent down to St. Albans for the purpose. The town was disfranchised, but unfortunately for his own comfort Mr. Bell could not be debarred from keeping his seat till the end of the session. He sat there like a Pariah among men of high caste. He was a bird whose plumage had been bedaubed with mud among an unpolluted flock; like a school boy sprung from lowly parents among the sons of aristocrats. No one would take his cause. None would countenance him. He had been detected in doing that which so many around him had been clever enough to do without detection, and was consequently beyond the pale of mercy.

Mr. Bell's bribery, however, was clear, and his punishment, though sufficiently ludicrous, not quite undeserved. But in what language sufficiently strong shall we speak of the far different case of Mr. Stonor?[6] If any man was ever wickedly sacrificed to the clamour of a false and prurient purism, it was Mr. Stonor. Let us first put forward his fault in as glaring a manner as it can consistently with truth be made to appear.

A publican's or agent's bill at an election has been refused payment; and at a subsequent election Mr. Stonor suggested that the question of the payment of this bill so repudiated might be reconsidered, his object no doubt being to secure the support of

[4] The Carlton was a leading club for Conservatives; the Reform for Liberals.
[5] Jacob Bell (1810-59), founder of the Pharmaceutical Society; he was returned as a Liberal for St. Albans in 1850.
[6] On Henry Stonor's bribery conviction and subsequent recall from Australia, see Introduction, p. xxii.

this person on behalf of the friend in whose cause he, Mr. Stonor, was interested. This we believe is the very worst that can be made of the charge against Mr. Stonor, and, if we are not mistaken, more than was proved against him. But this if proved may probably be taken to amount to bribery. It was so regarded by a committee of the House of Commons, and Mr. Stonor was declared to have been guilty of bribery or of some one of those adjacent sins which are similar in their result, and supposed to be nearly equal in their turpitude. Mr. Stonor, it will be remembered, was not a member of the House, and the friend for whom he was interested had of course to pay the penalty.

Let any one who may wish to weigh justly the extent of Mr. Stonor's sin presume himself to be engaged on a friend's canvas.

"Come Mr. Boniface," you might probably say, "you must let my friend again have the benefit of your vote and valuable interest."

Boniface crams his tongue into his cheek, winks his eye, sticks his left thumb over his left shoulder, and civilly asks you if you don't wish you may get it.

"But Mr. Boniface," you would continue to argue, "you were always a friend to the good old cause! You who have taken such a manly interest in the welfare of the borough. You who—"

Boniface winks again—and mutters forth with beery voice from lungs replete with double stout—"Did you ever hear, Mr. Thingumbob, of any man as didn't like to have his little bills paid? I never heard tell of such a one as that. I an't such a one myself—not by a long chalk."

"Oh—ah—yes. I think I heard there was a bill," you say. "Well, Mr. Boniface, we can make that all right—you understand me. We can make that all right."

Boniface does understand. He votes as he is desired, or does not as the case may be. He receives, however, the amount of his little bill; and then comes up to London to give his evidence before the committee of the House of Commons.

Oh, my reader, if such has ever been or if such could ever be your conduct, far be it from me to defend it on any abstract principle of right or wrong. But much further be it from me to animadvert upon it with severity, judging you, as I must do, by the habits of those around you.

When we hear of some fast young gentleman who has ordered

more coats from his tailor than he is exactly able to pay for, we cannot commend his conduct; but we do not therefore turn him away without contumely from our houses and tables, treat him with scorn as an impostor, and declare ourselves unable to breath the same atmosphere with such a villain.

But with such severity as this was Mr. Stonor treated on account of his fault, and was so treated by men in whose inmost heart no real horror could be felt for such conduct. Some time subsequent to this election inquiry, Mr. Stonor was appointed to a colonial judgeship and was positively sent to the Colony on his mission. As soon as he was gone, it was discovered that his appointment was fair ground for a ministerial badger bait.

Not from any disgust at Mr. Stonor's appointment, not from any high toned feeling at the iniquity of that gentleman in having secured to Mr. Boniface the payment of his bill, was the attack made. Not from any pure desire to preserve the rising Colony from the impurity of Mr. Stonor's morals was all this done; but because it gave to one party an opportunity of damaging another.

This of course may be denied, and cannot be proved; but the fact may be safely left to the conscience and conviction of all those who were in any way conversant with the matter. It may safely also be left to the understanding of those who know the character of the persons concerned and watched the affair in its progress. The government of the day was accused of sending out as a judge a man convicted of bribery, and a committee was instructed to make inquiry into the matter.

It appeared that a certain sort of legal excellence had been asked for, and that Mr. Stonor had been highly recommended as possessing that kind of excellence; that the circumstances of the appointment were not such as to secure a lawyer of higher merit, and that when Mr. Stoner's testimonials were submitted to the minister with whom the appointment rested, this affair of bribery, if it can be called bribery, was not kept in the background. The minister, it appeared, remembered nothing about the bribery when appointing Mr. Stonor, but the Deputy Minister had mentioned the fact when suggesting the appointment to his chief officer.

Such having been the discovered facts in the matter, Mr. Stonor was recalled, and recalled as is believed without any compensa-

tion for the cruel hardship of his position. It is not too much to
say that by such a course a man's prospects in this life must
probably have been ruined.

That Mr. Stonor should be ruined would be nothing to the
nation if his ruin had been accomplished in the true pursuit of
virtue. However hard might be his case, his misfortune would be
utterly unworthy of consideration if it had been consequent on
the adoption of true principles of national right and wrong. But
can any one say that such was the case? In attacking Mr. Stonor,
the government was attacked. And in throwing over Mr. Stonor,
the government threw over the Jonah which for the time
embarrassed it.

Let those judges now sitting on the bench who have heretofore had seats in Parliament put their hands on their hearts if
they can, and say they have never been as guilty as was Mr.
Stonor. Let the learned gentlemen who are now Attorneys and
Solicitors General, and those who have been so under other
ministers, do the same. Mr. Stonor's fault was committed in
Ireland. Mr. Stonor was attacked by an Irish member.[7] Can the
law officers there say that such doings are uncommon, or held
to be unclean? The attack was abetted by English conservatives.
Can the law advisers of that party say that election jugglery,
even in England, is abhorrent to the feelings of a gentleman and
the high principles of those who would be judges?

It is not the person or persons who made the attack on Mr.
Stonor who should be blamed for this. Nor is it mainly the
minister who appointed, and then dismissed him; though probably he would have played a more manly part had he supported
his absent nominee. The fault is with the feeling of the time.
That feeling as exemplified in the case of Mr. Stonor is neither
manly, nor true, nor just. It delights in the display of a false
purism before the eyes of the public, and delights no less in the
fruition of lax principles within inner and closed circles.

This feeling is like the religion of Imperial Rome. The senators
were priests and augurs. The Emperor himself was an high priest
of the Olympian Gods. They read auguries, performed sacrifices,
and did solemn rites in gorgeous temples before the eyes of the
people. But what Emperor, what senator, believed in the Olympian Gods? To them religious belief was a portion of statecraft

[7] G. H. Moore. See Introduction, p. xxii.

very useful for the governance of the lower orders.

Such is the purity of our House of Commons. A victim now and then is required, and some Mr. Bell or some Mr. Stonor is offered up as were the white bulls and birds of the pagan sacrifices. We get no nearer to virtue than we were before, but depart daily further from the truth.

From what lips do we not daily hear accusations of inconsistency, dishonesty, and self-aggrandisement brought against the best of our public servants! Men whose whole political lives have been passed in doing the work of a weathercock, turning ever which ever way the breezes of patronage may blow, men who have always been up for sale, like some old screw well known at Tattersals;[8] men who in every phase of their political career have ridiculed the very idea of purity, men by whom scruples have been regarded as follies and public truth as at best a political dream, come down to their places in the House, and, with the practised thunder of parliamentary eloquence, denounce their rivals with the vehemence of a Demosthenes and the patriotism of a Brutus. Till at last the Omega of Impurity attacks the Alpha of British statesmanship, and some modern Verres accuses a modern Cicero of dishonesty and selfishness!

The virtue of a Cicero has since the world began been the sure mark of attack for the venality of a Verres, and it may be supposed will be so till the arrival of the Millennium. But such attacks have generally secured the sympathy of public men for the Ciceros, and not for their opponents. At present it would seem that in public estimation all public men are equal. The nation would feel no disgrace if Verres should be seated on the Treasury bench. They feel no sympathy when Cicero falls from it. In fact neither public vice nor public virtue are believed in. There is much cant of such things, but it is only cant. When we see the august high priest solemnly sacrificing his white bull in honour of Jove's majesty, we know that to him Jupiter is no God, but the picturesque and useful creation of wise men of old.

We were told of an eminent statesman in the last century that he "gave up to party what was meant for mankind."[9] The same thing may now be said with equal truth of the House of

[8] *Tattersals*: the celebrated London horse auction rooms; *screw*: a worn-out or worthless horse.

[9] Edmund Burke, so described by Goldsmith, 'Retaliation', l. 32.

Commons. There was much eulogy in the sentence when spoken of an individual, for it declared that the man was possessed of qualities sufficiently large to be of general benefit to his fellow men. But it contains no praise for a national assembly. Of course such an assembly is meant for mankind, is intended to guard the welfare, and watch the best interests of a whole nation; and if such intention be lost sight of in individual antagonism and party contests, the assembly, let it be ever so national, ever so great in character and privilege, is neglectful of its highest duties.

Who ever cares to listen to any debate in the House of Commons that has not arisen from some party accusation and that is not carried on with gladiatorial skill and internecine malignity? Indeed there are no other debates. It is true that a long evening may be consumed by a diffuse exposition of financial matters; or once or twice in a session a minister may produce and explain some new plan for the government of a colony or the management of criminals. But the House of Commons debates of which we hear so much, which we read so often, never arise from dull matters like these. No, they are personal conflicts, in which the Achilles of opposition is anxious only to damage the reputation of Agamemnon, caring nothing whether Troy shall stand or fall. In which Agamemnon can think but little of the Grecian army at large, fully occupied as he is with repressing the insolence of Achilles.

It is fearful to hear the denunciations which one member of a British Parliament can nightly make against another, and that other a chosen ruler of the people. We should rather say that it would be fearful did we for a moment think that the indignant orator believed or could induce others to believe any of the evil things which fall from his mouth. But he believes none of them. He is practising his trade as did the gladiators of Rome, when one old friend in his professional duty would slay the other unless kind spectators mercifully declined to turn down their thumbs.

In our arena no thumbs are ever withdrawn. There is no mercy for the fallen combatant. Let the hero of a hundred successful struggles once bite the dust, and the sword of his rival will thrust through and through his breast. Let his foot slip so that he once lie prostrate, and he will neither expect nor ask for grace. Parliamentary duellists are like the wild Indians. In their warfare quarter is neither asked nor given. Such are the debates of the House of Commons. Such are all debates to which any interest is attached. And it is by sedulously asserting in such debates, and by manfully taking a part in such battles, that would-be statesmen get themselves lifted up into the Elysium of government places.

"And very naturally," would say a stranger to our constitutional practices. "Whom should a minister of the Crown gather under his banners for his support and service but those who have shown themselves able and willing to fight in his behalf?"

Softly, my friend. That apparently self-evident method of yours is by no means the way in which our parliamentary tacticians recruit their ranks. Not those who have shown themselves able and willing to fight on their behalf do they choose. Why pay for services which are their own without payment? Not those do they enroll in their regiments, but such as have shown themselves sufficiently able and sufficiently willing to fight on the other side. A double benefit is secured by the possession of such services. It is not only that Bernaldus may be useful in the corps to which he is now attached: useful indeed he is, but that is of less account than the withdrawal of that quick sword of his from the ranks of the enemies. How bitter was Bernaldus, how deliciously sarcastic to the ears of the opposition, how cruelly severe to the nerves of the minister before his services were secured! By no one's prowess was the gladiatorial contest more enlivened. It was a pity that Bernaldus should have been draughted into a steady body guard of non-combatants, and thus become as dull, as silent, and as safe as a common well drilled Treasury hack.

Look too at Llanebicus, the touchy Welshman now chief of Adiles.[10] And at the classic Candidus, to whose versatile mind Railways and Coal Exchanges are doubtless dear. How odious was Llanebicus to all who loved church and state, till in happy hour he also was induced to open his palm and take the Queen's shilling. Now he trails his musket like a quiet good old soldier, and has quite forgotten his war dance. How fearful was the pen

---

[10] *Adiles*: from *ædilis*, Roman magistrate in charge of public buildings, games, and police.

of Candidus till he also took in his hands a pen of regimental colours, and now how useful!

And what shall we say of the fierce Namsrok, that worse than Persian persecutor of all Christian churches? Namsrok the bishop hater, Namsrok whose name was terrible to deans and prebendaries once as was that of Amurath[11] to the priests of the Eastern Church in the days of the feeble Emperors? Namsrok is now Deputy Governor of a province. He sits well pleased at the same board with an archbishop, shares his venison with court divines, and hob-nobs over his champagne with the chaplain of the royal closet.

And to thee, great O'Fighe, what credit is not due for dexterous management of such small parliamentary advantages as have been vouchsafed to thee? Soon shalt thou sit high on the honoured bench of justice, a sight horrible to those who in thy early days thought thy services not worth the purchase. Where now would have been O'Fighe had he trusted to the support of those whose policy he professed to adopt? Defending ribbonmen[12] in Cavan, or prosecuting breaches of marriage contract in Galway, and receiving in return a most moderate honorarium. O'Fighe has fought his battle better than that. He has known how to make himself feared, to prove that he could do mischief, to secure payment like the organ grinder if not by his harmony then by his discord. He is now therefore the great O'Fighe, and will soon be my Lord.

Indeed so common has become this mode of entering into the sweet sanctum of government, so clearly has it been proved that fear and not love teaches the minister where to look for supporters, that a great mind has conceived the idea that the very citadel of the fortress may in this way be stormed, and the Cabinet achieved in one leap by a bitter tongue joined to a bitterer pen. There is Hevenin who has tried it. Hevenin, who since the war began has clearly looked on himself as a minister sent from heaven for the removal of all difficulties. Hevenin who knows so well the wild paths of Assyria that he alone of men was able to conduct the war which we unluckily have had to wage

---

[11] Murad I, or Amurath (1319-89), Sultan of Turkey. He led the Ottomans to considerable military conquest in the Balkans and Asia Minor.
[12] Members of the Irish anti-Protestant 'Ribbon Society'.

in Russia.[13] Hevenin who has at his beck the only thunderbolts to which an Englishman in these days will listen. Hevenin has tried it,—and almost succeeded.

Whether Hevenin has not gone a little too far for his own success; whether his courage may not have carried him a step beyond that point at which his services to a government would appear in the most desirable light, may we fear be doubted. Hevenin was quite right when he conceived that to become one of a ministry it was necessary to attack it. But there is a kind of attack which even ministers will not forgive.

As long as men are better treated for indiscriminate abuse than indiscriminate support, the cleverer of our rising politicians will naturally begin life by opposing the ministers under whom they hope ultimately to act. It is grievous that it should be so, but so it is, and so it will be till human nature is altered. The effect, however, in the House of Commons is anything but salutary, and certainly anything but dignified. All men through the Kingdom are taught to look upon political support as an affair of expediency, and of course all confidence in the leading principles of our leading men is lost. One would say that in such an assembly as the House of Commons, an assembly of men which all but deifies itself by the more than human privileges which it assumes, no word should be heard to fall in the slightest degree antagonistic to the truth. Members on the different sides of the House may differ; but truth is always the same to Whig and Tory.

But is truth thus adhered to in the House of Commons? Does common report in England attribute to members generally that positive assurance of veracity which in the world at large one gentleman attributes to another as a matter of course? No man accuses any individual member of falsehood, but every man feels that the aggregate of untruth is very large. This is so completely the case that truth is not even expected. It is known that men will argue, debate, and vote, not according to the facts of a case, but according to the political view in which party requires that they should regard those facts. If it be necessary to decide

---

[13] *Hevenin*: presumably a reference to Sir Austen Henry Layard, excavator of Nineveh, and Liberal member for Aylesbury 1852-7. In 1854 Layard personally observed operations in the Crimea and later testified before the Parliamentary Committee investigating the conduct of the war.

whether Black be Black, or whether it be not rather in all respects White, men will go into different lobbies on the matter; and according to the power of parties at the moment, Black shall be declared to be Black, or to be the opposite of it.

And indeed this is so notorious, the conviction that such is the practice of the House is so fixed in the mind of men, that better conduct is not looked for, and the practice is not regarded as disgraceful. If Mr. Smith out of the House states that Black is White he will lose his credit for veracity, and men will gradually know him for a liar. But if he merely votes Black to be White within the House, no one on that account accuses him of untruth. Did he not do so, he would be as a public man impracticable, unmanageable, useless, and utterly unfit for any public service. There are still a few of these foolish fellows in the House—men who have never been able to distinguish truth that is esoteric from truth that is exoteric. Such men can do the state no service.

So grave an accusation may to many seem startling and incapable of proof. But it is the daily recurrence of the offence which hides the enormity of it. It is because men are habituated to the practice that they will be slow to acknowledge that any such practice exists. If you tell a Londoner that London is a dirty town, he will not credit you. He has become so used to the dirt of London that he does not know that it is dirt.

When a new House of Commons first meets, many petitions are brought before it with the object of unseating certain of the members who have been returned. These petitions are referred to committees. Why are men so anxious to ascertain what are the political bearings of each member of the committee, if it be believed that those who compose it will decide assuredly according to the facts, and in no way be guided by party feeling? Would any Whig member choose to have his case judged by an exclusive committee of Tories? And yet the facts of the case must impress the minds of Tories and Whigs in the same way. If the same gentlemen were sitting as a jury on a charge of murder, these political feelings would not bias their verdict. The verdict they have to give in the one case depends as entirely on facts as it does in the other.

It very frequently happens in every session that a committee has to be selected to inquire into the facts of some matter which has been represented to the House as being important. All such committees have to inquire into facts, not into political opinions. And yet how distrustful of itself is the House in such matters! A committee is named, probably by the government, perhaps by the private promoter of the inquiry. In either case it is demanded that men shall be selected so as to balance with exact equality the partisans of each great political division of the day. The committee, however, is probably not so balanced, and hence arise violent denunciations from that party which conceives itself to be unduly represented. What need that any party should be represented, when men are assembled together to gather facts from evidence? Each party must, however, be represented, or the committee would be useless. If composed wholly of members supporting the government, the verdict would certainly be as the government would wish. If composed wholly of members of the opposition, the verdict would certainly be the other way.

Let any man conversant with the politics of the day see the names of a committee, and be made acquainted with the subject of inquiry, and he will be able to place the ayes and the no's on every subject on which the committee may divide, without any reference whatsoever to the evidence. He will so place them with tolerably sure accuracy unless indeed one of those few impracticable members shall have crept in, of whom no party is able to make any use.

Let us suppose that a committee has been demanded and granted to inquire as to the expediency of the Crown advancing a large sum of money, a quarter of a million we will say, towards building a huge bridge across the Thames, from Limehouse to the opposite shore of the river in such a manner that the ships of all nations may pass under it. We will suppose that the government are determined if possible to refuse the money, that considerable agitation has been made on the matter, and that the Limehouse Bridge Committee is to take evidence as to the national value of such an undertaking, and advise the House either to vote such a sum for such a purpose or not to vote it. The committee has of course been opposed by the ministers. But advantage has been taken of the Newmarket Spring meeting, when no less than fifteen government votes were at the races.

The Honourable Member for Limehouse, who lives somewhere in Scotland, and never visits his constituents except during an election, or on an occasion when he wishes to achieve a little popularity by coming out with his opinion on the War, has promoted the matter. Of the probable real value of the desired bridge he knows as little as any man in the Empire. But he has a due appreciation of the value of his seat, and also of the very great influence in the borough of the firm of Blocks, Piles, Cofferdam & Co., who hold a vast quantity of the bridge shares, and who are also to be the contractors for building it. The Member from Limehouse is consequently to be the chairman, and he proceeds to name his own committee.

He first places on it some members of the Treasury. This is of course a necessity. Would that he could dispense with doing so! But he well understands how far he can go with any chance of success. He names the Treasury gentlemen, and sundry other supporters of the government; some members also of the opposition, and fills the list with certain others, who may not be looked on as sure supporters of one side or the other, but with whom for certain reasons he thinks he may be safe.

The Member for Limehouse may be sharp, but the Treasury gentleman is much sharper. His object is, in fact, merely to do his duty to the country by preventing a profuse and useless expenditure of money. His anxiety is a perfectly honest one—to save the Exchequer; but the circumstances of the case require that he should fight his battle according to the tactics of the House, and he well knows how to do so.

When the committee has been named, he objects to two or three names—only to two or three. They are not those of staunch enemies of the government, and therefore less suspicion is excited. Nor does he propose in their places the names of staunch supporters of the government. He suggests certain gentlemen who from their acquaintance with bridges, tolls, rivers, &c. may be of use. He also is sure of his men; and as he succeeds with two of them, he is also tolerably sure of the committee.

The committee meets, and a host of witnesses are in attendance. The chairman opens his case, and proceeds to prove by the evidence of sundry most respectable men connected with Limehouse, and with the portions of Surrey and Kent lying immediately opposite to it, that the most intense desire for friendly and

commercial intercourse is felt. But, that though absolutely close
to each other, the districts are so divided by adverse circumstances which are monstrous considering the advance of science
in the nineteenth century, that the dearest friends are constrained to perpetual banishment from each other; and that the
men of Kent are utterly unable to do any trade at Limehouse,
and the Limehousians equally unable to carry on traffic in
Surrey.

It is wonderful that that narrow river should be so effective
for injury. One gentleman of Poplar proves that, having given
his daughter in marriage to a man of Deptford two years since,
he has never been able to see her from that day. Her house by
the crow's flight is but seven furlongs off; but as he keeps no
horse, he cannot get to her residence without a four hours' walk.
He is too old to walk eight hours a day, and therefore cannot see
his daughter without being a night from home, which in his
case is impossible. He is able, however, to visit his married
daughter at Reading and be back to tea. The witness declares
that his life is made miserable by his being thus debarred from
his child, and he wipes his eyes with a red pocket-handkerchief.
In answer to the Treasury gentleman he admits that there may
be a ferry, but he does not know. Having had from his childhood
an aversion to the water, he has never inquired. He is aware
that some rash people have gone through the tunnel, but for
himself he does not think the tunnel a safe mode of transit.

Another gentleman belonging to Rotherhithe, who is obliged
to be almost daily at Blackwall, maintains two horses for the
express purpose of going backwards and forwards, round by
London Bridge. They cost him £70 per annum each. Such a
bridge as that now proposed, and which this gentleman declares
that he regards as an embryo monument of national glory, will
save him £140 per annum. He then proceeds to make a little
speech about the spirit of the age, and the influence of routine,
which he describes as a gloomy gnome. But his oratory is cruelly
cut short by the gentleman from the Treasury, who demands of
him whether he ever uses the river steamers. He shudders fearfully as he assures the committee that he never does, and refers
to the "Cricket" whose boilers burst in the year 1842;—besides
he has things to carry with him.

Another witness tells how unsafe is the transit of heavy goods by barge from one side of the river to the other. He had had a cargo of marine stores which would go to sea before their time. The strong ebb of the tide, joined to the river current, had positively carried the barge away, and its course had not been stopped till it drifted on shore at Purfleet. He acknowledged, in answer to the Treasury gentleman, that something had been said of the bargeman being drunk; but he had no knowledge himself that such was the case. His own cargoes, he admitted, had repeatedly gone over safe; indeed they had generally done so; he could not at the moment remember any other cargo of his own that had gone down to Purfleet or elsewhere; but he had frequently heard of such cases. He thought that a bridge was imperatively demanded. Would the tolls pay for it? He had no doubt they would. Why then should not the bridge be built as a commercial speculation without government aid? He thought that in such cases a fostering government was bound to come forward and show the way. He had a few shares in the bridge himself. He had paid up £1 a share. They were now worth half-a-crown each. They had been worth nothing before the committee had been ordered to sit. He declined to give any opinion as to what the shares would be worth if the money were granted.

Ladies at Limehouse proved that if there were a bridge, they could save thirty shillings a year each by buying their groceries at Rotherhithe; and so singular are the usages of trade, that the ladies of Rotherhithe could benefit their husbands equally, and return the compliment by consuming the bread of Limehouse. The shores of Kent were pining for the beef of the opposite bank, and only too anxious to give in return the surplus stock of their own poultry.

"Let but a bridge be opened," as was asserted by one animated vendor of rope, "and Poplar would soon rival Pimlico. Perhaps that might not be desirable in the eyes of men who live in the purlieus of a court, and who were desirous to build no new bridge, except that one over the ornamental water in St. James Park." Upon uttering which the rope vendor looked at the Treasury gentleman, as though he expected him to sink at once under the table.

Mr. Blocks, of the great firm of Blocks, Piles, and Cofferdam, then comes forward and declares that a large sum of money is necessary before this great national undertaking can be commenced in a spirit worthy of the nineteenth century. It is intended to commence the approaches on each side of the river a quarter of a mile from the first abutment of the bridge, in order to acquire the necessary altitude without a steep ascent. He then describes what a glorious bridge this bridge will be; how it will eclipse all bridges that have ever yet been built; how the fleets of all nations will ride under it; how many hundred thousand square feet of wrought iron will be consumed in its construction; how many tons of Portland stone in the abutments, parapets, and supporting walls; how much timber will be buried twenty fathoms deep in the mud of the river; how many miles of paving stone will be laid down. Mr. Blocks goes on with his astounding figures till the committee are bewildered, and even the gentleman from the Treasury, although well used to calculations, can hardly raise his mind to the dimensions of the proposed undertaking.

The engineer follows and shows how easily this great work may be accomplished. There is no difficulty—literally none. The patronage of the Crown is all that is required. The engineer is asked whether by the word patronage he means money, and after a little laughing and a few counter questions the engineer admits that, in his estimation, patronage and money are synonymous.

Such is the case made out by the promoters of the Limehouse bridge question, and the chairman and his party are very sanguine of success. They conceive that Mr. Blocks' figures have quite cowed their antagonists.

The gentleman from the Treasury then takes the case in hand, and brings forward his witnesses. It now appears that the intercourse between the people living on each side of the river is unceasing. It would seem that Limehouse has nothing to do but to go to Deptford, and that all Deptford consumes all its time in returning the visits. Little children are sent across continually on the most trifling errands. They can go and come for one halfpenny. An immense income is made by the owners of the ferry. No two adjacent streets in London have more to do with each other than have the lanes of Rotherhithe and the lanes of Limehouse. Westminster and Lambeth are much further apart, and much less connected by friendly intercourse. The frequenters of this ferry are found to outnumber the passengers over Waterloo Bridge by ten to one.

Indeed so lamentable a proposition as this of building a bridge across the river was never yet mooted by the public. Men conversant in such matters give it as their opinion that no amount of tolls that can reasonably be expected will ever pay one per cent on the money which it is proposed to expend. That sum however will, as they state, not more than half cover the full cost of the bridge. Traffic will be prohibited by the heavy charges which will be absolutely necessary, and the probability is that the ferry would still continue to be the ordinary mode of crossing the river.

Another gentleman, who is accustomed to use strong figures of speech, declares that if such a bridge were built, the wisest course would be to sow the surface with grass and let it out for grazing.

Such is the evidence which is collected by this committee, who devote three weeks to the purpose. The expenses of witnesses, short hand writers, and printing cost the Crown about £30 a day. And worse than this, the valuable time of the gentleman from the Treasury is taken up in a manner that nearly drives him wild.

At the close the members meet to prepare their report. It is now their duty to decide on the merits of what they have heard, to form a judgement as to the veracity of the witnesses, and declare on behalf of the country which they represent whether or not this bridge should be built at the expense of the nation.

With his decision each is ready enough; but not one of them dreams of being in the slightest way influenced by anything that has been said before them. All the world, that is, all that are any way concerned in the matter, know of course, that the witnesses for the bridge are anxious to have it built, and that the witnesses against the bridge are anxious to prevent the building. It would be the worst of ignorance, ignorance of the ways of the world we live in, to suppose that any member of Parliament would be influenced by such manoeuvers. Besides, was not the mind of each man fully known before the committee met?

Various propositions are made by the members among themselves, and various amendments moved. The balance of the different parties had been very nearly preserved. A decided

victory was not to be expected on either side. At last the resolu-
tion to which the committee comes is: "That this committee is
not prepared under existing circumstances to recommend a
grant of public money for the purpose of erecting a bridge at
Limehouse; but that the committee consider that the matter is
still open to consideration should further evidence be adduced."

The gentleman from the Treasury is perfectly satisfied. He
does not wish to acerbate the Honourable Member for Limehouse, and is quite willing to give him a lift towards keeping his
seat in the borough, if able to do so without cost to the public
Exchequer. At Limehouse the report of the committee is declared by certain persons to be as good as a decision in their
favour. It is only postponing the matter for another session. But
the gentleman from the Treasury knows that he has carried his
point; and the world agrees with him. For the bridge shares,
which were worth half-a-crown, become literally valueless. A
huge blue book is printed which nobody reads, and so the matter
terminates for ever.

The gentleman from the Treasury has done his work successfully, and, considering the circumstances of his position, has
done it with credit to himself. But the House of Commons has
not been creditably employed. Their work has been a mummery.
There has been no truth in the presumed investigation which
they have been making. No possible evidence would have made
that Member of the Treasury Board vote for the bridge. No
possible evidence would have made the Member of Limehouse
vote against it. The followers of each were as decided as their
leaders. The conclusion was foregone. Or if not so, it depended
solely on the relative strength of two declared parties. To the
outer world the publication of a blue book about the Limehouse
Bridge may show evidence of national care, but in the inner
world the matter is fully understood.

If it be the fact that no work can be well done that is not done
with truth, then can not such work as that above described be
well done. The House of Commons may boast its omnipotence
never so loudly, and prove that its boasts are not vain by never
such manifestations of its power, and yet lack the elements of
permanent strength. It will lack those elements as long as
pretence and show are among the recognised tactics of Parliamentary life; as long as purism prevails to the exclusion of

honesty, and men allow themselves to profess one code of morals for the public, and a far different code for their private circles.

Each honourable member who is induced by any circumstances to vote that Black is White does whatever in him lies to destroy the honour of England, and hasten the coming of the New Zealander. And unfortunately every honourable member that does so vote has it in his power to do much.

Drogheda.
2 March 1856.

[manuscript draft in cursive handwriting]

1. A page from the manuscript of *The New Zealander*

2. Board of Trade, Whitehall, from Downing Street
Lithograph by Thomas Shotter Boys

THE SUCCESSFUL CANDIDATE.—DRAWN BY PHIZ.

THE USE OF ADULTERATION.

Little Girl. "IF YOU PLEASE, SIR, MOTHER SAYS, WILL YOU LET HER HAVE A QUARTER OF A POUND OF YOUR BEST TEA TO KILL THE RATS WITH, AND AN OUNCE OF CHOCOLATE AS WOULD GET RID OF THE BLACK BEADLES?"

3. Elections
Drawing by Phiz,
The Illustrated London News, 24 July 1852

4. Adulteration of Food
Punch, 4 August 1855

HYGHEST·COVRT·OF·LAW·IN·Yᵉ·KYNGDOM. Yᵉ·LORDS·HEARYNG·APPEALS.

5. House of Lords as Court of Appeals
Richard Doyle, *Manners and Customs of ye Englyshe in 1849*

BONNETTING THE NEW BOY PARKE.

6. The dispute over Life Peerages
Lord Lyndhurst leads the attack against a life peerage for James
Parke, Baron Wensleydale. *Punch*, 16 February 1856

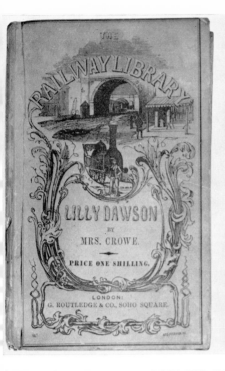

7. Railway fiction
From the Michael Sadleir Collection

THE CHURCH OF ALL SAINTS, MARGARET-STREET, REGENT-STREET.——Mr. Butterfield, Architect.

8. All Saints Church
The Builder, 4 June 1859

9. Trafalgar Square and the National Gallery
Watercolour drawing attributed to Thomas Hosmer Shepherd

10. The New Zealander
Gustave Doré, *London*, 1872

CHAPTER VIII

The House of Lords

THE House of Lords has of late years been rather snubbed.
Peers have been at a discount in England as well as in France.
Their work as a branch of the legislature has dwindled down to
inconsiderable proportions; and little more is now left to them
than to look to the administration of the laws, and reform the
practices of those courts inferior to their own to which the
general administration of the laws is delegated.

A certain amount of confusion arises from the common use of
the words law and laws. The making of new laws has but slight
connection with the reformation of the practice of the law. The
repeal of the Corn Laws was a great new law, but it has probably
given little or no work to lawyers. The establishment of the
County Courts[1] was not a great law in the eyes of the nation. Yet
it has had very great effect and will have greater on the practice
of lawyers.

Such acts as that which repealed the Corn Laws must be, as
we all know, according to constitutional theory the joint act of
Crown, Lords, and Commons. In fact, however, such acts almost
always spring from the House of Commons. Such legal reforms
as the establishment of the County Courts appear now to be
regarded as the legitimate work of the House of Lords, and the
only legitimate work on which that august assembly can safely
employ itself.

Our theory in such matters is so different from our practice,
our old constitution has undergone so many imperceptible
changes, our doctrine is so completely at variance with our
doings, that it may be as well to ascertain if possible what are
the functions absolutely and in truth performed at the present
day by each of the three parts of the legislature.

There are but few educated men in the country who are not

---

[1] The jurisdiction of these courts, established in the face of considerable
opposition from high judges and law officers in 1846, was chiefly limited to
matters of petty debt; in 1850 this jurisdiction was extended to cases involving
as much as £50.

well aware how these functions are practically divided. There can we imagine be no educated man in the country who does not well know what is the constitutional theory on the subject. But gradual use and daily habit has made this present practice so much a matter of course that men do not observe or consider the discrepancy between that which we do and that which we affect to do.

That no law can be carried out but by the joint consent and united act of the Crown, Lords, and Commons, that it is open to the Lords and Commons to propose any new law, and to the Crown, or to the Lords, or to the Commons to reject any new law, that no new law can emanate direct from the Crown, the power of which in the legislature is thus confined to a veto, this is our great theory, and this theory is known to all men.

The practice is as opposite to it as are the antipodes to each other. New laws require only the joint action of the two Houses of Parliament. The Crown has in fact no veto. But in lieu of this, it will be found that almost all laws emanate from the Crown. This is so much the case that members of both Houses are apt to look with much suspicion on any important law which does not so emanate.

Perhaps in alluding to the three parts of the legislature it would have been more constitutional to speak of the King than the Crown—or, at this present day, of the Queen. The phrase most common to our ears is King, Lords, and Commons. The word Crown has, however, been used because it more aptly typifies the real power to which reference is made. We all know that in fact as well as in theory no political responsibility is attached to the Crown. It is the happy lot of our sovereign to fill a throne as far divested of the usual cares of sovereignty as a throne can be. The individual King or Queen of England can certainly interpose no veto on any law, can certainly initiate no law. Whatever power now rests with the Crown of doing either the one or the other rests in fact with the Crown's ministers.

By the ministers, who are the personifications of the political power of the Crown, are originated nearly all the important laws which are passed in England. These ministers, however, never dare refuse the Crown's sanction to a law which has received the sanction of the Lords and Commons. Instead of doing so, they resign, and other ministers come in. It is now acknowledged by all those who write or think on the subject that any edict which has passed through the two Houses of Parliament, and obtained the assent of both, must become the law of the land.

Dearly therefore as we all cling to the old constitution under which we pride ourselves in living, it is tolerably clear that in the most important points which that constitution affects to regulate, we have found it practically impossible to abide by it. In truth our constitution is a fiction, and from the nature of things it must be so. The habits, rules, and laws of one century cannot suffice for the next. The world in this respect has been constantly changing, and the faster is the progress of science, the quicker such changes will follow each other. We still talk of our constitution fondly. We still love it, venerate it, admire it, laud it, and fight for it. But we cannot live by it. The marrow has gone from its bones. The pith has died out of its trunk and branches. The spirit has evaporated. It is an old banner under which warriors formerly fought—useless now, but of infinite value to the memories of men. It is as the yule log which is never allowed to be consumed. It is an old knife which now receives a handle anew and then a blade. Who will be so cruel as to deny to the owner of it the possession of the thing which his father used? It is as the wall of a city which once was service-able for defence but which now only encumbers the streets of the overgrown modern town. The walls of Derry still stand, those walls which the historian of today has made so memor-able,[2] and the citizens still talk of them with respectful love. But as walls their day has gone by. One cannon shot, as cannons are now cast, would shatter their bravest front. They stand, however, in the middle of the town, and the ladies of Derry walk on them comfortably and with dry feet.

The operation of the Crown has been completely changed in this constitution of ours; and the operation of the House of Lords is quickly changing. This House is in truth becoming like the old Parliaments of Paris, which were in fact an upper court for the administration of laws, which were empowered in certain

[2] The Third Volume of Macaulay's *History of England* appeared in 1855 and contained a stirring account of the defence of Londonderry in 1689 against the siege of James II. Macaulay concluded: 'Five generations have since passed away; and still the wall of Londonderry is to the Protestants of Ulster what the trophy of Marathon was to the Athenians.' C. H. Firth ed. (Macmillan, London, 1914), III, 1524 (Chapter xii).

cases to advise the King, a seat in which conferred much dignity, but which had little, if any, legislative power.

It cannot be said that such at present is the state of the House of Lords. Its independent action in the legislature is still used. It has within the last few years proved its power by rejecting on more than one occasion a bill for the admission of Jews into Parliament;[3] and is by no means contented to consider itself as a dead letter in the passing of laws in general. But no one who watches with care its present operations can fail to perceive how little is done therein towards the general work of legislation, and how sleepily that little is performed.

In truth a politician is all but unfitted for any active part in politics by assuming a seat in the House of Lords. A peer may be a useful servant of the Crown, and the Cabinet is still mainly composed of such. But though they are Cabinet ministers they can hardly be called political leaders. It may perhaps be said that one great party in the state, which at the present moment is supposed to act under the guidance of a noble earl, proves the incorrectness of such an assertion. It rather proves its accuracy. During the short time that Lord Derby was Prime Minister,[4] he was obliged so to lean on the services of a Commoner in the Lower House that the servant became a greater man than the master. The Earl was doubtless Prime Minister of his party, but Mr. Disraeli was the prime mover of their politics: can anybody believe that had Lord Derby's father been still alive, the relative position of the two ministers on the Treasury bench would have been the same?[5]

Since that time Lord Aberdeen has been Prime Minister.[6] But who will say that he was in truth the leader of the government? The result of such an arrangement was that there was

[3] Baron Lionel de Rothschild was returned as a Liberal for the City of London in 1847, but the Christian nature of the oaths required of a member of the House of Commons prevented him from taking his seat. Almost yearly until 1858 the House of Lords voted against bills passed in the Commons which would have obviated this difficulty for Jews.

[4] Derby was Prime Minister of a Conservative administration from February to December, 1852.

[5] On becoming Fourteenth Earl of Derby after his father's death in June 1851, Derby necessarily had to vacate his seat in the Commons and take his place in the House of Lords. Disraeli was Chancellor of the Exchequer during Derby's administration.

[6] From 1852 to 1855 Aberdeen headed a coalition government of Whigs and Peelites.

no leader, and consequently no public confidence in any man.

There is still occasionally a political field day in the House of Lords. Such days occur generally at the commencement or at the close of a session, and seem to make promise of unaccustomed vitality either for the session then commenced, or for that which is to come after the approaching vacation. But such promise is not kept. The field day goes off with some set speeches, some courteous attack, and more than courteous recrimination. The noble earls and noble viscounts warm for a few hours into political life, fancy for the period of an evening or two that they will give themselves up to oratory and opposition, and then become again dormant, not to be aroused till some other chance speciality may awaken them.

It is in the House of Commons that the government of the Crown must fight its battles. It is in the House of Commons that they who are in fact the chief political ministers of the Crown must sit. And it is in the House of Commons only that the rivals of those ministers can successfully oppose them. It may probably be prophesied with truth that no member of the Crown need in future be much afraid of any opposition which is mainly confined to the House of Lords.

Such appears to be the present tendency of the political power of the English peerage. A tendency much perhaps to be lamented, but hardly now to be avoided. The Reform Bill opened the arena of political strife to a set of men who had been before that all but excluded from Parliament; and those men with their ready wit and rough usage have been too much for the House of Lords. They have, as it were, dragged every subject of political discussion into their own ground, and assumed the all but exclusive right to be indignant, vehement, disgusted, shocked, excited, and patriotic.

The majority of the House of Lords have no cause for desiring to be either indignant, or disgusted, or excited. Some few may desire political place and patronage; but even they are not anxious to encounter political badger-baiting. Why should any man choose to submit to the virulence of political abuse as at present administered who has £20,000 a year to spend, and that position in the world which the possession of an English peerage still gives?

But the House of Lords still has work of its own. It is a pity that out of something less than five hundred members, there should not be more than five who are able to do it.

There is no stronger proof of the pertinacity with which Englishmen cling to institutions which are no longer fit for their use than the fact that the House of Lords is the last court of appeal to which in England questions can be referred for decision. We all know with what difficulty cases are decided on in our Chancery courts—but even when a decision has been thus obtained, it is but of small use for the successful litigant. If his rival have but a sufficiently long purse, or if the stake be of sufficient importance, the question runs through the gauntlet of various courts, goes from the Vice Chancellor to the Lords Justices and Lord Chancellor, and from the Lords Justices and Lord Chancellor to the House of Lords. Having received the full attention of those learned pundits who have been appointed to their high places as being peculiarly fit to decide in such matters, it is referred at last to the House of Lords, who, as all the world knows, are no whit more learned than their ordinary neighbours, and are by no means fitted even to understand the subject in dispute.

These questions are referred to the House of Lords as a body, and their decision is final. The House of Lords as a body never meddles with such matters. Were any foolish earl, or pigheaded baron not learned in the law, to insist on taking a part in these decisions, the constitution affords no means of putting an end to so manifest an absurdity. Ten or twelve pigheaded barons leagued together could, according to the constitution, upset all the learning of all our ancient pundits.

But, it will be said, ten or twelve pigheaded barons never do league together for such a purpose, and practically never can do so. As a fact the House of Lords is a tolerably safe court of final decision. As a fact the awards of the court below are very seldom meddled with. This is all true—as is the case in so many of our institutions, our practice is better than our theory. But nevertheless the practice itself is so awkward that we can only make apology for it by pleading that it is somewhat better than our theory.

Our last resource in cases of legal difficulty is a reference to the House of Lords, in which there may perhaps be on an average five members fitted by the habits of their lives for the required duty. Of these five one is already employed elsewhere, as he holds the situation of Lord Chief Justice. One is Lord Chancellor, who sits, or should sit, in one of the lower courts from which these appeals are made. The other three are necessarily aged sages who have filled high legal appointments, and should be looked on as already *rude donatos.*[7] There are now in 1856 three such who grace the House of Lords. Three men of whom as judges no evil can be said but that their ages average some 80 years for each.

We believe that lawyers, that is, successful lawyers, work harder than any other men: and yet they outlive all their neighbours. They are among men as crows are among birds. Sombre habiliments, long winded cawing, and grave faces tend to longevity. And it must be owned that lawyers live longer than other people not only in body but in mind also. And of all lawyers Lord Lyndhurst is in this respect, as in many others, the most wonderful. Who can believe that the man who the other day spoke for hours on the subject of Lord Wensleydale's peerage, and spoke so that even on so dry a matter his speech is light and easy reading, who can believe that that man is 84 years of age?[8] Why ask for more law Lords, argues Lord Lyndhurst, while I am here? I and my learned brethren, who were nursed in law, who have rendered ourselves memorable by Herculean feats of legal prowess? This House, says the venerable Baron, never possessed more legal strength than it now possesses.

What an argument is this against our constitutional theory that the House of Lords should be our last court of legal appeal! Exclusive of the Chancellor,[9] who sits and should sit elsewhere, Lord Lyndhurst names two Lords besides himself, two venerable Lords whose names are entitled to every honour that England can pay them, two venerable Lords, the elder of whom is 78, and the younger 75 years of age![10] No further legal assistance is necessary while such towers of strength belong to us!

It would be monstrous indeed to speak aught but praise of men whose only fault is their age; of men who are willing in the long evenings of their lives, when others look for rest and

[7] *rude donatos*: honourably discharged.
[8] Lord Lyndhurst gave this address 7 February 1856.
[9] Lord Cranworth (1790-1868), created Lord Chancellor under Aberdeen in 1852.
[10] Lord Brougham (1778-1868), and Lord St. Leonards (1781-1875).

dignified ease, to work gratuitously for their country! Let all honour be paid to such men. Let them be regarded as wondrous ornaments of their age. But we must not on that account forget that wonders are not often repeated; or calculate that all ex-Chancellors will be serviceable at 80.

We of course make use of fiction, one of those legal fictions of which our constitution is so fond, when we talk of referring law questions to the House of Lords, or of going to the House of Lords for a bill of divorce. We mean that we will refer to a court presided over by ex-Chancellors or some other occasional legal sage whom chance may have brought into the House of Lords.

The difficulty into which an arrangement so absurd must often result is now felt; and consequently another sage has been called from the judicial bench to assist his aged brethren. Has been so called, but hitherto called in vain. An attempt has been made to create a law peer for his life only. An attempt which hitherto has failed all but ludicrously.[11]

The minds of noble lords were shocked by such a creation. Such a step has not been ventured on by any King or Queen since the dark ages. Even if within the ancient privilege of the Crown, such a doing is not within the constitutional use of such privilege. The minds of peers have been in a state of ferment and the matter has been debated.

Whether the Queen's ministers were right or wrong to recommend such a measure we will not debate here. But this, at any rate, is clearly shown, that the House of Lords as it existed was not found to be sufficient for the work assigned to it, and that some measure was necessary to enable it to get through its duties. As a sufficient number of lords are not lawyers, it will be necessary from time to time to turn a certain number of lawyers into lords; and as the sons of lawyers may not be so useful as their fathers, such peerages might conveniently be conferred for life only.

Let us presume that the Crown exercised an undoubted right

---

[11] In January 1856, the Crown issued a patent for a life peerage for James Parke, Baron Wensleydale. Lord Lyndhurst, opposing life peerages, moved (in the speech referred to above, p. 137) to submit the matter to the Committee for Privileges, which in turn decided against the patent, urging that the Crown had through disuse lost the power of creating life peerages. Wensleydale was then made a peer in the usual form, July 1856.

in doing this. Let us acknowledge that the Crown was judicious in attempting to supply the amount of legal acquirement that is necessary. Still it cannot but be felt that such an arrangement is a most clumsy recourse for getting over a difficulty which admits of a practical and easy solution.

The House of Lords in their debates have not admitted, and are not likely to admit, that this jurisdiction of theirs is altogether an anomaly. But such to a plain thinking man will be the result of the discussion. The ancient constitution of the realm requires that the House of Lords should be the last court of appeal in legal matters, and in order to fit the business of the age to the ancient constitution some pieces of patchwork must be done. The idea of remodelling the constitution and changing it so as to suit the work to be done has not occurred to any of the noble lords who have taken up the matter.

It has been duly shown that the practice of making peers of Parliament for life has not prevailed, and that if made to prevail it would alter the constitution of an assembly which in its general features boasts to be hereditary. It has also been duly shown that in order to enable the assembly to do its allotted work more legal assistance is necessary, and that the sons of legal pundits are frequently without the means of maintaining an hereditary peerage. Hence the nation is at a dead-lock. What if we were to absolve the House of Lords of duties which as an assembly they don't pretend that they are able to perform? What if we should cease to use any fiction in the matter and boldly declare that legal questions must be settled by lawyers and institute accordingly some court of appeal?

That is the last thing which we should think of doing. Let this constitution of ours die by degrees, if die it must. Let our ancient usages wear themselves out and become abolished by their own utter impracticability and unsuitableness. But let no sacrilegious hand touch it or them. Let it be the adored Lama to which crowds of worshippers attribute the continued vigour of beautiful youth. How often the object of adoration is changed is known only to the priests.

But to the Buddhist priest it is known that when the beauty of their young god begins to pale, his godship is got rid of, and another substituted in his place. It is only for the political priesthood of England to ignore so palpable a change. It is only for the great statesmen of this country to endeavour to guide their countrymen by rules which were made to suit a people as different from ourselves as they again were different from the ancient Britons who coloured themselves with woad, and lived like beasts in the woods.

It is impossible not to smile when we are told that worthy Baron Parke cannot be a Peer of Parliament for his life only, because some wretched French renegade who was made a baron by Richard II never was known to sit and vote among the barons of England! But what if this Frenchman had so sat and voted? Would it then have been quite clear that Baron Parke might do so too? If not, the argument is worth nothing.[12]

Is my Lord Lyndhurst anxious to regulate the privilege and restrictions he is under by the privileges and restrictions of a baron in the days of Richard II? It would be as unreasonable for my Lord St. Leonards to paint himself from head to foot and walk through Westminster with a club in his hand, as it is to argue that Baron Parke may not sit in Parliament because Guishard d'Angle seems never to have done so.

It would be singular that learned men should utter such mildewed sentiments, such moth-eaten shreds of arguments, should refer to such dusty forgotten chronicles, or rake up the reminiscence of such obsolete usages as precedents for our present governance, were it not that other men are willing to listen to them and be guided by them.

Englishmen will not understand the full necessity of changing their customs as the circumstances of the world change, till it be too late. Our lords still strive to guard their privileges by those barriers which guarded the rights of the barons of King John, our commoners still claim the privilege of voting by payment of scot and lot,[13] and by burgage tenure.[14] Property is

---

[12] In his 7 February speech to the House of Lords, Lord Lyndhurst mentioned Guishard d'Angle as the first recipient of a life peerage patent; but, since Guishard was not allowed to sit in Parliament because he was a foreigner, Lyndhurst claimed he was not using this argument against Parke's life peerage. Lord Granville, however, thought Guishard's case germane. See the entire debate, Hansard, *Parliamentary Debates*, 3rd Series, CXL (1856), 363-83.

[13] *scot and lot* (usually 'lot and scot'): duties which in certain cities and boroughs had to be paid before electors were entitled to vote.

[14] *burgage tenure*: a kind of tenure whereby someone held lands in ancient boroughs by payment of rent to the king or other lord.

still held on payment of heriot fines[15] and other similarly absurd conditions. And there is, we believe, still in existence a legal officer who by right of his appointment claims to be called Mr. Deputy Chaffwax.[16]

The names in themselves are of little moment; but when we are told that the ancient things so named must impose on us restrictions in making arrangements for our better convenience, we cannot but feel that we are paying worship to the dead at the expense of the living. It is this worship of the dead, of things that are dead as well as men, that has so often been the ruin of nations. It may be possible to exclude Baron Parke with his life peerage from the House of Lords; but it may not be found possible to exclude from London Bridge that gentleman from the Pacific, who is, as we are told, to visit us in our decadence.

---

[15] *heriot fine*: a customary tribute in goods or money to a lord on the occasion of the death of a tenant.

[16] *Chaffwax*, or *Chafewax*: an officer of Chancery whose duty it was to prepare wax for the sealing of writs and other documents; the office was abolished in 1852.

CHAPTER IX

The Crown

MR. MACAULAY has described this New Zealander who is to come as standing on a half ruined arch of London Bridge. That picture is sufficiently trying to the nerves of an Englishman; but the stranger might be worse placed even than on London Bridge. The last spot which we would desire to imagine as desecrated by his presence is the throne of our sovereigns. We certainly do not wish to see him, even in our mind's eye, lolling in the House of Lords on the seat of our Queen; or wondering at the obsolete regalia of our past royalty, as we wonder at the hidden jewels of the Three Kings, when in our autumn tours we visit the Cathedral at Cologne.

To us Englishmen our throne, and our Crown, and our Monarch are matters all but sacred. And this feeling is anything but the same as that which induced so many good men to advocate the doctrine of the divine right of Kings in the days of the four Stewarts. Nay, the one feeling is directly antagonistic to the other. The two are, as it were, each the antipodes of the other. We recognise no divine right in any one to reign over us. We proclaim that the sovereign is the servant of the people, and not the people the servants of the sovereign. We insist that the King and Queen shall reign in order that we may be advantaged thereby, not that he or she shall be benefitted. She is our Queen rather than we her people. We have so arranged that she can hardly reign so as to inflict injuries on the country. But were it possible, and did she do so, we should undoubtedly put a stop either to the injuries or to the reign. Our Queen has no recognised right from heaven to the place she fills. But on that account we are the more chary that the right given her by the powers on earth shall be fully respected and strictly guided.

There is true chivalry in this. As long as we had rulers over us who claimed our fealty by a right inherent in themselves, not given to them by us and not within our power to remove, it was neither cowardly to rebel against such a claim, nor false to deny the truth of it. Now however, we, having set aside such a doctrine as utterly untrue and inefficacious in this England of ours, have nevertheless chosen to perpetuate a throne and a monarch, not for his purposes but for our own. His dignity is to be supported for our advantage. His greatness is to reflect the grandeur of our nation. His rank is to be supreme, in order that our country may be supreme also. Having thus ascribed to our sovereign dignity, greatness, and rank, it becomes us also to ensure to him security, respect, and the full enjoyment of his high place.

This too we have done and done thoroughly. The divine right of Kings, though so firmly believed in by many of the subjects of the House of Stewart, could not keep one of that House out of danger. Gunpowder plots, beheadings, exile, and abdication attested the falsehood of this divine right. Security than which nothing human can apparently be more secure attests the truth of that right which depends solely on a people's choice.

There is in England no feeling of antagonism to the Crown. Of all our institutions it is the most popular. Not only does it not meet with antagonism, but antagonism to it may be said to be hardly possible, as it is thoroughly understood that the Crown can oppress no one.

It is so arranged that the highest political office in England is wholly divested of political power. By a happy conceit (for at first it was but a conceit) the Crown is divested of all responsibility. And as no duty can exist without responsibility, so the Crown has gradually become free from political duty.

This was at first but a fiction created to guard the Crown, if possible, from the serious dangers which encompassed it. As long as Kings stood on their divine rights, and so standing conceived themselves to be endowed with the power of annulling laws, deposing judges, or even of going to war at their own discretion, it was idle to say that the King could do no wrong. As long as our sovereigns acted in any political emergency according to their own judgement, such an assertion could be but a fiction. Were our Queen to assume for a moment the power of acting either in opposition to the advice or without the advice of her ministers, this rule, which has now become a great constitutional dogma, would again become null and void. The power of action without responsibility belongs to no human creature, cannot belong to any human creature.

No law, no set of laws, guarded with ever such ingenuity by hosts of legislators, can bestow such privilege on any monarch. We do not speak of the responsibility which the creature owes to the Creator, but of that which every governor here on earth owes to those whom he governs. Let us try it and we shall find that this doctrine that the King can do no wrong applies and can apply only to the King who holds, or at any rate assumes, no power of doing anything. Were our Queen to insist on appointing some unseemly reprobate to a bishopric, would it be held that in doing so she did no wrong? But it will be said the Queen could not make such an appointment without her minister, and he would be impeached. The minister of course would not consent, and if pressed by Her Majesty would of course resign. We will imagine that other ministers would be summoned to her Councils, would remonstrate, resign, and take themselves out of harm's way, finding that their mistress was firm to her unwise purpose. Will any one declare that in such event as this the Queen would be held to have done no wrong?

But such an event would be impossible. All the world knows that the Queen does not make the bishops. It is the Prime Minister who makes them. True: and the Queen, having no power to make a bishop, cannot be held to have done wrong if bad bishops are selected. As it is in the making of bishops, so it is in all other matters of governance. As regards our monarchs it is now, happily for them, no fiction that the King can do no wrong.

The course of our sovereign in all political emergencies is plain and must be followed. There is no choice, no doubt, no room for tyranny, no scope for ambition, and consequently, there is no fear, no enmities, no hatred, no danger.

It may be said that all forms and all manners of government whatsoever do and must in effect resolve themselves into oligarchies. The few best men of a people are always those who should rule. An attempt is always made to get at these few best. Sometimes successfully—sometimes also so unsuccessfully that it would appear that the few worst have been selected. But in the one case or in the other, and indeed in all cases, one result is invariable. The power of ruling becomes the privilege not for one man, even though a despot may reign, not of 20 million, even though a republic may exist, but of some few who are specially chosen with reference to their presumed power of governing their brethren.

In nations over which a despotic monarch reigns, a Napoleon, or a Nicholas, this fact is hidden with more or less skill. Everything is done in one man's name. All political facts are presumed to emanate from him, and it is probable that no great political act is accomplished without his cooperation. But not on that account can he be said to rule a great people alone. He also has his councillors, his few best men, by whom he must be led and guided. He also must often be a puppet in the hands of his ministers, and walk as they would have him walk. To walk, or else disappear rapidly from the stage with tragic catastrophe, as has happened before now to so many despotic monarchs.

The result is the same in a republic. Five million of adult male citizens may be much flattered by the feeling that each is as powerful to rule in his own country as any of his brethren. But each knows in his own heart that by such an illusion he does but flatter himself. An oligarchy is here also chosen in some fashion. The few best are again looked for, and proclaimed with much noise and tumult, and many doubts. But they are looked for, and in some sort found. And so the government goes on and is conducted, in the one only way in which the government of a great people can be managed.

In England we do the same. The question is whether we have not ascertained the best known way of doing it. In our method there is at any rate no pretence, no sham, no make-believe that all rule emanates from one bosom or from five million. Every Englishman knows, or may know, that a dozen gentlemen leagued together, and forming one council called here a cabinet, do rule the country. Their rule is supreme, open, and without appeal. If they declare that the country shall go to war, the country goes to war. If they deem it right to make a treaty, the treaty is made. They appoint judges, bishops, admirals, and generals. To them belongs the privilege of pardoning criminals, and rewarding merit. To them is attached the responsibility of failure. To them belongs the praise of success.

All oligarchs are in some way removable. Men who have been reputed to be the best will occasionally lose their reputation. Their faculties will pale, and younger and better men will grow

up round them. Our ideas as to the requisite accomplishments
of a best man will change. And here as elsewhere virtue and
wisdom themselves will in time render their possessors unpopular. In Russia the Czar gives his unpopular best man his
congé in a very unceremonious way, and sends him about his
business without much apology. Here our sovereign, if allowed
to retain her ministers, would probably never change them.
A change of ministers is to her her only political trouble. But
such changes are unavoidable, and we all know how they are to
be effected and how avoided.

But though the power of ruling thus rests with a small council
of chosen oligarchs, to them belongs none of the grandeur of
reigning. The majesty and dignity of the throne is at least as
high with us, at least as far above the majesty and grandeur
of any subject, as in any country in which the responsibility of
political power is still attached to the sovereign. Our twelve or
thirteen governors do not sit on thrones, glorious with jewels,
and bright with scarlet raiment. No lictors go before them, no
guards do them honour, no flourish of trumpets is heard as they
pass daily from their office to their seats in Parliament. In the
hot sultry days of July one may often see a respectable gentleman in the decline of years, shuffling along rapidly between
Downing Street and Westminster Hall. He has probably a
bundle of papers under his arm, and is accompanied by some
friend into whose ear he is pouring rapid words as he walks. He
looks neither to the right nor to the left. He regards neither
cabs nor crowd. He leans somewhat heavily on the arm of his
companion, well skilled to get assistance of some kind from
every one that is near him.

He is one of the rulers of England. He is one of those few
best men to whom have been entrusted the duties of governing
the subjects of his Queen. Visit him in his own house, and you
will find a quiet, sedate gentleman, apparently fond of ease, and
guided in most domestic concerns by his wife and children.
Look at him in the presence of his sovereign, and you will perceive him to be actuated by the most profound respect for the
high majesty of the throne. But watch him in the management
of that office over which he is set, and you will be made aware
that none can be more autocratic than he. Not for a moment
would he allow his sovereign to interfere with those privileges

which are attached to the station which he fills. To her belongs the splendour and majesty of reigning. To him belongs the power and patronage of ruling. Each knows what is his own. Each is careful to give to the other all that is due.

There is a peculiar safety in this method of separating power from grandeur, the power of the ruler from the grandeur of the sovereign. By it we are enabled to secure the throne from those tumultuary throes to which political power must ever be subject; and also to secure our statesmen from those temptations to which new fledged splendour is always exposed. Our sovereigns in these days may probably not be better men than was Charles I, but they are guarded from the rock on which Charles was shipwrecked. Our ministers may not probably be by nature more virtuous than was Wolsey, but they are safe from the evils by which Wolsey was overcome.

We have been told more than once lately that this cabinet, with the name of which every educated Englishman is so familiar, is unknown to the constitution;—that though it is so important in our scheme of government, and so powerful in its councils, it has never been recognised as belonging to the constitutional policy of the country. The same thing may be said of so much of our present plan of legislating and governing that it would appear that the constitution does not recognise half the things that our rulers do.

Who can tell what the constitution does recognise, or what ceremony is necessary to make any change in our constitution? According to the constitution no person who has been sent up to Parliament to represent a constituency can divest himself of the burden of his parliamentary duties till that Parliament shall have been dissolved. And yet we all know that any member who wishes to resign his seat does so. The constitution also requires that any member of the House of Commons appointed to a place of profit under the Crown shall vacate his seat. We all know how the members are enabled by the latter named constitutional edict to break through the former. We all know how by a childish fiction any gentleman who wishes to resign his seat pretends that he has accepted a place of profit, and that he is thus disqualified. We all know that there is no place, no profit, no disqualification.

It would be well if some great constitutional pundit would tell us what the present constitution of the realm does really require in this matter of members vacating their seats.

Again according to the constitution the Queen is the head of the Church, and it is her duty as such to nominate the bishops. To the dean and chapter and diocesan authorities is delegated by the constitution the right of choosing the bishops—under this condition however, that they always choose the one person named by the Queen. The Queen, however, is also very much constrained as to her choice, for she can only name the person named to her by her minister. This minister selects the bishop exactly as he would his own gardener. At least he should do so. He finds the best man he can, having due regard to certain opinions and principles which he thinks it well that a bishop should hold; and the man so chosen by him as a matter of course becomes bishop. This practice is probably good, but it is hardly constitutional.

In the beginning of every session, the government has in a certain measure at its disposal three parliamentary nights a week; whereas private members have two. It generally happens that towards the end of the session, private members have to give up one of their two nights. This is a most important and necessary arrangement. But it may well be doubted whether it has ever been recognised as constitutional.

The constitution says that the debates in Parliament shall not be published. But they are published daily. Is the doing so now constitutional or the reverse?

The constitution says that the House of Peers is the final court of appeal in law courts. We have seen to what this constitutional edict has now come. It could have hardly been originally intended that by appeal to the House of Lords it was meant that appeal should be made to three or four ex-judges—all in extreme old age.

Examples of the same kind could be multiplied without end. Is it not therefore clearly the fact, that our constitution changes itself from day to day, as do all human institutions? that any plan which is brought into use in the state becomes by that usage constitutional?

Absurd fictions are employed, and antiquated theories, by which it is endeavoured to show that the constitution of England is a scheme of governance not subject to decay as other schemes have been, not proper only for a season, but enduring from age to age, gifted with fitness for all times, endowed with a finality, a political wisdom, and capable of carrying us on with security from generation to generation.

It has never carried us on with security from one generation to the next, not even from father to son. Such security as we have enjoyed has sprung not from our adherence to a fixed constitution, but from the various changes we have made in it. And if we are to enjoy security, we shall achieve it by the mutability, not by the immutability, of our institutions.

The cabinet has now in very fact become a part of our present constitution—and by no means an unimportant part. One may say that there is no more important part. It is well known that the throne cannot be vacant. Such at least is the constitutional theory. It will soon become a constitutional necessity equally strong that the cabinet shall not be empty. A King or Queen who can do no wrong cannot exist without a cabinet.

A republican on reviewing this form of government would be apt to say that if such, such and no more, be the extent of the actual duties of the Crown, the Crown itself might be dispensed with without danger to the government. A utilitarian might as well declare that Salisbury Cathedral would answer all its legitimate purposes just as well if deprived of its steeple. He might argue that the spire contributes neither to the solidity, nor to the size, nor to the convenience of the church. That it is expensive in its repairs, dangerous in its height, and pernicious to the country as being a vain, useless gewgaw. Such a man had, however, better keep his opinion to himself if he chooses to sojourn in the County of Wiltshire. There the lovely spire of this magnificent cathedral is held as of great price by thousands who are unable perhaps to argue justly as to the true use of the beautiful and decorous in church architecture; or as to the substantial effect which elevated grandeur will always have on the minds of men.

The throne is the apex of the building in which we Englishmen delight to dwell. Among other people the throne is the strong centre column on which the whole weight of the edifice is supposed to rest. Such have been the seats of European despots. Among others again the throne is the nucleus of the temple of the nation, a temple which appears to have been created merely as an accessory to the majesty within, as a protection for one man's ease, as the means of gratifying one man's pleasure. Such have been the thrones of Eastern Kings.

We do not treat our monarchs as though they had no appetites higher than those of a brute; nor yet do we look to them for the omnipotence and wisdom of a God. With us the throne is the beautiful spire which completes the symmetry and constitutes the grace of the building. We do not, however, expect that the building if inverted should stand on its spire, nor is it necessary that it should do so.

Poets have often told us of the miseries of royalty, and have not infrequently put their sentiments into the mouths of Kings. How often has the Crown been apostrophized as lined with thorns, and the throne as being the seat of wretchedness!

Uneasy lies the head that wears a crown. Let us hope that it is not so now in England. Perfect happiness, as we all know, is not the lot of any human being. But let us hope that we have done all that subjects can do to ensure happy hours, quiet slumbers, and easy dreams to the Majesty of England.

CHAPTER X
Society

A MAN in his short sojourn here on earth has mainly three things to do; and he should endeavour to do them all well. He has to say his prayers, he has to earn his bread, and he has to amuse himself. The latter of these occupations is the least important; nevertheless, it is the one to which among educated people the most time is devoted; and it is undoubtedly the one in which we Englishmen most signally fail.

Let a man say his prayers truly and he will say them well, whatever be his special creed. Let a man work truly, and he will not work amiss. It is the same with our amusements. If a man truly enjoy himself in his leisure hours, he cannot be said to have chosen wrongly his mode of diversion. Whether his pursuit be in itself good or evil, it will have been well chosen as regards its purpose, if it succeed in relieving his spirits, delighting his mind, and exciting him without fatigue.

Of all kinds of amusement that which we call society is what we men and women most desire. Indeed it may be said as regards nearly all mankind that amusements and society depend altogether one on another. It is but here and there that a man exists of a mind so constant that he with his books can be all sufficient to himself; and such a man when met with is not enviable. With most of us society is considered to be not only desirable but indispensable. It is a necessary to our existence to be purchased at any price, almost at any sacrifice. To it we look for most of our pleasure. To the want of it we attribute most of our disappointment.

If this be so we should be very careful to see that society does do that for us which we look to it to do. We should ascertain with much certainty whether we are amused when we seek to amuse ourselves; whether we do succeed in throwing off our cares, in diverting our minds, in making the hours fly lightly, at the periods in which we specially devote ourselves to doing so.

Foreigners say of us that we fail signally. They declare that we go to our theatres without even a hope of diversion, and sit there sadder even than we do at our sermons. That our dinner parties are so insufferably dull and cold that they are, as it were, the periods of confinement with hard work to which the upper classes from time to time condemn themselves; that our evening meetings are held that we may scowl at each other with disgust, and show each of us with what power of pride we can outscowl one another; that no man addresses a woman unless it is that he does now or may at some future time require a wife, and that our ladies with much perseverance reciprocate the custom; that in studying how to speak we have forgotten how to talk; that our daily work is the pastime in which we delight, and our evening amusement the great labour of our life; that we congregate in clubs to escape the horrors of society, and retire to an armchair and a newspaper from sheer want of energy to endure them.

Such are the charges brought against us by others. It is for every man's conscience to say whether as regards himself such charges be true. It may be that for many of us, nay, for all of us, society truly has no charms; that the disposition of an Englishman is such that that easy interchange of ideas, that light communion of spirit which is so natural to a Frenchman, neither delights him nor becomes him. In this, if the fact were so, there could be no disgrace. But there is a certain disgrace in attempting that which is never achieved. We know the fate of the foolish frog who would blow himself out to the dimensions of the bull; also that of the donkey in the lion's hide; and of the jackdaw who put on the peacock's tail.

Let no bird wear any tail but his own, or attempt to fly in other guise than that intended by God for him. So shall he fly with most admiration from beholders, and most satisfaction to himself.

Every man should ask himself whether the society in which he moves is truly and thoroughly to his taste, and every woman also. How many are there who have ever seriously put such a question to themselves? They fall into habits to which chance directs them, and pass their lives not only without enjoyment, but without discovering whether to them God has vouchsafed a mind capable of enjoying anything.

That this is the rule with Englishmen is thoroughly proved by the exceptions to it. Look at any man who has discovered within himself a true taste, who has learnt to have a pursuit which he can follow with excitement, and see how different to him is life than it is to those around him. The difference is that between life and vegetation, between the sweet rose that from month to month puts forth her precious buds and the dull aloe that has the name of flowering once in a hundred years. See the man to whom music is really dear, who has a true love for art, a true love if it be but for hunting or shooting. On what quick wings of joy does life float away with a man so blessed. A true love, though it be for eating and drinking, would be, one would say, better than no true love at all. If a man can find within himself no power of enjoyment of a higher scope than that, if after diligent search so much must be confessed, in God's name let him to himself confess it; and, with due aid from medical skill, eat and drink what he may, so that his gastric juices be not overtasked.

Montaigne insists on this with his usual practical wisdom, but the wisdom of Montaigne is not at the present moment much in vogue. He advises us to look carefully to our mode of living and see that we learn what it really is that we like to do.[1] My reader, have you ever done this? Doubtless you have your dress coat, and other becoming aids from the tailor's art; or, if it be my lot to be blessed with such an audience, you have all your woman's weapons ready at command, all that millinery can do for you to assist you in your struggle. Have you ever, when bedecking yourself for the world's gaze, asked yourself the question whether you are going to do that which will really be to you a pleasure or a benefit? From time to time you go to dinners and routes, to balls and parties, music parties and the like—do you really know whether in doing so you truly follow the bent of your own inclination, or go there because as a matter of course it is necessary to go into society?

In looking at you when there, oh my friends, one cannot but think that the bent of your inclination has little to do with it. To speak the truth, you too often seem as though in sitting there so silently, so tranquil, so impassive, you had not obtained for yourself, nor were prepared to communicate to others, much intellectual gratification. Why, oh my female friends, not sit at home without the cost of such expensive millinery production?

[1] See, for example, *Essais*, III, xiii, 'De l'experience'.

Or why, oh thou silent, sombre crowd, standing so uneasily round the doorways, why not stand at home, where thy comfortable old coats would have sufficed thee? Stand indeed! Each there might have had the luxury of his own armchair. Think, oh think my friends, how sweet would have been that nap which thou hast denied thyself.

It is so uncommon a thing now-a-days for a man to examine his own taste, and habitually to do that which he really likes, that any one acting in such a manner is considered eccentric, if not absolutely insane. Such a one we are told is mad about music. Such another is mad about pictures. That man is cracked because he spends his life in going up in balloons, and this other should be put under confinement because he squanders his fortune in buying china tea-cups. It is these men who are really sane. It is these, eccentric as they are, who have really learnt the secret how to live. That crooked little blear-eyed Nestor with his tea-cups is an Emperor, nay, a Demigod, when he acquires some new wondrous prize, old as the patriarchs, transparent as amber, thinner than the holy wafer, softer in its hue than cream, covered over with those sweet, uncouth Asiatic monsters which the eye of the connoisseur can recognise at a glance. Put him in confinement! No—but put him where the world may see him, and make a study of a man who has learnt to live.

And that mustachioed hairy man, the primary object of whose life is to make aerial ascents with Madame Quelquechose the Aeronaut,[2] and who, one may easily believe, has as often a second strong object of ambition in descending, even he can live without ennui. He also, descendant of Witless as he is, has contrived with that witless pate of his to find out the thing that he likes. To go up in a balloon with Madame Quelquechose, and, if lucky, to come down again, paying twenty guineas per trip, even that, if a man truly like it, is something. There are so many of us who have nothing that we like.

An Englishman appears to have a vague hope that if he goes among other men and women he will be diverted, just as he would be wetted, if he walked out into the rain. No action or

---

[2] Ballooning, long popular with the French, became increasingly so in England in the early fifties. *Punch* wrote: 'Balloon ascents are now so numerous that we expect the air will, before long, be navigated as much as the sea' (25 Sept. 1852).

effort of his own is considered necessary. He will not even do as apes do, who, fondly putting their heads each on the other's withers, kindly nibble away with agreeable exciting little nibbles, making each other happy. That is society. In that *tête à tête* meeting each has learnt what the other likes, and knows how to contribute to his friend's gratification. The two are better together than apart. There then is at any rate friendly intercourse, if not a feast of reason or flow of soul. A flow of soul is not possible to all souls; but by most of mankind some friendly intercourse of an agreeable nature might be found, if like the two apes they would look for it truly.

It is not often that the brute animals meet together without either good company, or good hostility. But there are instances in which they also are constrained and ill at ease. We have all seen geese on a pond the first morning after a hard frost. How they waddle on the ice, or mournfully stand still, expectant of the water. How they wonder why it is that they don't swim; how weary and woe-begone they are, how literally out of their element! Oh, my reader, have you not often seen a great mangander in black pantaloons standing as doleful on the hard cold ice of society; as doleful, as woe-begone, as silent, and as ill at ease? If the ice would but break and let him down quietly into the pleasant waters of his own feather-bed at home! What a release were that!

We have not very accurate means of knowing how folks lived together in the merry days of old England. Those days may have been merry, but we cannot now say of what kind the mirth was. A sort of flavour of strong ale with a floating apple has come down to us; a taste, as it were, of sack and spiced beef. We have heard of little of their gala doings but the eating and drinking.

> 'Twas merry in the hall
> When the beards wagged all.[3]

So much we know; and know also that beards will not wag for nothing. But whether it were wine or wit we cannot surely say. If the latter, then indeed have the days in England been merrier than they are now. And how goes that other old song?

[3] Thomas Tusser (1524?-1580), 'August's Abstract', *Five Hundred Points of Good Husbandry* (1557). Cf. *King Alisaunder* l. 1163. This was a favourite quotation of Trollope, see *Barchester Towers* (O.U.P., London, 1925), p. 364 (Chap. xxxviii), and *Doctor Thorne* (O.U.P., London, 1926), p. 15 (Chap. i).

Let back and side go bare, go bare,
Let back and side grow cold:
But, belly God send thee good ale enow,
Whether it be new or old.[4]

If such were the prayers of our ancestors, and the author of this song is said to have been a bishop, we can hardly venture to regret their more animated society, although we can conceive that they were merrier than their children.

But in truth we know little as to the manner in which barons and baronesses met each other, or the barons' retainers. Bulwer has indeed endeavoured to tell us, but we do not feel confident that his authority is good.[5] Much of social manners is seldom to be learned from poets; from Chaucer something may be learned, but that something is very rarely read, and less frequently understood. Perhaps Shakespeare's Merry Wives of Windsor gives as true an idea of English people in the fifteenth century as any work now extant. We must own that our matrons are hardly equal to Mistress Page and Mistress Ford; but we may boast that the gentlemen of the present day have not degenerated from Master Slender. Falstaff too, and Bardolph, Sir Hugh Evans, and dear Dame Quickly all truly lived, and still live to give us some little insight into the houses of our ancestors.

Social life in the time of Charles II has been described to us by perhaps the greatest masters of that style of writing that ever flourished. From the Memoirs of Count Grammont and the Diary of Pepys we have a perfect picture of high life and middle life in England two centuries since. And what a picture it is!

The sale of Dunkirk was disgraceful;[6] the political vassalage of the country was disgraceful, the falsehood of the King was disgraceful, but the disgrace of all these is as nothing to that which should be heaped on the nobility of that time for the quickness with which they adapted themselves to the heartlessness of the Court. There is a sort of prurient luxury in the immorality which must have been enticing to many after the sour

---

[4] William Stevenson (1530?-1575), 'Song', *Gammer Gurton's Needle*, II. 1-4. Formerly attributed to John Sills, who became Bishop of Bath and Wells; at one time also attributed to John Bridges, Bishop of Oxford.

[5] See *The Last of the Barons* (1843), *Harold* (1848).

[6] Dunkirk had been ceded to England after she had helped capture it from the Spanish in 1658, but in 1662 Louis XIV paid nearly £300,000 for its return to France.

rule of the Roundheads, but immorality to be enticing should not be systematic. There is a hard wickedness about the heroes and heroines of Anthony Hamilton which robs them of all charm and makes their loves disgusting. One is almost brought to excuse the heartlessness of the seducer, on finding that the women were fit for nothing but seduction. The society of the Court of Charles II was perhaps not dull (though even that may be doubted), but it was devilish. That we have changed from such manners cannot at any rate be regretted.

But Hamilton speaks only of the Court, of the courtlings, and of the courtesans. Pepys, though a courtier himself to the backbone, had a much wider field. When he strays away from home to sup with a favourite actress we see at a glance how in those days the domestic virtues of the people were first invaded by the vices of the fashionable world. Pepys also, though prone enough to a little gallantry, and eager after his worldly ends, had about him the feelings and affections of a man. He delighted to see a pretty foot and ankle even though it were not the ankle of his own sworn spouse, but yet he loved the wife of his bosom. He was glad enough to scrape together his few hundreds, and not so scrupulous as to his manner of doing it as in our days it behoves a servant of the Crown to be; but for his time he was more than common honest, and even had at heart the interest of the department which he served.

To him we can confidently look for the real manners of the people who then lived, for the manners of that class of which English society is mainly formed. Those among whom Pepys lived were the same in rank as the ordinary gentry of the present day; but the ordinary gentry of 1856 do not seem to relish the world with half the gusto of Pepys and his friends.

The change in this respect has been for the worse. Who would not wish to make one at such parties as those which Pepys gave in his comfortable little rooms in the city, with so much ease but so little pretence? There was then a truth about the manners of the people which seems now to be the great want of the age. Men did not pretend to be what they were not, or ape customs which to them were not customary, or affect enjoyments in which they found no true delight.

As we come down nearer to our own time we are again at a loss for any trustworthy views of general society. Fielding, though the first of caricaturists, was but a caricaturist. We do not quite believe in the Lady Boobys, and scarcely put full trust in the Squire Westerns. Squire Western and Allworthy could hardly have lived together, and, had they done so, Tom Jones, Sophia, and Blifil would not have been the product of their joint efforts at education. Richardson clearly knew nothing of the world of which he was writing. Had he been describing the loves of a true Mahometan with a houri in the seventh heaven, he could not have been less near the mark of reality than he has been with his English heroes and heroines. To have advocated virtue in pleasing but yet moral language and with some powers of imagination has been sufficient to give to Richardson the fame which he enjoyed. In these days few of us know much beyond the name of Clarissa Harlowe.[7]

Miss Burney's Evelina, though probably a copy from Richardson's mode of writing, is an improvement on it. But we can hardly trust even Miss Burney for a faithful delineation of society. She is also too stiff and constrained, too deficient in life, too much like an artist in wax work. But when we come to Miss Austen we fare much better.

Since the writing of Pepys' Diary Miss Austen has perhaps gone the nearest towards giving us a true insight into the houses of the people of her day. With Mr. and Mrs. Bennet and Lady Catherine de Bourgh we are quite at home. With the Bertrams and the Crawfords[8] we have our sympathies and antipathies as we have with the surrounding families in our own village or our own circle. The return of Sir Thomas is as when our own father came upon us in our juvenile delinquencies; and we can hardly help believing that we ourselves received Mr. Collins' letters each with one of Rowland Hill's penny stamps in the corner of the envelope.[9]

We will end the catalogue of these British painters of home scenes with the name of another spinster lady, who brings us

[7] In 1868 Trollope wrote a lengthy notice of E. S. Dallas' abridgement of *Clarissa*; he granted that the novel was moral and 'pre-eminently pathetic' but insisted that it was so prolix and improbable as to be unreadable even in its shorter form. See 'Clarissa', *St. Paul's*, III (November 1868), 163-72, and Trollope's letter to Dallas, 22 August 1868, *Letters*, pp. 226-7.

[8] See editorial note, pp. xliv-xlv.

[9] Rowland Hill (1795-1879), high postal official and father of the penny postage (1840). Trollope wrote of Hill: 'With him I never had any sympathy, nor he with me,' *Autobiography*, p. 133.

down to our own days. Miss Mitford has been with us quite lately,[10] and has moved and talked, and told her tales among the very circles of which we, still living units, now form a part. She also has described society as it is, but she has only described it as it is at its best. She told her tale as the world told it to her. She painted only the scenes which she herself saw.

Judging from what we can thus read of the manner in which our fathers and mothers lived we cannot but think that we have greatly retrograded and are still quickly retrograding. Look at that ingenuous youth, with head stiffly ensconced in a wondrous prison of starched linen, self-immolated, with his hideous trailing half monkish coat, with his listless swinging cane, and his lisping cockney twang. He is one of the curled darlings of the nation. Oh what a subject for national pride! Is he not a fit descendant of Master Slender? His gait indeed is somewhat slower, his language somewhat less intelligible, his clothes somewhat less comfortable, and he is wholly deficient in Master Slender's virtue of modesty. If there be one class of the Queen's subjects in these realms more deserving of pity than another, it is that class of young ladies who *malgré lui* are bound to fall in love with these wooden specimens of youthful manhood.

Things are much altered since the days of Horace. No Lydia need now be implored by the name of any God or Gods to abstain from destroying her Sybaris.[11] The brother of no Megilla need be asked to declare from what amorous wound he languishes.[12] A circular collar sufficiently high and sufficiently stiff, a coat trimmed with sufficient velvet, with tail of sufficient length, a cane that can be sucked with sufficient effect, make a man what he should be—sufficient in all things to himself. Add but a cigar and the blisses of this world are all within his grasp. To such no Lydia or Chloe is necessary.[13] The only love from which he suffers is love of self. The only arrow which can wound him is such as may come from his tailor's quiver. Yes, Master Slender if you please; with the character of Anne Page left out.

Is it not clear that English men and women when they do meet each other do so as a duty and not as a pleasure? A man

[10] Mary Russell Mitford died in January 1855.
[11] *Odes*, I. viii.
[12] Ibid., I. xxvii.
[13] Ibid., I. xxiii.

and his wife, in council perhaps with their grown up daughters, come to a conclusion that society is desirable. Going into society is the proper thing to do for people who consider themselves anybody. A residence has been chosen perhaps with direct reference to this. A great struggle is therefore to be made, and, let us suppose, a successful one. At the end of a dozen years what has been the result of this success? what amount of relief from the world's care has society afforded to his household? what balance of enjoyment has remained after the trouble and expense that have been incurred?

Alas, the worst of all the world's heavy cares has been the care of doing this work of society in a manner fashionably becoming. As to relief, that has been felt only when the duty has for a while been done; that odious duty which has so often to be repeated. The only enjoyment has been in the consciousness that no trouble, no expense, has been spared. Such and such refinements of fashion have been produced and displayed by Mrs. A.B., and Mrs. C.D., as she lays her weary head upon her pillow, either sobs to remember how far she has fallen short of her neighbour, or else remembers with exultation how completely she has eclipsed her.

As to that easy *laissez-faire* which should be the delight of society—as to that relaxation, and unbending of the bow which should be the special comfort of all social hours—who ever dreams of finding such in an English drawing-room? *Laissez-faire!* No—there is no permission to you to do anything that is agreeable, unless, being in want of a wife, it may suit you to make love. Relaxation! There is no period of your day at which your bow is so tightly drawn as in those hard hours of weary labour. It is bent, often to the breaking.

If a man goes into society expecting amusement to come down upon him like dew from heaven, how should it be otherwise? There is clearly no dew to be expected from heaven for these score of mortals who have thus assembled themselves together in Mrs. Gingham Walker's very elaborately furnished best drawing-room. Dew, if any be to be found, they must provide each for the other. An unfortunate score of mortals, totally unprepared to effect any such distillation! There is poor G.W., who, sitting at his counting house all the morning, did there with comfort his customary daily work. Hundreds of bales of goods he there disposed of, hundreds of others flew into his keeping. With quick pen, voluble voice, and cheery eye he did all this and was happy in the doing. But look at him now. Some idea he has that as master of his house he should entertain his company, and he strives with voice half choked to say a word to one, and a word to another, if it be but a word about the weather.

"We shall have more rain, I think, Shares."

Shares mutters an assent with his thumbs ensconced within the armholes of his white waistcoat, standing there silent on the hearth rug, gazing into vacancy. He has so stood for the last half hour. He is Shares the stockjobber, whose fat wife and round-faced daughters are sitting within that magic circle which seems to have been touched by the wand of the wizard of dullness! Shares, who is Walker's friend of twenty years, with whom in happier days he has fought so many a score of battles with a cribbage board between them. But then there was no ormolu clock, no mirrors nine feet high, no Bohemian glass making the room look like a German shop, no grand piano, no silk damask hangings, no ottomans, lounges, couches, and sofas covered with ruby silk, the pride of Mrs. Gingham Walker's heart, and the amazement of the upholsterer.

But the Walkers had no society in those days. To be sure, he liked his game of cribbage though he sat but on a horse-hair chair; and so did Shares, too. He liked his cards, and his glass of brandy toddy, and the easy way in which he was allowed to say "Two for 'is 'eels—hey my boy." But in those days Shares had no society.

"Nothing new from the seat of war, I believe," suggested poor Walker, going on to his next guest, the Reverend Elias Howle,[14] minister of the district church hard by. Mr. Howle is standing with his back to the large loo table, bolt upright—and he is very upright, with his hair as upright as himself, and his chin considerably prominent; his left hand is thrust into his waistcoat, and his right diligently employed in assisting himself in the consumption of pound cake. Mr. Howle bends slightly to catch the words, replies that as far as he knows the seat of war has no

---

[14] 'Elias Howle' is a curious choice of name for Trollope's purposes here, since Charles Lever had caricatured Thackeray under this name in *Roland Cashel* (1850). See *The Letters and Private Papers of William Makepeace Thackeray,* ed. Gordon N. Ray (University of Harvard Press, Cambridge, 1945), II, 451-2.

news, resumes his straightness, and helps himself to another piece of cake. Mr. Howle keeps all his eloquence for his pulpit. But his wife, who sits on the sofa there next to Mrs. Walker, is very fond of society—and he is apparently—very fond of pound cake.

Poor Walker still perseveres, and sidles up to Gibbs Sharpe, who is standing behind the sofa on which his hostess sits, hoping that in time the genius of conversation may illumine his thick darkness. He also is waiting for dew from heaven. Who so intimate with Walker as his own attorney, Gibbs Sharpe, the man who recovered every debt for him since he was master of a debt, the man who drew his marriage settlements, pulled him through that long law suit with the Manchester calico house, looked to the titles of his new bought properties, and made his will? And Sharpe is a clever fellow; he belongs to a West End club, can hold his own with most men, has a horse or two that he knows how to ride, and can tell a thing or two about the next Derby. When sitting behind his own office table in the Poultry he would not fear the Devil if he came to him with a sack full of law papers. But now he cannot think how on earth to get Mrs. Howle into chat with him, Mrs. Howle being in some unfathomable way related to an old baronet.

"Anything new at the clubs?" says poor Walker.

"Nothing particular," says Gibbs Sharpe, "except indeed that affair of Lord Vanity Ditchwater. You know, I suppose, that Lord Vanity has been pulled before the House Guards for throwing young Charley Gosling's breech—clothes, I mean, out of the barrack windows?"

Gingham Walker never went to the West End, and cared nothing about Charley Gosling's attire; but his little move had been so far successful that something like conversation had ensued.

"Do you happen to know the Ditchwaters, Mrs. Howle?" said Gibbs Sharpe, following up the happy lead.

"Not at all," answered she, scowling dreadfully beneath the unnecessary load of her auxiliary ringlets. Mrs. Howle's connections with the peerage, if not extensive, have been most decorous. The idea that she, a cousin of Sir Cloudy Cloumley's, should know anything of anybody who could amuse himself by throwing another man's breeches out of a window!

Mrs. Howle has a nephew, an offshoot of the great Cloumley

family, who has been standing all the evening by the door,
ornate with round collar, with peculiar dress coat, with immense
white tie, and quite motionless. It is with a feeling almost
amounting to pity, at any rate with true sympathy, that
Gingham Walker addresses him, assures him that the two Miss
Shares are most delightful girls, and suggests that there is room
between them on the ottoman. "You may be safe there," says
G.W., whispering slily. "There's lots of blunt[15] in that quarter."

"Oh—ah—eh—is there?" stutters forth the Cloumley scion,
moving round his head about an inch with great exertion, and
also his shoulders with it. "Ah—indeed—but I'm very well here
—thank you," and then again he slowly moves back the stiff
pivot on which the thing he calls a head is fixed. So much is the
share of refreshing dew which young Cloumley provided for
Mrs. Gingham Walker's guests that evening. But he also feels
how necessary it is to go into society.

Late in the following day he repeats with horror to a friend
similarly attired what stratagems had been used to induce him
to waste his sweetness on such females as the two Miss Shares.
"But old birds, you know, an't to be caught with chaff, eh?" and
he simpers with a miserable simper.

What hope can ladies have in company when men behave
themselves in this way? But the ladies hardly seem to expect
anything else. Those two Miss Shares, who would really be
pretty if everything about them were a little less round, seem
quite contented. To look at them one would say that the fact
of appearing there with dresses which cost ten guineas each was
to them quite sufficient. If that young Adonis of the doorway,
moved by sudden flame, should come and seat himself between
them, they would apparently be much alarmed by such an
extreme proceeding, and perhaps scream faintly for the assistance of their mother. What might not come next, were a strange
man to do such a thing as that? Poor girls, it would be hard to
say whether their amazement or his would be the greater.

The idea seems never to have occurred either to him or them
that they are all three there for the purpose of conversing with
each other: that they have come thither specially with the object
of enjoying each other's discourse, of being charmed with each
other's wit, of communicating each to the other so much of

---

[15] *blunt*: money.

thought and genius as each may have to dispose of. No—not of that has either the remotest idea. To communicate the sight of a dress which cost ten guineas, and a head of hair on which a hairdresser was employed for an hour, and of sundry brooches, gems, and jewels—with such object as that, one would say, have those daughters of the opulent Shares come into society. With what object he of the collar may have come out, it would be more difficult to define. Perhaps to his eyes that collar itself is as well worthy of notice as the richer adornments of the young ladies.

It must, however, be owned that English women generally are more disposed than English men to make some efforts towards accomplishing the true end of society. They will exert themselves more if any opening be made for them. The use of their tongues is not so completely paralysed. The flow of their thoughts is not so entirely stopped by the brilliancy of their neighbour's grandeur. But women are not fond of talking to each other in company, and it is hard for them to fight the battle unassisted.

There is that little Miss Sharpe, Gibb's sister. She is really not a dull person, and as she goes out somewhere every night of her life, she is not dumbfounded by being among strangers. Yet see how all her little efforts are in vain. She has tried Mr. Howle about the poor and the cholera, and the Broad Street pump;[16] she has tried Mr. Shares about Brazilian stock, and the Eastern Counties. She has tried Gingham Walker about his furniture. She has glanced with inviting eyes at the Cloumley scion, and laughingly whispered to a young lady at her side that Mr. Cloumley is astonished by so much beauty. It is all useless. From the men she gets nothing but monosyllables, and the young lady simpers and shakes a bit of lace which is dangling from her hand and which she calls a pocket-handkerchief.

What can one poor Miss Sharpe do against such a multitude? At last, having done her duty to the utmost, she sinks back in her easy-chair exhausted, and makes up her mind to rate her brother soundly about his friends, when the happy hour of escape shall have arrived.

---

[16] The cholera epidemic which struck London in the summer and fall of 1854 was particularly severe in the Broad Street area. See *The Times*, 27 Dec. 1854.

But why does cruel fate prohibit these unfortunates from amusing themselves as under other circumstances they might be able to do? Let us suppose for a moment that the thunder and lightning tapestry carpet was covered with its ordinary crumb cloth, that tea, and bread and butter, instead of being handed round by a couple of servants were served in the old fashion on the round table, that Mrs. Howle had brought with her a portion at least of the large quilt which she is making—there would have been room for it in the cab on young Cloumley's knees—; that Mrs. Shares was allowed to eat her fill instead of being limited to a mouthful snatched from the cake basket, that her daughters were divested of their ponderous finery, and girt round their heads with their usual simple *bandeaux*; that Miss Sharpe was listened to as she chattered over her tea-cup; that a whist table was permitted for Gingham Walker and his friends; and that Mr. Howle, *faute de mieux*, had ensconced himself in a corner with the notes of one of his extempore sermons in his hands for correction. Would not that be improvement? with such as that would not the hum of voices soon be heard? would not Mrs. G.W., under the press of her hospitable cares, talk and beg, and press and be busy? would not Mrs. Howle thaw with the warmth of her comfortable tea, and forget for a while Sir Cloudy and her dignity? would not Miss Sharpe talk till her tongue was tired? and the wooden youth, would he not be compelled to bring a chair to the table; and, encouraged by the contiguity of the circle, might not he be tempted, even he, to utter some platitude that good natured beauty could accept as a small social effort?

And as to those middle-aged gentlemen, their sorrows, burdens, and labours would be at an end. The vast load of their ennui, the intense weight of their weariness, would be dispelled in a moment, and in lieu thereof animated interest, and strong feeling would arise. "Walker, score that treble." "Sharpe, have you got that double safe under the candlestick?" "Why, Shares, man alive—in the name of common sense, why did you not trump the diamond?"

Mr. Howle would look on with envious eyes and watering lips, and before the evening was over he also would have cut in and taken his chance. And the younger Miss Shares on her retiring to her rest would whisper to her sister that, after all, that Mr.

Cloumley was not quite such a fool as people said.

But nothing on earth could be more vulgar than this, or less like those elegant reunions of the great which it is Mrs. Gingham Walker's special ambition to emulate. Such a party as that which we have described would much more resemble a meeting of German tradespeople than an evening assembly of English *comme il faut* people in London. Add but a large glass of beer to each guest, and we might fancy ourselves in Bavaria at once. Almost. Add a little more life to the young people, grant that some good music might be hoped for, deduct still a little from the arrogance of Mrs. Howle, let the hospitality of the hostess be rather less ambitious, and the gaiety of Miss Sharpe rather less affected, and then one might in truth almost fancy oneself in Bavaria.

What a change for the better would that be as regards all who are concerned! What a lesson one might learn from our German or French neighbours, were it not that we are too proud to learn anything.

"But," says Mrs. Gingham Walker, "the people who live in that style in Bavaria are not *comme il faut* people. The aristocracy there have their own manners, and the bourgeoisie have theirs. Why should you ask me to live like the wife of a German pastry cook?"

My dear Mrs. Gingham, every woman is *comme il faut* as regards manners who lives in the style that suits her. In doing so she is not only *comme il faut*, but also prudent and sensible. If that style of the tea-cups handed round, and of waiting for dew from heaven suits you and makes you and your husband happy, in heaven's name don't be laughed out of it. But if it does not—if rather it bores you till your back and heart be nearly breaking with the weight of ennui, then I would counsel you to try the fashion of Bavaria. I for one would rather be—oh how much rather!—the wife of any Munich pastry cook than of a London merchant, were I doomed by accepting the latter alternative to go through such troubles as yours.

It is doubtless very good for Lord Palmerston and his wife when entertaining diplomats, cabinet ministers, royalty, and bedchamber ladies, to have their coffee and tea handed round to them; and we can also easily understand that such very tip top people may have so much to say to each other that they really have no time for cards. They probably truly like the fashion in which they live; and the same fashion may also be very suitable to others near the top of the tree, though not perched quite on the highest branch.

It is for every man to judge whether fashions which thus descend through the different grades of society be or be not good for his use. If he hear of a custom which clearly is for his good, let him undoubtedly adopt it. There is no reason why that which suits Lord Palmerston should not suit Mr. Jones; but let Mr. Jones be studious to adopt no custom as his which is recommended only by its suitableness to Lord Palmerston, and not at all by its suitableness to himself. It is by this mistake mainly that Englishmen err so much in their search after social pleasure.

If a man do not like conversation, but be fond of threepenny whist, let him at any rate find that out, and confess it to himself. He may thus escape many weary hours, and finally also much self-contempt. It is impossible that any one should feel self-satisfied, should feel that as a man he is sustaining a manly part, who allows himself to stand sad, silent, and sombre in a neighbour's drawing-room for hours together. It need be no disgrace to him that such amusements as are to be found in drawing-rooms should not for him have charms; but it is a disgrace if he have not wit enough to discover this, and moral courage enough to withdraw himself from a pursuit that gives neither pleasure nor profit, either to himself or to others.

The amount of boredom which is inflicted on man by his fellow men in our so-called social meetings creates a feeling amounting almost to hatred. Who can regard as other than an enemy a creature that sits at one's table speechless and motionless —or, if in motion, only so with the object of taking in food? Who can have friendly sympathies with a man whose powers in society appear to be limited to those of digestion? What return is there in such meetings for the money spent? What excuse to be found for the time consumed? A man spreads his table and calls together his acquaintance; and then, when he sees them seated round the certainly not festive board, begins to count the minutes till they will leave him to repose.

"Whenever I give a party," once said Mr. Green to us—and Mr. Green does occasionally give dinner parties—"the one wish of my heart is always this—that the floor might suddenly open;

and the guests, table, and dishes vanish suddenly into the bowels of the earth."

But why give dinner parties, Mr. Green? That question Mr. Green has hitherto declined to answer. Had he said that he did so because Walker, and Shares, and Sharpe all entertained (?), he would have spoken the truth as honestly as he did in describing that wish of his, ever present to his mind on gala evenings.

It will probably be said that the views of our social manners here put forward are true, if they be true at all, only with regard to persons moving in inferior circles of society. Let us for a while presume that this be granted. It is of inferior circles, that is to say of the middle ranks, that we specially wish to speak. These circles, if individually inferior in wealth and rank, are not so in numbers and importance. Dukes and duchesses are not of so much moment to us as are retired tradesmen; nor do earls and viscounts with their wives spend on their costly pleasures half the sums that doctors and lawyers lay out in vainly looking for social joys. Let it be granted that men and women in Park Lane know how to amuse themselves, though even that we think is far from the fact. But let so much be granted. Park Lane, with all its adjoining vicinage from Belgravia to Baker Street, affords but a drop to the vast waters of English social life. What though men and women never yawn in Grosvenor Place, though dullness be banished from Piccadilly, and wit reign triumphant at Whitehall; what though peers can always joke, and members of the Lower House be never unprovided with small talk! It is given but to few to live in Mayfair, or to sit in either House of Parliament. If English society ever become worthy of the name it must be by the enjoyment of the bulk of the middle classes.

There is a class of the nobility in Austria who affect to call themselves the *crème de la crème*, the very first skimming off the milk pan of German social life. In Vienna such a class may be all important. In London it at any rate should not be so. If it be so, its importance is deserved from the very mean worship of its very foolish votaries.

If an Englishman, an Englishman that is not ashamed to confess to himself that he belongs to one of these inferior circles, if such a man wish to learn how society may be charming and yet inexpensive, how men may meet together and be neither surly, nor dull, nor ill at ease, let him look at some old French-

man as he talks to an old Frenchwoman between the acts of a
comedy. Here at home we are accustomed to think that an old
woman can never be worth the talking to, and that an old man
should never amuse himself at all. Or let him watch a family
party in a beer garden at Munich. There are no fine dresses
there, no stupendous achievements of the hairdresser, and as yet
we think of no circular collars. There is, however, an equal
absence of ennui. Or let him go into some sunny town of Italy,
and see how men and women there can meet together in the
piazzas and be happy. This in the open air would not perhaps
be as agreeable in Russell Square as it is at St. Mark's, but the
good humoured quiet mirth of the Italian might perhaps suit the
Briton better than the vivacity of the Frenchman, or the un-
exacting ease of the German.

But alas, an ordinary Englishman can hardly look amiss if he
desire to look for an improvement on his own idea of society.
If two Esquimaux meet together in the same wigwam, and meet
on friendly terms, we may presume that they talk together without difficulty in such lingo as it is given to them to utter. An
Englishman under such circumstances holds his tongue. Not
voluntarily, not of malice prepense, nor yet from prudence.
It is not that he remembers Solomon; and saying to himself,
"he that refraineth his lips is wise," refrains therefore from
speech. No, he would talk if he could. But the fountains of his
speech are dried up. In this respect, at any rate, we may believe
that the New Zealander who is to be the heir of our wealth and
industry is already in advance of us.

And must then an ordinary Briton abandon all hope of being
happy in society? Must he devote himself to the life of an owl?
Or live like a pelican in the wilderness, happy only in such
sacrifices as he can make for his domestic circle? We should say
by no means so. The idiosyncrasy of an Englishman is not more
antagonistic to social life than that of a Frenchman. He has only
to change his method of performing his social duties.

Social dew will not fall on him from heaven. Let him above all
things remember that. No man can be made happy by the fact
of walking into a crowded drawing-room with a better coat on
his back than that usually worn by him. We should say that so
much as that and no more can contribute to the happiness of
neither man nor woman. We go into society with the hope of

obtaining much. We can obtain there nothing but what others bring, and are therefore bound ourselves to bring something as a contribution towards the enjoyment of others.

No heaven sent dew will be forthcoming. But a man must be very stupid if he have not some dew within himself. It may cost him an effort to produce it, but that effort he is bound to make. No work can be done, no pleasure received, no content obtained without an effort. To stand on the rug before the fire without any effort, looking at the pattern on the paper, as our friend Shares does, thinking that thereby he achieves society, is, one may say, as grievous an error as any into which a poor mortal can well fall.

Oh my reader, let me think it improbable that to thee is given no better method of social conduct than that adopted by poor Shares. If, however, such should be thy forlorn condition, if such thy fate, at any rate let so much be known to thyself, and in such case cease to trouble either thyself or thy friends.

CHAPTER XI

Literature

I T is not very easy to decide whether an Augustan age of literature should be taken as a sign of national strength or national
weakness. To many such a question will appear to be most preposterous, nay, almost blasphemous. Such persons will assert
with confidence, and not improbably with truth, that all tokens
of increase in a nation's genius must be synchronous with the
nation's vigour. They will declare that all true strength must
come from strength of mind, and that high efforts of literary
labour are the surest proof of mental power.

The matter, however, is one that might well become the subject of academical discussion. If we look to the experience of
past nations we shall see that the laurels of their poets flourished
best when the leaves of the tree of liberty had fallen, when its
branches were draggled in the mud, and the sap of its trunk
dried up.

The very name of the Augustan age of Rome tells us that the
Roman poets who formed so grand a galaxy were the children
of the Empire, and not of the Republic. And in the modern
nations around us we can also trace the same connection between
literary excellence and political vassalage. It appears necessary
that a Horace should have an Augustus as well as a Mæcenas;
that high strains as to moral worth and the beauty of freedom
should swell forth from beneath the shade of a tyrant's throne.
Racine, Molière, and Boileau graced the court of the Grand
Monarque; and it was the Grand Monarque who paved the way
for the vileness of his next descendant, and the iniquities of the
Revolution.

Even Dante was forced to act an ingracious part as a graceless
courtier at a foreign court. And when Dante began to write, then
also began the long and yet incomplete servitude of Italy, a
servitude which in its early days was graced by the names of
Tasso and Ariosto, Pulci and Boiardo. Cervantes, Lope de Vega,
and Calderón were servants to those worst of throned imbeciles,
the latter Philips of the house of Hapsburg.

But if we look at those spots in Europe in which freedom has been preserved with the fondest care and the proudest success, how small an amount of literary excellence shall we find in them? How many great names has Switzerland given to European literature; or the Tyrol, which is really free in its customs and government, though belonging to a despotic empire; or Sweden and Norway, proud as they are of their ancient privileges and constitutional liberty?

Can it be then that excellence in literature is inimical to the best interests of the human race? By no means. But the best interests of the human race do not depend on the continuance of this or that dynasty, or of this or that special phase of government; no, nor on the continuance of this or that nation. It may be that a nation must be in its decadence before it can reach its greatest literary glory, but mankind at large, to the whole of whom such glory appertains, will by such effects be soaring higher towards perfection. It may be that a people shall swan-like sing and die; but the song shall be immortal, and the poet's name, as that of the prophet, shall be greatest far away in years as in space from those among whom he sang.

It must, we think, be clear to any thoughtful mind that no true poet knows aught of the extent of his own importance, or dreams of the distant ears to which his song will be delightful. Indeed it may be questioned whether a poet is personally more entitled to the full possession of his own glory than were the inspired prophets, who, with solemn words mysterious to themselves as to others, foretold the will of God. Indeed the highest flights of the poet may reflect but little honour on the man.

With what delight do we read the fulsome flatteries addressed by Horace to Augustus.[1] How nauseous would these be now addressed by Mr. Tennyson to the Queen or to Prince Albert! How sad it is that genius should ever thus stoop! But now, after the lapse of years even flattery is delightful, and the meanness of the poet adds a grace to the poetry.

The same may be said with some modification of that name of which all Englishmen are so immeasurably the proudest. If we run the plays of Shakespeare through, there are no sweeter lines than the following.

---

[1] See Appendix I, p. 214 for a lengthy Latin quotation from the *Odes* which Trollope deleted.

That very time I saw, (but thou could'st not,)
Flying between the cold moon and the earth,
Cupid all arm'd: a certain aim he took
At a fair vestal, throned by the west;
And loos'd his love-shaft smartly from his bow,
As it should pierce a hundred thousand hearts.
But I might see young Cupid's fiery shaft
Quench'd in the chaste beams of the watery moon;
And the imperial votaress passed on,
In maiden meditation, fancy-free.[2]

Can words be sweeter to the ear than these? can poetry be more preciously delightful? would not the loss of that short passage as it stands be one that a nation might deplore; one that critics and commentators might worthily spend their lives in recovering? Yet it was but false flattery as it fell from the poet's pen, and as such unworthy of the man. But the all but divine inspiration which graced the poet turned vilest dross into purest gold. If we look at it justly, Shakespeare was responsible for the adulation, but the heavenly melody of poetry was a gift from God to all the world.

The literary giant of one age is sent for the advantage of many ages following. His efforts of genius, unlike those of the great soldier, the great divine, or the great mechanic, do not act with a tenth their power on those among whom his lot is cast. He is essentially working for posterity, and too frequently for posterity alone. It may therefore be doubtful whether the great literary strength of any period should be taken as proof of the nation's strength. It has hitherto most frequently been the fore-runner of a nation's decadence.

But whatever may be the law on the subject, which wise men should be able to deduce from the experience of past times, it will be very difficult to apply that law to England. It can hardly be said with truth that there has been. an Augustan age of literature in England.

Everybody is of course aware that the reign of Elizabeth is so styled. But as well might the time of Homer, if Homer ever had a time, be by an allowable anachronism called the Augustan age of Greece. In the true meaning of the word, the glory of one man cannot be said to entitle any age to such an honour. If it

[2] *A Midsummer Night's Dream*, II. i. 155-64.

could, we might well allow that the glory of Shakespeare should do so. Had the literary pre-eminence of the reign of the second Caesar depended on the merits of one poet, the age might have been called Virgilian or Horation, but certainly, as regards literature, not Augustan. And we should therefore repudiate the name as attached to the period in question.

The minor giants of the reign of Queen Elizabeth have been out topped in height and overborne in strength by many a huge son of Anak who has since appeared upon the scene. Indeed we have rarely, if ever, been without our giant. Few men who care for poetry could now be inclined to rank Spenser above Dryden, or even to compare as poets the lettered Ben to our dear unlettered Burns. Even Beaumont and Fletcher, who among the old dramatists should certainly be ranked next to Shakespeare, do not please now as Goldsmith pleases or Cowper. The readers of Massinger, Ford, and Marlowe are, we believe, not numerous, and were they to become so the readers would be astonished to find how few and far between are their beauties, how monstrous and irredeemable are their faults.

In coming to Milton we come altogether to a later age, to altered style and altered tastes, altered morals and altered manners. If the age of Shakespeare be an Augustan age for us, Milton, at least, is excluded from it. With us the rival competitions for the laureateship of the nation did not grace the same period.

In fact, literature has from the commencement of its palmy days in England always fairly flourished. In the following list no name we think is included, not in itself sufficient to sustain the credit of the nation; and this list brings us down in an uninterrupted succession to the days in which we now live.

Spenser	Swift	Burns
Shakespeare	Pope	Scott
Fletcher	Thomson	Byron
Milton	Johnson	Southey
Dryden	Goldsmith	Taylor
Defoe	Cowper	Tennyson

In this list all are poets; all but two are famed as such. Defoe and Johnson are better known to the world as writers of prose, but the labours of each have been so influential on the literary history of England that it has been impossible to omit their names when a list of such worthies is given.

There have been different periods in which we need not fear to compare ourselves with the Augustan age of Rome. Is Swift less venomous or less powerful than Juvenal? Is Dryden in his occasional highest flights less majestic than Virgil? Is Burns ever less sweet than Horace, or less witty? To whose efforts shall we compare that one, long, sustained and precious song of Henry Taylor,[3] or the mysterious, heavenly melody of Tennyson? Of that poetic electricity, felt but indefinable, with which Tennyson touches, and but touches, the chords of the heart, the utilitarian Romans knew nothing.

It may probably be said with truth that we Englishmen have had no Augustan age of literature, and that therefore the rule which has apparently prevailed in other nations, and which seems to imply that high literary excellence is incompatible with great national strength, does not apply to us. We need not surmise that we are in our decadence if it so happen that our nightingales are now singing with unwonted excellence of melody. Nor can we boast that we have safely passed the climacteric which has been so fatal to so many nations, and therefore conceiving ourselves to be governed by safer laws than those which have governed them, take heart of grace, and defy the coming of the New Zealander.

But it is not of the merits of authors living or dead that we would specially speak, but rather of the effect of their productions on the present race of Englishmen. Whatever award may be due to the literary products of the times, of this at any rate Englishmen conceive that they may be allowed to boast: that such as they are, they are placed within the reach of all who can use them; and that they are used by thousands and tens of thousands who five and twenty years ago would never have dreamed of buying a book, and rarely have thought of opening one.

We may well surmise that in the days of Augustus those who could really enjoy the poetry of Virgil were very few. Those even who in the reign of Elizabeth or James I read the plays of Shakespeare were also few. What was known of him was mainly known from the performance of his plays on the stage; and, strange as

[3] *Philip Van Artevelde* (1834).

it may appear, Ben Jonson was often the greater favourite of the two. Now, however, readers are counted by tens and hundreds of thousands. We hear of 30,000 copies of one new work being carted at once out of Paternoster Row;[4] and we all know how often we are told of the sixty or seventy thousand copies of a morning newspaper which are daily required for the voracious appetite of Englishmen of the present age.

Whatever effect literature may have on the national glory and strength, its effect on individual happiness cannot be doubted. It may be that the enervating influence of imperial luxury in Rome was necessary to produce the Aeneid, the Fasti, and the Odes; but whether this were so or not, no one will deny that men whose minds had become open to the appreciation of such works were in a happier condition than their less intellectual, though more independent, ancestors.

National glory is a great matter; but national education, if it can be accomplished, is surely a greater matter. It is well to beat the Russians; but this beating of the Russians, be it ever so complete, will go but a small way towards accomplishing the happiness of Britons. A month's excitement will end that happiness. But the happiness of any man to whom has been imparted the power of reading and enjoying a song of Burns' is to a certain extent ensured for his lifetime. And not only for him is this done, but probably for his children, and his children's children. As regards education a man's offspring do not frequently retrograde from himself.

An educated people, though they be in their decadence, may probably possess more happiness and higher virtues than their ancestors with all their rising martial glory; and may also do much more for the benefit of the world at large. The idea of national pride has been inculcated in our breasts with too much vehemence, and those who have preached the lesson have not always been actuated by the most disinterested motives. There is no source of true happiness to the multitude in the idea of their belonging to the biggest of nations. The happiness arising from this, if any happiness do arise from it, is to the few. The glory and sense of greatness are to those who are concerned in

---

[4] 'It is by no means difficult to dispose of 30,000 to 40,000 copies of a popular novel.' 'Railroad Bookselling', *Saturday Review*, III (31 Jan. 1857), 102.

great things. It is necessary for such that the multitude should support them, and therefore a pæan as to the continued strength and immaculate power of England is so often sounded into the ears of Englishmen.

But who would not sooner look forward to seeing his son a shoemaker at Melbourne, if as such he could be educated as becomes a gentleman, than contemplate his living as a gentleman in London with no better education than that becoming among shoemakers? We wish our children to be pious and happy. Such are generally our aspirations for them, whatever impurer wishes we may entertain as to our own pursuits. If they can be pious and happy on some foreign shore, to which as yet no national glory is attached, which knows nothing of the honour of maintaining the balance of power, why for their sake should we be so anxious to assure ourselves that in England's constitution alone is there no principle of decay?

The honour and glory of the throne of England, dear as it should be to all who live subject to its splendour, should not be half so precious to any Englishman as the education of his countrymen. Much as he may desire the success of her policy, it should be as nothing in his mind as compared to the success of her literature. The one must die, the other may live. The one can serve but at most for a few years. The benefits of the other will endure for all time short of eternity.

Whether will it be better for that son of thine, thou sturdy labourer of the soil, that unkempt, flaxen little boy who now paddles barefoot through the village gutters—whether will it be better for him to tend his sheep in foreign lands, and in his old age hear from *his* son words of wondrous import read from wondrous books; or else, to stand the brunt of some future fierce Crimean winter now in the womb of time; and, returning legless or armless to his virtuous country, enjoy there as in such state he best may the shilling a day which that country will vouchsafe to him? For the country this latter alternative may perhaps be the better. "And for thy lad, too," will the recruiting sergeant boldly say, and swear to it.

Recruiting sergeants, let them recruit for regiments of the line, or parliamentary votes and political support, will doubtless always swear to as much as that. National honour and military glory are fine subjects for the eloquence of a recruiting sergeant.

Dulce et decorum est pro patria mori.[5]

Yes. Death in the path of duty is doubtless decorous. If a man elect a path of duty in which death may meet him, being a man he will not shun the encounter. But in this bargain between him and his country he is so likely to have the worst of it, that he should think twice before he makes it.

If then it could be proved beyond a doubt that the furtherance of literary habits among a people would lead to national decadence, no convincing argument against literature would thence arise. If called on to decide between the two, between literary excellence and national grandeur, the philanthropist could hardly fail to give the preference to the former. But in giving such a decision it would specially behove the philanthropist to promise that the literature be excellent. We cannot but respect a people who, when ceasing to govern themselves, found consolation in the Odes of Horace—and those Venetian Gondoliers, who, as we are told, solaced themselves through their labours with songs from Tasso;[6] for them also and their love of verse one cannot but feel sympathy and respect. The man who has daily sung, though it be but one stanza of Tasso, and that in the roughest cadence, will not have gone down to his grave with a heart altogether unawakened.

Alas, from the labourers in our mines, from the children who bend over their work in our factories, from our cornfields and huge workshops no song of Tasso is heard to come, in ever such rude cadence. No song of Tasso, of other poet national to us, as was Tasso to the Italian. But a song, if song at all, verily of the Devil's inspiration. In such song as that, too often heard, one would say there is no sign of literary excellence, and but small token of national grandeur.

The amount of books printed by us annually, the tonnage of paper, the acres of type, the rivers of ink, are facts which cannot be refuted. That we have achieved a vast mass of literature, and that we get that mass sold, no man can doubt. It is printed and sold, and, as we must presume, in some sort read. But as yet the effects of literature are hardly as visible as they should be, even

[5] Horace, *Odes*, III. ii. 13.
[6] That Venetian gondoliers sang songs from Tasso was proverbial; perhaps the most familiar reference is in Byron's *Childe Harold*: 'In Venice Tasso's echoes are no more,/ And silent rows the songless Gondolier.' Canto IV. iii.

in those classes among whom the greater portion of these myriads of volumes must circulate.

We write our books too quickly, read and digest them too quickly, and of course forget them too quickly. We are so very anxious to walk the way of knowledge, if we can but find a royal way, easy, short, exciting, and fashionable. Take any subject, poetry, politics, history, romance: it is very expedient that the young men and women of our large towns should know all that can be known of these charming subjects, and it is so easy to teach them. Only let some great man, lord or other, some man who has devoted years to such matter, come down from town and tell these young people all about it. In two hours the precious vial of knowledge has been poured forth, and things hitherto recondite, mysterious, known but to the pale student or long-lived man of genius, become the common property of common people. The royal road has been discovered. It consists in an evening lecture at a mechanics' institute.

Let us at any rate pay honour to the great man who makes the attempt, be he a lord or not. As far as they go lectures such as these can do nothing but good. They may induce high tastes; by such employment one evening at least is rescued from the huge cesspool of misspent hours; and the communion thus brought about between the great lecturer and his modest hearers is of the noblest kind.

Nevertheless, there is no royal road to learning, neither now, nor ever was, nor ever will be. One man cannot pour out the vial of his knowledge into the brain and mind of another. Only by slow deglutition and mastication can such food become wholesomely nourishing to any mortal man.

In striving after such a royal road, the inclination for study, the taste for literary labour, is lost. We have got to think that nothing is worth our notice that cannot be produced, enjoyed, and disposed of with the utmost imaginable despatch. Some short half century since, when our two great quarterly reviews were first established,[7] the literary world conceived that such productions, appearing as they did at every three months' interval, and discoursing as they did on every subject incident to literature, gave sufficient evidence of rapidity of performance.

[7] *The Edinburgh Review* began publication in 1802; *The Quarterly Review* in 1809.

But how is the world changed now! We were amused the other day by a description of the heavy Edinburgh and its awful period of three months' gyration.[8] What value can be attached to an opinion for the maturing of which a quarter of a year has been found necessary? The world and the world's way of thinking will have changed between the time when the author dipped his pen in the ink, and the far distant day on which his lucubrations see the open air. A quarterly indeed! Are not monthlies stale before they appear, unless indeed they can forerun their own dates? Is not a weekly newspaper so heavy an affair that its present use is confined to ladies in distant counties?

Now-a-days a daily newspaper is the only pabulum sufficiently new, and sufficiently exciting for the over-strained public mind. That too will soon fail to satisfy the craving of the British public for news. It is positively a fact that the London morning newspapers are becoming antiquated. The Times, if it intend to hold its own, must publish itself at least three times a day, and each time with new matter. At every meal we must have our literature reeking wet from the steam press. The tidings of each morning will soon be utterly obsolete and forgotten before the sound of the dinner bell shall have greeted our ears.

We are all now so anxious to live fast, to live up to the pace of the times, that we never pause sufficiently to enjoy those good things which by our industry and ability we collect around us. Our English life is becoming like an American hotel dinner. The table is covered with every thing that is good and presents the fairest hopes to the hungry guest. The servants are sufficient in number. The dishes are well cooked. No expense has been spared. The doors of the banqueting room are opened, and those who are to enjoy the feast swarm in. And then how fares the banquet? It is as though a legion of starved tigers had rushed through at their food. In ten minutes the human beasts of prey have doubtless fed themselves in the scramble. The viands are gone, and the cravings of nature are appeased. But it can hardly be said, if we use the word in its proper acceptation, that any man has dined.[9]

---

[8] *The Times*, 19 Oct. 1855. A leading article called the quarterly reviews 'ponderous and antiquated ... both in style, tone and form'.

[9] Trollope, who had not yet visited America, may here be echoing his mother's famous *Domestic Manners of the Americans* (1832). She speaks, for

So it is with many of us at present. When a man dies, it can hardly be said that he has given himself time to live. We are so anxious to do more than others before we have done, to live up to what is called the spirit of the age, that we allow ourselves no time to ascertain whether what we are doing be good for ourselves, either for our souls or bodies. If a man be not up to the times he is nothing, and in order to be up to the times, he is obliged to abandon all hope of ever really being anything else.

This is perhaps more essentially true of us as regards literature than in any other matter; but in nothing is this superficial rapidity so dangerous as in literary pursuits. The mind, when once allowed to skip lightly from subject to subject, to dwell on nothing that requires either an effort or a pause, and to abandon all tasks of real investigation, soon loses its best powers; and the faculty of thought perishes from want of practice. How many a man who regards himself as sufficiently educated, and knows himself to be a sharp man of the world, never truly thinks at all. Of such men it would be too much to say that they have no mind, or that they never use the mind which they possess. But it is only too true that the noblest mental faculty given to every such man by God dies within him wasted and untried.

We have all been told how uselessly small are the feet of Chinese women. How they are crippled, deformed, and made unfit for their intended purposes by some accursed shoe into which they are crammed in early years. Is it not true that many men cram their minds into similar small receptacles with the object, as it appears, of saving them altogether from the trouble of work?

It is almost as much out of the question for an Englishman to think deeply as for a Chinese woman to walk alone. Have we not indeed got a first rate thinking machine to take all that labour handsomely off our shoulders?

We greatly admire the power of thought displayed by our greatest men. Bacon, Newton, and Locke are held in the highest

---

example, of a hotel dinner at Memphis, where the guests ate 'in perfect silence, and with such astonishing rapidity that their dinner was over literally before our's was began; the instant they ceased to eat, they darted from the table in the same moody silence which they had preserved since they entered the room.... The only sounds were those produced by the knives and forks, with the unceasing chorus of coughing, &c.' ed. Donald Smalley (Random House, New York, 1949), p. 25 (Chap. iii).

reverence—and in our own days we are disposed to pay all honour to such men as Lord Brougham and Sir David Brewster.[10] But we do not honour them as we ought to do for that which is most honourable in them. Such men as these have not so far excelled all their countrymen in the magnitude of their mental faculties as given them by God as they have done in the intense labour to which those faculties have been subjected, and the acuteness of thinking which that labour has produced.

When seeking shelter from a storm in some rural smithy, who has not wondered at the brawny muscles of the blacksmith's arm? has not thought of his own comparative feebleness when watching the huge hammers thrown with ease round the man's head? And yet it is competent to most men to become a blacksmith, or was so at one period of their existence.

To have become the equal of Bacon or Newton has not probably been within the compass of many minds; but to be immeasurably nearer to them than it often occurs to men to think possible for themselves is within the compass of most minds. We see daily how great is the difference between the absolutely unlettered clown, whose mental faculty has, alas, never been awakened further than to the necessity of a straight furrow, and the educated gentleman who appreciates the majesty of Milton's epic and the sweetness of Horace's ode. It is not in the quality of the mind that the difference so materially lies as in the discipline to which it has been subjected.

The educated gentleman is to Newton as is the clown to him. The deep thinking of the sage is caviare to him, as are his dilettante readings to his ploughman. The gentleman will confess as much, and will modestly decline to assimilate in any degree his own mental gifts to the huge powers of the philosophic giant. Such modesty will generally be considered commendable. But had there been less of it in the world, the infinite purpose of God's best gift to man would have been more generally appreciated than it now is.

In truth few men will be at the pain of thought; and, to an unaccustomed thinker, thought is painful. We read books without thinking, and then complain that our memories are so

[10] Sir David Brewster (1781-1868), Scottish physicist, renowned for his work with light and optics.

treacherous to us that reading is useless. We write books without thinking, and wonder that what we write makes no impression. Literature such as this, whether we speak of the efforts of the author or the reader, can be little less than useless.

We are a locomotive people, and during these last twenty years in no way has the national taste for literature been so developed as in the arrangements made for facilitating railway reading. Railways have done much for the world; but in no respect have they more essentially benefitted the constant traveller than in allowing him to save from loss the hours spent on the road. A man's seat in a railway carriage is now, or may be, his study; and to men obliged so to pass a considerable portion of their existence such a facility as this is a vital benefit.

And not only has the power of reading been thus brought within the reach of travellers, but the literature for their enjoyment on the road is handed to them with their tickets. It is not necessary that a man should provide himself, that he should come with a volume of Gibbon in his greatcoat pocket, or a small edition of his favourite poet in his travelling bag. A bookseller's shop at each principal station is prepared; where books may be bought at the cheapest rate, and where those which are found specially fitted for such purposes are kept in abundance.

We have heard, but now forget, the statistics of this railway book trade. The numbers of volumes sold annually, the numbers of hands employed, the capital turned, the net profits, and the amount of rent paid for stalls, are expressed in very astounding totals. The business has become a large trade.

Such signs of the times as these must at any rate be tokens of improvement! The establishment of such a trade as this must surely be taken as a proof that the march of intellect is no fallacy! As a proof of the increase of reading of some sort this fact must certainly be taken. And as the mere technical capacity to read is among the masses an improvement on olden times, we are entitled to rejoice at so wide-spread a display of this capacity. But when we come to examine the quality of the literature our satisfaction cannot but be considerably abated.

That travellers should read little else but novels was perhaps to be expected. But why should the very worst that can be culled from our huge receptacles of such wares be those specially adapted for railway reading? Wretched translations of French romances—and such romances! unintelligible decoctions from the prolific shop of Dumas, stories of Sue's which in losing their native language lost every charm which they ever possessed.[11] American tales, wordy past all belief, trashy beyond all description, one would say unreadable were it not that there exist such signs of their being read. Piles upon piles also of truly English production are to be found; novels we believe written specially for railway sale, and, as far as we can judge, wholly confined to railway stalls. Let any one anxious to satisfy himself on this subject look over the volumes which he may find at an ordinary railway station ticketed at a price not exceeding 1/6, and then form his opinion as to the kind of literature that is becoming popular in England.

But it may be said, a good article cannot in literature be supplied at a low price. That in no trade can this be done. A good volume in one sense cannot of course be sold cheap. As regards the material portion of the book, this rule must hold good in the business of the booksellers as in all others. When we furnish our libraries at 1/6 a volume, we of course are prepared to put up with vile paper, vile printing, to sacrifice our eyes, and refuse to ourselves indulgence in the *petit maître* luxuries of reading. Excellence of this description we might gladly see dispensed with, rejoicing that the true production of the author's brain might be put forth without those comfortable but expensive appendages. But excellence of another kind, that excellence which in literary productions one may say is the only excellence needful, may for the most part be produced as cheaply as mediocrity. It is the taste of the public, and not the necessary price of the article, which rules the choice of the vendor.

The most popular authors of the present day are those who content themselves with writing up to what is called the spirit of the age. That is, with feeding popular feeling, and acting as a reflex back upon the people of the latest opinions engendered

---

[11] Trollope is probably referring here to cheap editions (which became synonymous with 'railway novels') especially as issued by Simms and McIntyre in 'The Parlour Novelists' series (Belfast, 1846-7) and the 'Parlour Library' (London and Belfast, 1847-63), as well as the very successful imitation thereof, 'Routledges Railway Library' (London, 1851 onwards). See Michael Sadleir, *XIX Century Fiction: A Bibliographical Record, Based on his own Collection* (Constable, London, 1951), Vol. II, for a comprehensive treatment of 'Yellowback', cheap, and railway editions.

among themselves. Such an occupation is the special work of a certain class of writers and of a certain class of publications. Our good friend Punch could not exist another month if he were to abandon his diligence in this respect; and perhaps also such should be the task of most writers for the daily press. Their productions are necessarily ephemeral, and, being for the day and the day only, need hardly look beyond the interests and feelings of the present moment. But no man who writes for any age beyond his own, nay, for any day beyond the present, can safely trust himself to such a task.

As a commercial speculation it may pay well to write for the people such matter as they may willingly read. We have in these days more than one conspicuous example of the prudence of such a course. That an author, when the career is open to him, should devote himself to so profitable a trade cannot be a matter of wonder. But the effect of such literature on those who so greedily devour it can hardly be beneficial.

Vox populi vox dei. The voice of the people has in itself a divine truth which cannot be led astray. Such now is the received opinion of the world with reference to the multitudinous mutterings of the many headed monster; and it may be that a true philosophy is expressed therein. The tides of the sea, which hurry hither in currents and thither in strong eddies, which now beat with angry violence against the affrighted shore, and anon creep up with a smiling ripple and gently caressing touch; which at one hour leave bare, hideous, slimy rocks and dark putrescent holes, and then again swell up to their extremest limits with a full crest, run ever true to their appointed course. Such also is the truth of popular opinion. It veers hither and thither, and fluctuates with gigantic motion for ever and a day. That which at present receives its assured mark of approval will soon be reprobated and condemned; today's hero will be to-morrow's victim; opinions which are now regarded as the rhapsodies of a few eccentric enthusiasts will in a few years be popular with the world, and then again, in a few years more will be scouted out of countenance. Such is the voice of the people. And in the end it expresses truth, for it is made up of true units. The thing uttered at the time of uttering is the true belief of the single human being who so expresses what there is in him to be expressed. Be he right or be he wrong in his thought, he is at least so far right that he truly says what he truly thinks. And as the ingredients of which public opinion is formed are thus true, so will the result be true. It will possess at least a rough average of truth sufficient to justify its claim to that divinity which it is supposed to possess.

But the voice of the people is infinite. The voice of the author, let it be never so harmonious, is but finite. That which is true in coming from a multitude is too often false when reechoed by him. To him can be allowed no rough average. The word as it falls from his pen must be true or false. To him is given in a certain degree to guide mankind; and he must either guide them as best he can by the light which he may have from God; or leave their guidance a matter of mere chance, using no light whatever, but hurrying them on by whatever path may best suit their own pleasure to follow.

Great is the gift of that man to whom it is permitted to create public opinion. Great the gift and noble the purpose to which it may be applied. It is far otherwise with him who is content to put forth the opinions of others, and write up to the popular feeling of the time. From such at any rate can no truth be expected. A foregone conclusion, a well known result, a decision on any matter easily anticipated may perhaps convey no falsehood. But neither for his truth nor his want of truth is such an author to be held accountable. If he express the opinion of the day he does his appointed work. He is but a trumpet into which the people may blow, a drum on which they may beat their rough music with such approach to harmony as may be possible to them. The true writer, be he poet, historian, romancer, or what not, is the true leader of the people. But such a one as this is the last of their followers.

On the whole, England has no cause at present to blush for her literature; indeed it may be doubted whether she ever had need to do so. The obscenities of some past times were disgraceful, and the puerilities of the present may scarcely be more honourable; but the literature of every age must be judged by its highest, not by its lowest efforts. To have one giant always with us is much, and who can say that at the present moment we have not even more than one or two? Let it however be matter of devout prayer to all of us that we may have grace to worship the giants and not the pigmies.

CHAPTER XII

Art

IN looking back to the histories of past times it certainly appears that the fine arts have best flourished among people and at periods not conspicuous for political grandeur or aspirations after liberty. The noblest buildings of Rome were built under the Caesars. Raphael, Michael Angelo, and Leonardo Da Vinci adorned an age and a country in which petty tyrants were allowed to rule with iron hands. Velasquez and Murillo were the servants of the Philips of Spain. Naples and Rome in their modern abject states of political vassalage have been prolific in music and statuary. And the architectural splendour of Paris, which was commenced under one despotic Napoleon, is being consummated under another.

Art has certainly thriven best under the wings of tyrants. It is not only that such sovereigns have been best able and most willing to reward the labour of the artist; but that the subjects to such sovereigns, debarred as they have been from the arena of politics, have sunk from sheer leisure into the dilettante pursuits of promoters of art. And tyrants have been wise to encourage this propensity. The man who could satisfy all the energies of his soul with a disputation as to the correctness of a torso, or the authenticity of an all but obliterated fresco, would not probably rise in rebellion against his master, or evince much anxiety to fight for his liberty.

And yet we should be all but broken-hearted, we Englishmen, if it were proved to us that an increasing love of the fine arts is a sure sign of a decreasing political importance, or even of a decreasing aptitude for national aggrandisement. That a love for the fine arts is gradually becoming a strong passion among us may be regarded as certain. This is shown in nothing more clearly than in the daily improvements in our ecclesiastical architecture. We are now building churches which in beauty, though not in size, may be compared with the best Gothic structures of the Gothic times. It is shown also in the general architecture of our towns, and especially in many of the new buildings in London. It is shown in the avidity with which pictures by the hands of masters, modern as well as ancient, are bought among us. It is shown by the increased number of our public statues; by our opera houses which alone among our theatres can get themselves filled, by the brass bands which have banished hurdy gurdies from our streets, and are making the livelihood of the organ grinder so precarious. But most of all is it shown by the ready sale which books on art now find in England. Some knowledge of the first principles, or at any rate of the history of the fine arts is now as essential to the education of an English gentleman as is an acquaintance with Horace and Virgil, or a familiarity with Hume and Gibbon.

But does it follow that a true love of art is incompatible with a true love of free institutions? Is it the case that an Englishman who becomes energetically anxious for the erection of some fitting National Gallery will also become indifferent as to the extension of the franchise, or the attitude of Russia? Let us hope, if we can hope, that it is not so, and each at least endeavour that it may not become so as regards himself.

The histories of past times are written in pages open for us all to read. But who can read the history of this time in which we live ourselves? The Romans under Augustus regarded themselves as the masters of the world. But even in the days of Augustus the seed from which grew the decline of Rome was already germinating. The Spaniards under Philip II thought themselves the first among educated nations. Nevertheless, the subjects of Philip had already fallen into habits which were soon to make others regard them as the lowest.

When the New Zealander on his return to his own country shall write, as he certainly will write, his "Impressions made by a ten days' sojourn among the ruins of London," he will doubtless attribute the fall of our nation to the wealth and luxury of the people.

"They had become infatuated," he will say, "by a passion for all that is rich and rare. The enormity of the price of that which they coveted served only to stimulate their desires. Had St. Cecelia deigned to play for them at a free concert they would not have listened to her. But a moderate disciple of the Saint would often receive for a few songs money sufficient to maintain a gentleman's family for a year. Terpsichore in a few years danced herself into possession of ingots of gold. Pictures which in the lifetime of the artist were worth perhaps one hundred shillings of the money of this people were sold for ten times as many hundred pounds. All the paintings of all the masters of ancient and modern days would not satisfy their craving for these toys. A gallery of pictures had become the necessary appendage of a rich man, and all who could appear to be rich felt themselves bound to possess a gallery. Houses were built of which the deserted walls, and the grass grown courts, still show the extent and the folly of the builders. Houses in which the courts of Kings might have been held were built for the use of private men; or rather for their ambition. All the wines of all the vintages of Europe were insufficient to supply the needs of this luxurious city. And yet while thus revelling in wealth, they were fast sinking into deep poverty." &c., &c.

It may be difficult to name a date for this interesting volume, but sooner or later such a volume will appear; and the same edict which we have so often pronounced on other people will be as freely pronounced upon us.

Art no doubt is a luxury, but it does not necessarily follow that all lovers of art must be luxurious. It is more than a luxury. It becomes a necessity to him who has once received it into his understanding and his heart. He who has habituated his ears to sweet sounds will live without delight if forced to live without music. He whose eye has become accustomed to forms of beauty, to artistic groupings, and to grand designs, will look on his life as robbed of half of its joys if he is debarred from the exercise of those tastes which he has acquired. Many among us now have acquired such tastes and have subjected ourselves to this necessity. It will be the same with our children, whom we educate by our own standard. And it should therefore be with us a duty to see that this great enjoyment be not allowed to sink into sloth or mock dilettante energy.

Of the four fine arts three are decidedly popular with us. In spite of our many statues and great fecundity in busts, Englishmen do not generally appreciate sculpture. Our public statues are regarded more as ornamental structures than as individual works of art. In erecting them we think rather of the position, the size, and the general effect than of the work of art itself. Busts too are valued not so much for their intrinsic merits as for

their likeness. In that treasure room at Florence, for one Englishman that is entranced by the Medician Venus, there will be
found ten who stand gazing with delight at Raphael's picture of
the youthful Baptist.

Music, architecture, and painting are as a rule appreciated by
the educated in this country; and the two latter arts are not only
enjoyed here, but are prosecuted probably with as much success
as in any land under the sun. And yet by the vehemence of our
own abuse of our own productions, strangers might be led to
think that our artists are inefficient, tasteless, ignorant, and barbarous.

In this respect the peculiar idiosyncrasy of an Englishman
brings about most singular results. In fine arts as in religion, as
in politics, and as in science, an Englishman must belong to a
party. He will not recognise merit as meritorious unless it be
meritorious according to his side of the question. He is always
a Jansenist or a Jesuit, be the matter in dispute what it may.
And if he chance to be the latter, all the grace and all the truth
of a Pascal will be to him but as so much atheistical ribaldry.[1]

We show this propensity almost equally with our buildings
and our pictures. We can do nothing as a nation that we do not
ourselves as a nation most emphatically abuse. And yet we
entrust to our architects enormous sums for the erection of
churches and palaces, and give even for modern pictures prices
which fifty years since would have been thought high for the
Italian, Dutch, and Flemish productions of the sixteenth
century.

We hear it constantly said that England never produces a fine
building. This is constantly said by Englishmen, but we imagine
rarely repeated by foreigners who know the country. And yet in
what class of buildings are we deficient? These critics will say
that they do not refer to the peculiar ages of Gothic architecture;
and will admit the beauty of Salisbury, Hereford, and Westminster, unequal as they be to Strasbourg or Antwerp, Milan or
Pisa. But they assert that we have failed in all our modern
efforts, and have gone on failing till we have reached a bathos, of

---

[1] Jansenists (after Cornelis Jansens, 1585-1638, Dutch theologian) and Jesuits
were rival schools of theology, the former espousing very rigorous moral
standards. Pascal was at least unofficially within the Jansenist camp, and his
writings, especially the *Lettres Provinciales* (1656-7) were highly and effectively critical of the Jesuits.

which Buckingham Palace and the National Gallery are presumed to be the lowest depth.

We will not now raise a comparison between Salisbury and Strasbourg, nor attempt to whitewash those two unfortunate blackamoors which have been treated with such universal contumely. But we would ask those who are so ill-satisfied with the buildings of their own country whether they are really acquainted with the church architecture and house architecture of England. Men who know Florence and Rome as well or better than they knew London; who are closely intimate with the stones of Venice,[2] who have almost watched the building of the palaces of Munich, and who rave of the extensive effects of French designs, have never visited Somersetshire and Dorsetshire, and know nothing of the quiet gems which are there embosomed among the finest trees of Europe, the productions of all but unknown English names in the sixteenth century. Such men have heard, and probably only heard, of Hatfield and Longleat and Montacute. But Hatfield and Longleat and Montacute are, if equal in beauty, not more than equal to scores of mansions and modest country houses which are to be found almost in every parish of our western counties on this side the Tamar.

One in these days is almost ashamed to say a word about St. Paul's or Somerset House or Whitehall. Reprobation is so much more attractive than eulogy that the friends of these noble buildings have almost been silenced by their enemies. Young men are now instructed to look with anything but admiring eyes on structures which Englishmen used to regard with pride as the grand productions of English genius. And yet young men of these days are more open to pleasure from such sources than were their grandfathers and great grandfathers. But in their judgement St. Paul's must be translated over the Alps before it can be of value, and Whitehall repeated in Vienna in order to secure due appreciation.

But what will such critics say of the Bank of Ireland in Dublin?[3] If they speak truth, they will most of them declare

---

[2] An allusion to Ruskin's *Stones of Venice*, the first volume of which appeared in 1851 and the last two in 1853.
[3] Originally the Irish Parliament House, designed by Edward Lovet Pearce, and completed in 1739. The Bank of Ireland purchased the building in 1802.

that in their wildest dreams of architectural pursuit the idea of looking for a building in Ireland never occurred to them. And yet it may almost be said that in no capital of Europe is there a finer specimen of Grecian architecture, or one more effectively placed. We know of no modern building of the class completed before the commencement of this country that excels it.

But in coming down to later days, to the present century and the present days, how much have we to be proud of, and yet how constant we are in speaking ill of ourselves! It is alleged that we do not make grand streets, produce fine effects, and throw our metropolis into attitudes. But people who make this allegation forget that it is impossible to do this in a country where the government has no power of doing away with a dozen streets in one district, of opening a square in another, and of ordering what style of architecture shall be chosen, what cost shall be incurred, and what scheme adopted in replacing what has been torn down.

Nor is it so certain that this attitudinizing is successful in its result. For no town in this respect has so much been done in modern days as for Munich, and it may be doubted whether the effect there is such as to create much envy in other nations.

"It is very nice," said one traveller to another.

"Very nice," said his friend, "very nice indeed. But it looks a little as though the buildings had been ordered from the manufacturers a month since, and had been sent home clean in bandboxes last Saturday night."

The new streets of Munich do look as though they had been sent home in bandboxes, and he who gazes at them is forced into the consideration whether buildings of architectural pretence do not lose more than they gain by being erected in close proximity to each other, and in arranged order. It may be a question whether the whole effect of the Louvre will not be lessened by the completion of the Rue Rivoli.

In London we have no Ludwig Strasse and no Rue Rivoli, but we have erected finer buildings than are to be found in either. Now that our Houses of Parliament are nearly completed it is of course the fashion to abuse them. They are too low, too much burdened with decoration. Perpendicular ornamentation is found to be unsuited for so long a frontage. The towers are, or will be, too heavy. There is no point from which to see it, and nothing worth looking at if such a point were found. Such are the judgements pronounced by architectural critics of the present age, and yet it may be doubted whether many nobler piles have ever yet been built by the hands of man, or blessed with a better site than this will be found to have when the bridge over the river shall have been finished,[4] and St. Margaret's and other adjacent buildings removed.

But English critics of this age are indignant if ready made palaces do not fall from heaven into grounds prepared for them in a night by legions of angels. It is not some twenty years since the plans for the present Houses of Parliament were approved of, and men seem to think it wondrously shameful that everything belonging to the building is not completed.[5] Do they ever reflect how long it took to build St. Peter's? How long the Duomo of Florence? How long it has taken and will take to finish the cathedral of Cologne?

Let us grant that the National Gallery is a poor erection, but if so let us also confess that the facade of the new Treasury offices is very beautiful.[6] How few, however, are ever heard to express such satisfaction. Let the fastidious man of taste declare himself unable to be pleased with Buckingham Palace, if such be his judgement; but let him also declare that he is pleased with the City Post Office.[7] But the fastidious man of taste in England has no wish to be pleased with any modern English building. How heartrending must be the business of an English architect of the present day, unless indeed money can supply the want of praise!

Has the fastidious man of taste who looks for architectural beauty only out of England ever seen the interior of the new church in Margaret Street—unfinished, and alas, we fear for the

[4] Westminster Bridge, built 1856-62, was designed by Thomas Page.

[5] In 1836 Sir Charles Barry, with whom Augustus Pugin had collaborated, won the competition for the new Houses of Parliament. Above-the-ground construction began by 1840, and in 1852 the new House of Commons, although still unfinished, was used for the first time.

[6] The National Gallery, completed in 1838, was the work of William Wilkins. The renovation of the Treasury Building, also known as the Board of Trade, was completed in 1847 by Sir Charles Barry.

[7] Buckingham Palace, begun by John Nash and completed by Edward Blore, was ready for occupancy in 1837; Blore added the Eastern Facade in 1846. The General Post Office in St. Martin's-le-Grand, finished in 1829, was designed by Sir Robert Smirke.

present to remain unfinished?[8] Had such a gem been constructed five centuries since on the other side of the Alps,
thousands of English tourists would yearly make pilgrimages to
the shrine even though it had been left all incomplete as it still
is; and coloured bricks would now be as natural to the eye as
painted glass. Any one may see the church in Margaret Street
without payment of a penny, but few if any go to look at it.
Margaret Street is so much less attractive as a site than the bank
of a Venetian canal, or a narrow lane in an old worn-out Tuscan
town!

But of all the fine arts, painting is the most popular in
England. So much so indeed that it may be said that now at the
present moment there is a rage for pictures. The rage for the
possession of pictures of course produces an equal rage for
getting rid of them. Men who have bought doubtful Dutch land-
scapes for thirty or forty pounds are naturally willing to sell
them for three or four hundred. And three or four hundred
pounds is at present by no means an extraordinary price for a
doubtful Dutch landscape.

How Messrs. Christie and Manson get through their work is
a mystery to an uninitiated man; for the Dutch landscape would
be of comparatively little saleable value unless it were made to
pass under their hammer. The multiplication of these pictures
is an equal mystery. It would seem that the artists of Brabant
and Flanders can have never died, and that Cuyp and Hobbema,
Gerard Dow and Jan Steen must be yet alive and yet at work.

It is the fashion now of all trades to sell false articles in lieu
of true;—chicoree, for instance, instead of coffee, and horses'
liver instead of chicoree; and in no trade is the fashion more
prevalent than in that of the picture dealer. The worst of this is
that one cannot but believe that the artists who fabricate the
false pictures are too often aware of the purpose for which they
are working. That Jew brokers should buy in Brussels for a few
hundred francs clever copies which they can sell in London for
four times the price if unlucky, and forty times if lucky, is a
matter of course. But it is matter of deep lament that men who
are truly worthy of the name of artists as regards their art,

[8] Begun in 1850 and completed in 1859, the Church of All Saints, designed
by William Butterfield, was notable for its use of 'polychrome' brick and its
elaborate and rich tracery and gilding. See Introduction, p. xix.

should be so unworthy as regards their practice.

But the most wonderful fact in the history of art of the present day is not the avidity with which are bought pictures by old acknowledged masters, or pictures passed off as being their works. The eagerness which is shown for works by English painters still living, and the prices given for them is much more miraculous. It is said that more than one small picture painted within the last five years has been bought off the easel for fifteen hundred pounds, a price which a century ago would have been large for a masterpiece of Titian's; and it was not long since it was announced that two pictures which were submitted to sale, the one painted by Etty and the other by Maclise, were bought in at prices over eight hundred guineas for the one and a thousand for the other!

We would counsel those who have pictures to sell, and to whom the result of such sale may be important, to make their hay while the sun shines. Such a state of things will not be permanent. At the present moment there is, as it were, a mania for pictures, for pictures almost of any sort and certainly at any price. There will come a reaction, and then a man will dispose of any chattel easier than of a picture. It is like the tulip rage in Holland. It is now past our understanding how industrious Dutch burghers brought themselves to invest the savings of half a life in a few flower roots; how they gave over half a dozen such as a rich dower for a daughter, who so bedowered stept proudly into her new home; how at last it came to pass that the favourites among tulips became unpriceable, above all price, more precious to the Dutchman than any money, more costly than any jewels. But the passion died as it sprung up.[9] And so will it be with pictures in England. The passion will evaporate, but not the taste. It will not be that Englishmen will in fact take less delight in works of art. Nor are we aware that tulips are less appreciated in Holland. But the mania will pass by and we shall be more chary with our money.

And yet we can not but be proud to feel that this practical appreciation is given by Englishmen of the genius of English artists. It is our only mode of bestowing praise. We read in the history of Italian art how Cimabue was made to walk in glorious

[9] The Dutch tulip fervour reached its greatest heights in the 1630s; the crash came in 1637.

procession through the streets of Florence when one of his great
works was carried home to the church in which it was to be
hung; but nobody clothes Mr. Millais in white garments and
leads him in triumph from his house to Charing Cross.[10] It suits
us better to give him fifteen hundred pounds for his five or six
months' work, and then to abuse him roundly. Perhaps it is
better so for Mr. Millais, but it is not better for the country.
There is a want among us of any general and enthusiastic appreciation of genius. We do acknowledge the talent; we do by
degrees give status and wealth to the artist; we make him in our
own way perhaps as great a man in London as Cimabue was in
Florence. But he is made so by one party in the world of art;
and he is consequently little better than a dauber, or else a mad-
man, in the eyes of the other.

We walk through roods of canvas every year in our exhibition of modern pictures, all of which are glaring with new
varnish, and how seldom do we stop to praise any picture with
enthusiasm. We perhaps repeat the visit three or four times in
the year, and then declare that it is just so so—very moderate—
perhaps not bad as a whole—not discreditable to the nation—
but nothing to be wondered at. And yet probably there will be
hanging there some Tragic Queen, some Market Cart, some
Blind Fiddler,[11] which, when a score or two of years shall have
given it value, the nation will hang with pride among its choicest
treasures.

And how proud the nation should be of that collection which
is now hanging in Marlborough House![12] How little shame need
be felt in placing it under the same roof with the works of the
old masters! It seems that Englishmen generally are hardly

---

[10] Trollope, while speaking of his villain Tom Towers in *The Warden* (1855),
remarked condescendingly that 'a singularly long figure of a female devotee,
by Millais, told ... plainly the school of art to which he was addicted.'
(O.U.P., London, 1918), pp. 174-5 (Chap. xiv). Trollope later came to know
Millais, and in the *Autobiography* paid him the highest tribute both as man
and artist. Millais eventually illustrated four Trollope novels.

[11] Sir David Wilkie's *Blind Fiddler*, Gainsborough's *Market Cart*. By *Tragic
Queen* Trollope presumably refers to Reynold's *Death of Dido*.

[12] The Vernon Collection, presented to the nation in 1847 by Robert Vernon
and containing 154 pictures by British painters, was kept at Marlborough
House because of problems of space at the National Gallery. For the same
reason the huge Turner Collection, which the artist had willed to the nation,
was housed at Marlborough House.

aware how far they have advanced in painting. They do not know that they have already rivalled some of the old schools which stand high in the annals of art, and have even surpassed others. Our collectors are very fond of Teniers and Dow, but surely Hogarth and Wilkie are as artists, at any rate, their equal. The Fleming and the Dutchman may have understood more thoroughly the mechanism of preparing and laying on their colours, but when do they tell a story as do the Englishman and the Scotchman? Inner design they have none. The man who sits and smokes does sit and smoke very perfectly. The girl who gapes listlessly out of the window is excellently painted.[13] But in neither the one nor the other is there either wit, or feeling, or attempt at reading the mind of the figure on the canvas.

Teniers is regarded as a great artist. We believe that Sir Joshua Reynolds declared that from no one's works could be better studied the mechanical art of painting.[14] Nevertheless, an Englishman should be forgiven for boasting that Hogarth is the greater artist. No one surely can say that any Flemish or Dutch pictures of genre have exceeded those of Wilkie or Webster in the plain telling of a good story.

And now we will venture to touch on a matter bearing so closely on the subject of fine art in England, that our remissness in this particular has done more injury to our character among nations than the genius or skill of our artists has been able to redeem.

We have more pictures of worth in England than there are in any other one country. Were we to go much further than this and declare that we have a greater value of easel pictures in England than are to be found in any other two kingdoms—than there are, for instance, in Tuscany and France together, or in

[13] It is difficult to determine precisely which pictures Trollope had in mind. A young girl at a window is a very characteristic subject for Dou. His *A Man with a Pipe* was purchased by the National Gallery in 1844. Teniers painted numerous genre scenes of men smoking.

[14] Reynolds said: 'The greatest style, if that style is confined to small figures ... would receive an additional grace by the elegance and precision of pencil so admirable in the works of Teniers ... the school to which he belonged more particularly excelled in the mechanism of painting ...' See Allan Cunningham, *The Life and Writings of Sir Joshua Reynolds* (Barnes & Burr, New York, 1860), p. 105 ('Sixth Discourse').

Saxony and the Papal States—we should startle our readers, and be unable to prove our assertion; but the credible catalogues of known pictures would seem to show that such is the fact.[15] And yet a foreigner on his arrival in England has wonderfully little means of bringing home to himself the truth of such a fact. He goes to Rome, Florence, Bologna, Venice, Milan, Munich, Vienna, Dresden, Berlin, Paris, Antwerp—and to places even of much less celebrity in repositories of pictures, and sees without difficulty, and generally in such fashion as pictures can best be seen, all that those towns have to show. After that he comes to London and sees our National Gallery. The contrast cannot be favourable to England.

This is of course mainly owing to the great wealth of individual Englishmen, and the inability of English governors to spend public money according to their own discretion. The great wealth of pictures in England is in private collections, many of our nobles and great commoners possessing galleries equal to those in which some foreign states rejoice as sources of national glory. Such galleries, though in most cases very easily accessible, are generally beyond the reach of strangers. They are not visited except by those few who care to make themselves intimately acquainted with the subject of pictures. Our national deficiency is also owing in a great measure to the very recent date at which we commenced to form our collections; and also, we may add, to form our taste.

But still the question remains whether or no we are able to put together a worthy collection of pictures belonging to the nation, and so to place them that they may be seen with pleasure both by ourselves and others.

The first thing necessary for such a desideratum are the pictures. The next is the fitting building in which to hang them, together with the fitting appliances for their enjoyment. Then we require the necessary knowledge for their hanging and preservation, and a proper set of regulations under which they shall be visible.

We cannot but repeat once more the very old joke of Mrs.

---

[15] Trollope may have had in mind (among other titles) the recently published three volume work of Gustav Friedrich Waagen, *Treasures of Art in Great Britain* (London, 1854).

Glasse's hare, which must be caught before it be cooked.[16] The pictures must be had before they be hung. But if the hare has been caught; if the pictures are in hand, one would say that that difficulty were over. Not at all. The hare has been caught and has been got so far as the skinning. But unfortunately the hare and the cook are in different places, and cannot be brought together. The pictures are in our possession, and are indeed to be seen; but though belonging to the nation they cannot be brought into a National Collection.

In our Gallery, such as it is, no one doubts that there are works of art of the very highest value, that some of the highest artists that ever lived are there represented by some of their finest works, that but few pictures are there of which we would desire the absence, and that, on the whole, the collection is good. It is, however, very small considering the purpose for which it is intended, and it must also be admitted that some schools of art are but indifferently represented.

In the first place our own school is not represented at all, if one except the two pictures which the somewhat egotistical will of the artist and donor has placed there.[17] This we all know has arisen from our want of room. But whatever be the cause we cannot but lament that a National Collection should exclude all national genius. Such is not the case in other countries. And surely if the French can feel a pride in covering a whole wall in the Louvre with the works of La Tour, we need feel no shame in hanging those of Reynolds, Wilson, and Callcott. However, we may presume that the time will soon come when the Vernon Collection and the National Collection will be under the same roof and in the same rooms.

Most people are aware that there is a huge collection of pictures at Hampton Court. And most people are also of opinion

[16] The popular saying, 'First catch your hare,' was perhaps a conflation of 'Take your Hare when it is cas'd [i.e. skinned] and make a Pudding ...' and 'Get some Rabbits ...', Hannah Glasse, *The Art of Cooking made Plain and Easy* (London, 1747), pp. 6 and 51.

[17] Turner in an early will (1831) left to the nation two pictures, *The Sun Rising through Vapour* and *Dido Building Carthage* on condition that they be hung, as it were in rivalry, between two paintings by Claude, *Mill* and *Seaport*. Trollope evidently thought that Turner lived till 1853 (he died in 1851), and that he presented the pictures to the National Gallery while still alive, for he says precisely this in his article 'The National Gallery', *St. James Magazine*, II (Sept. 1861), 167-8.

that with the exception of Raphael's cartoons there is little there worth looking at. And no wonder that such an opinion should be general. There are, we believe, more than one thousand frames hung up in those ill-lighted, ungainly, and unsuitable apartments—and of these three fourths contain pictures which are certainly not worthy of a place in any nation's picture gallery. How few of the picture-seeing world in general will go to the trouble of ascertaining that among the other fourth there are sixty or seventy works of art which would be a valuable addition to the best collections in the world, and an invaluable addition to our own.

But it will be said: why destroy one public gallery to improve another? We would answer that as a public gallery Hampton Court has no value which can be destroyed. Its distance from the Capital, its ill-adaptation for the assigned purpose, its great extent joined to its limited worth, conspire to divest it of any national value. Lovers of art accordingly visit it to see the cartoons, which are hung in the worst light which could perhaps be found for them in England. Great crowds of Londoners visit Hampton Court on Sundays, to roam at will through the pleasant gardens, to walk through the courts and also through the picture rooms, to eat their dinners on the grass in Bushey Park, and enjoy their Sunday out. God forbid that their pleasure should be injured. Were those sixty pictures necessary to their enjoyment, did they indeed add any appreciable zest to it, we would not wish them for the National Gallery. But they contribute in no way to this enjoyment. No London trade mechanic could be less happy on his Sunday at Hampton Court if those pictures were removed to London. We earnestly hope that they may be so removed.

As to the cartoons of Raphael, it may perhaps be doubted whether they would stand the atmosphere of London. That, if possible, they should form a part of our National Collection no English lover of art can doubt. In fact as regards the Roman school such an addition would altogether change our comparative poverty into comparative wealth.[18] These drawings might now be glazed, a method of protection which their size would have prevented a few years since; and if glazed we should think

[18] Raphael's cartoons, seven in number, were removed on permanent loan to the South Kensington (Victoria and Albert) Museum in 1865.

that they might be hung with safety in the new gallery which, it is to be hoped, we are going to build.

We then come to a more difficult matter. There is in the vicinity of London a spot of deep retirement—a silent, secluded, desolate spot, undisturbed by the sound of omnibuses, and in which the noise of cab wheels is seldom heard.

Est in secessu longe locus.[19]

Here the hum of men and the glib chatter of the aristocratic female tongue are unknown. And yet it is strange that it should be so lonely. Near to it are the busy streets of Camberwell, near also the popular shades of Norwood, and also near is the large glass roof of the Sydenham Palace.[20] These places are frequented, but Dulwich is always desolate. It is of Dulwich that we now speak.

In this retirement there is an inner recess, a sanctum, as it were, of inexpressible desolation and dull, deserted, deathlike silence, which is called a picture gallery. You think as you enter it that you are going among some catacombs of the dead, to which you are ushered by one who has already crossed the Styx, and been allowed to pass back again to Dulwich, in order that a fitting minister might be there for so sombre a purpose.

For desolate as the place is, it may be entered by those who choose to go rightly to the task. As Aeneas, carrying in his hand the duly acquired branch, was allowed to wander through the abodes of the dead, so may any enterprising lover of art, armed with a ticket to be acquired at a certain shop in Pall Mall,[21] demand to pass by that unearthly janitor. Such attempts are occasionally made; and men so making them have been known to return, as Aeneas did, in safety to the upper air.

Such is Dulwich Gallery—such as to its aspect, such as to its situation, and such as to the frequency of its visitors. And yet here are deposited some most valuable works of art. The Dutch and Spanish schools are better represented than they are in the

---

[19] *Aeneid*, I, 159. 'There is a place in a deep cove.'

[20] Norwood, originally named for its woods, still had a sufficiency of trees to attract Londoners for rural outings. In the 30s and 40s Beulah Saline Spa and its wooded environs were very popular; but the great attraction of the area after 1854 was Joseph Paxton's Crystal Palace, which was moved to Sydenham after the close of the Great Exhibition of 1851.

[21] These admission tickets were obtainable at Colnaghi's in Pall Mall.

Gallery in Trafalgar Square, and here also are works of many of the Italian schools which would be to the English world at large acquisitions of the highest value. Singular as is the locality, deserted as is the gallery, a large proportion of the pictures are in truth of the highest order.

But they are by no means in the best condition. One may almost say in the very worst. How can it be otherwise with them, left deserted, uncared for, unnoticed as they are. They have long been in bad order, and are quickly becoming so much worse that their condition if not soon attended to will be past cure.

Such is Dulwich Gallery. Our object should be to transfer the pictures to our National Collection. Our difficulty in doing it is the fact that the nation is not the owner of them—a difficulty not unfrequently felt when men covet that which is not their own. But to whom do these pictures belong if not to the nation? They are not like those in the Marquis of Westminster's house, or those in the Stafford Gallery,[22] the property of a single individual, who can, if he pleases, shut them up, or burn them, or sell them. There they hang, not for the benefit of any individual, but for the benefit of all Englishmen and foreigners who can learn how to get at them and will take the trouble of doing so. They are, we presume, legally the property of certain trustees under the will of old Mr. Alleyn, the founder of the Gallery and of the adjacent College.[23] That something is to be done to change materially the management of the College all the world now knows.[24] Surely something also might be done which would empower these trustees to make a better use of this property in pictures than is now done.

It will be asserted that Mr. Alleyn by his will ordained that these pictures should be hung at Dulwich. But surely Mr. Alleyn's will would not be the first which has been set aside and altered by Act of Parliament for the good of the nation. Surely the trustees, assisted by an Act of Parliament, might

[22] The home of the Marquis of Westminster contained the Grosvenor Collection. The Stafford Gallery was in the home of the Duke of Sutherland.

[23] Edward E. Alleyn (1566-1624), Elizabethan actor and founder of Dulwich College. The Gallery of which Trollope writes was designed by Sir John Soane and opened in 1814.

[24] Education as such was negligible at Dulwich until the Dulwich College Act of 1857. (In fact, the circumstances of the College bore strong resemblances to those of Hiram's Hospital in *The Warden*.) For some particulars, see *The Times*, 4 and 29 Jan. 1856.

authorize the removal of these pictures to Kensington-Gore without injury to any interest or damage to any right.

Such additions as these to our National Gallery would make it in truth a fine National Collection of pictures. One other addition we would propose. How rarely now are visited the magnificent works of ancient sculpture which lie in the rooms prepared for them beneath the British Museum? how rarely at least are they visited by the lovers of fine art? In fact there is too much now collected at the Museum; and the immense variety of subjects which are there to be studied makes it to a certain extent an unfit repository for sculpture. If such a gallery be built for us as we all hope to see, surely it should be enriched with the marbles which are now half lost to the world in Great Russell Street.

As to the gallery in which the country would wish to see its pictures hung, there can, we would fain hope, be no doubt that with such care as will now be devoted to the subject, an appropriate building will be erected, and one of which the nation need not be ashamed. The proposed site is excellent.[25] It is removed from the densest smoke and damp of the level of the river, and is not too far from the thickest haunts of that portion of the population which rejoices most in works of art. This however is acknowledged, and loudly exclaimed by all men: that the five dark rooms which we now call our National Gallery are disgraceful to us, that they are in some way ill-adapted to the preservation and exposition of pictures, and that no further time should be lost in rescuing such treasures as we have from their present unfortunate position. Something also we hope will be done towards the true, and let us confess if we must, the luxurious enjoyment of our pictures. When we sit in a small cane-bottomed chair on a dirty floor in Trafalgar Square, we are not comfortable. In the great room at the Louvre we are very much so, and also in the new salons at Venice. Velvet, and polished floors, and ornate cornices may perhaps be the devices of the Devil to lure us from our pristine energy into luxurious sloth and rapid decadence. But if so, so also are pictures themselves. And if so, we have now gone too far for retreat. Let us

---

[25] Kensington Gore had been chosen in 1853 by a Select Committee of the House of Commons as the best site for a possible new National Gallery.

hope, however, that a man may sit at ease, and yet care for his country.

There have been great contests of late as to the steps taken for the preservation of our pictures, and, as is the case in all matters in England, two parties wage an internecine war. The one declares that those who have it in charge to preserve such pictures as we possess and to buy others know nothing of their business; and the other affirms that in these matters the most perfect judgement has been shown.[26] It will require a God to decide between the combatants. This much however may be said, that to the eyes of ninety-nine lovers of pictures out of a hundred, a cleansed picture is preferable to a dirty one, even though in the cleansing something of the original surface may be lost; and that a picture though considerably overpainted is more valuable to the world at large than one that is half obliterated. It is only by those who are extremely skilled in the history and in the technical knowledge of art that the unrepaired ruins of an ancient master are appreciated; and those who are so skilled are few in number. Were all the pictures in the galleries of Europe now left in such state as they would be, had they never been retouched since they left the easels of the masters whose names they bear, the pleasure which we now take in art would be sadly diminished.

But on this account it behoves us to be the more careful to whom we entrust the task of preserving what we value so much. At present there are pictures in our Gallery which are so covered with dirt that they are all but invisible; and yet our custodians do not dare to touch them. And those others which have been cleansed, of which we are told that they are ruined. Between the dirty pictures and the clean, there will soon be none that we can look at with confidence. Our object in this, as in every other task which we have to see done, is to get the best men we can for the doing of it, and then to trust them entirely, let the cavillers say what they will.

One word let us add as to the right of entry to our Gallery. And here we are aware that we tread on dangerous ground. At

---

[26] The advisability of expensive purchases was warmly debated in the 1850s. On the controversy over the preservation of paintings, see, for example, *The Times*, 28 Dec. 1852, where it is claimed that in the process of 'restoration' a canvas by Claude had been partly obliterated.

present during the greater part of the week the National Gallery is open to all the public indiscriminately; on Sunday, and on two other days it is closed to all the public. We do not mean to allude to the vexed question of the Sunday admittance, but to express an opinion that for the sake of art, and the true taste for art which is springing up in this country, the National Gallery should be closed to the public except on payment for a certain portion of every week. It will be no matter at how small a sum such payment be fixed. Sixpence will suffice. Let the Gallery be open as it now is for three days to all the world; and then let it be open for the first two days of the week to those who choose to pay whatever sum may be stipulated for admittance.

Those who have lately frequented the Gallery in Trafalgar Square cannot but acknowledge that much true enjoyment would thus be secured to many, from which they are now precluded. There would doubtless be many to declare that those who object to come in contact with the poorer of their brethren should not come at all to a building which is emphatically the property of the nation, of the poor as well as of the rich—that the fastidious, and the affected, and the arrogant have no right to injure the working classes by their meanness, their affectation, and their arrogance—and that the fustian coat and the silk mantle may well look at the same picture together without detriment to each other.

Were any injury to be done to the poor man, any real harm, by his exclusion from the Gallery for two days a week, there would be something in this argument. It shall be admitted that the fustian coat had better be allowed to have the Gallery entirely to himself than be hurt by the proposed rule.

But no injury would result to the fustian coat, who is in truth remarkably indifferent as to the pictures before which he walks. And great advantage would accrue to that class which does care very much about them. The National Gallery now is a place of assignation, a shelter from rain, a spot in which to lounge away an idle ten minutes, a nursery for mothers who are abroad with their infants, a retirement for urban picnics. The place cannot be said to be often crowded, but it is always clear that of those who are there four fifths care nothing for the pictures.

Such uses for a picture gallery do rob those who really love the pictures of much of their pleasure. That the poorer classes, that is, those who are comparatively uneducated and who are doomed to lives of manual toil, should really care for pictures, we believe to be impossible. We believe that some carefulness of education, some of that refinement from which we all know that the mass of the populace is debarred, must be necessary to the appreciation of a work of art. This is not at present a popular doctrine. It is now in vogue to speak of the poor as if they were in all things equal to the rich except in their poverty. But even those who go with the fashions and teach this doctrine know that it is not so—that it cannot be so—and that the saying that it is so will not bring the poor nearer to so desirable a result.

The friend of the working classes may advocate in his newspaper or in his place in the House of Commons the ennobling result of opening our picture galleries to the lower orders; but let him go to the Gallery and watch the result! Let him speak to a journeyman shoemaker as he leaves the building, and judge of the impression made on him!

God forbid that we should use such an argument to the injury of the poor. But God forbid also that we should injure any class by a false argument in favour of the poor. Let the Gallery be open to all the world for three days, and let us and all men have such good results as may be procured thereby. But also let those who wish to see the pictures in comparative quiet be enabled to do so at a small expense. There would be no invidious class admission. The sixpence of the mechanic would be as operative as that of the peer.

In this way we think that England may be enabled to boast of a great National Gallery, as well as of those wonderfully rich private collections which are so peculiar to England. And here a word of thanks may be not ungraciously given to many of the owners of these noble private galleries. Their treasures of art are very generally open to the public, if only application be made in proper form and with due notice. By Lord Ellesmere,[27] Lord Ward,[28] and the Marquis of Westminster[29] are the thanks

---

[27] Francis Egerton, Lord Ellesmere (1800-57), built a gallery in his Cleveland Row home for the Bridgewater Collection.

[28] William Ward, later Earl of Dudley (1817-85); his generosity in making his collection available to the public drew special notice in Waagen (see above, p. 198), *Treasures of Art in Great Britain*, II, 230 ff.

[29] Richard Grosvenor, Marquis of Westminster (1795-1869), was heir to his family's Grosvenor Collection.

of the public peculiarly deserved. And here it may be observed that no one looking year after year at the Grosvenor pictures can understand why the pictures of our National Gallery cannot be well preserved in London. How is it that the Grosvenor pictures are preserved?

It is, we believe, understood that the Queen is willing that her private pictures shall be seen by due application through the Lord Chamberlain's office. It may, however, be observed that sometimes from one cause and sometimes from another the Lord Chamberlain is generally prevented from carrying out the Queen's permission in this particular.

CHAPTER XIII

Conclusion

O h, thou New Zealander, my enterprising polished friend, I pray thee do not hurry hither too fast. Not yet at any rate can we bid thee welcome, if thou comest in search of ruins, and desirous of relics of thy Anglo-Saxon progenitors. Neither by thee nor by thy prototype and forerunner of Yankeeland shall it yet be boasted that the remnants of the British constitution afford matter of speculation to the antiquarians either of the East or of the West. Not yet, let us say, by many untold centuries.

It is impossible not to be hopeful for one's country. Let reason tell us with never such unanswerable arguments that countries and nations will be alike to man, if man will but be virtuous; let history assure us with facts never so unanswerable that the father country must die so that its offspring colonies may have room to live, still we cling, cannot but cling, to the hope that these very fields, which are so smiling for us, shall smile also for our children's children and their children's children; that these very laws which we make for our governance may serve also to assist in governing those who for centuries to come shall bear our names, and dwell where we have dwelt before them.

Let him reason as he will, it is not sufficient to the content of an Englishman that England has been great, and is great. It is necessary for him that he can also hope that she shall remain so. Tell him that the decadence of England will come, and he will admit it as he will the coming of the millennium and the final resurrection of the dead. He will admit it as he will the approach of the day of judgement, the certainty of which is fixed. But in each case the intervening time is so indefinite that he can make no calculation on the matter. He sees nothing to warn him that the unexpected period is at hand.

It is impossible not to be hopeful for one's country. The Italian, the Hungarian, even the Pole hopes. The Greek imagines that prosperous commerce shall again make him as great as freedom made him in days long past. And the Jew looks forward with pious certainty to the coming of his Messiah, when he again shall be a united people, openly enjoying that pre-eminence in God's favour which he still regards as his own.

And if the citizens of other states, if people so fallen in the world's esteem, are still trustful in the destinies of their country, can an Englishman fail to be so? No. That idea of a future stranger interesting himself in the ruins of England is one which his mind refuses to receive. It is useless preaching to him on such a text. Tell him of the future glories of England and you may move him to increased exertion; but you cannot frighten him out of his self-complacency by any record of her faults. If such shall appear to have been the attempt of the Essayist, he must own that his labour has been in vain.

The self-confidence of an Englishman is invincible. It is in this that his great strength lies. He is able, because he makes others think that he is able. Out of this no sermon will shake him. No latter day pamphlets[1] will drive him to despair. No essays, were they as forcible as language can make them, would cause him to believe that the end of his dominion is nigh at hand.

This is his great strength. And without such strength no man, no nation, has ever been powerful. But his very strength if not well directed will be the forerunner of his weakness, and the cause of his fall.

It is impossible for an Englishman to be hopeless of his country. Industry and genius belong to him, indomitable industry and undying genius. Courage and perseverance are among his virtues. He has practical good sense, and sound knowledge of the rules of nature. He has an eye to see, an ear to hear, and a mind to understand. What does he lack of the attributes of strength that he should be thus warned of evil days to come?

All that he wants, all the counsel necessary for him is contained in the one short line of the old Scotch song with which we have ventured to grace our little page.

It's gude to be honest and true.[2]

---

[1] *latter day pamphlets*: this casual allusion is the only reference in *The New Zealander* either to Carlyle or to the work Trollope had been accused of imitating.

[2] 'Here's a Health to them that's awa', James Johnson's *Scots Musical Museum*, vol. V (1796), No. 412. See Introduction, p. xxxvii.

That truth and honesty are in the abstract loved and honoured here in England, no man can doubt. That they have been the characteristic marks of individual Englishmen history affirms. But is or is it not the fact that though the abstract love remains, the individual practice is changed?

What if the verdict of all nations could be taken as to our character, and that verdict should be that an Englishman is the strongest citizen of the world, the strongest and the most prosperous, but also the most dishonest? Would such a verdict satisfy us as to our present and future state? and would such a verdict be according to the evidence?

Unless we look to it, it would appear that such a verdict is not improbable. The pity of it is that our aptitude for dishonest practices has grown so homogeneously among us all that we fail to recognise the fault not only in ourselves but even in others. We do not perceive what is honest and what is the reverse, what is false and what true, unless we stop to inquire more curiously into matters than the fast race of life among us will often allow us to do. We practise that which others practise till we learn to regard dishonesty first as necessary, and then as honourable; and at last we teach it to our children as a virtue.

It's gude to be honest and true.

No Englishman will gainsay the truth of that assertion. There are but few who do not aspire with more or less earnestness to rule their lives by the wisdom therein taught. But it is needful that they do more than aspire. It is needful that each individual shall in the common words and acts of his life know whether or not he be speaking and acting with honesty and truth; or whether he be not rather speaking and acting in a manner which decorum is unwilling that we should specify by its plainer name.

It is on this point that counsel is so necessary to a young man entering life, ay, and to an old man leaving it if there were but hope he would accept it, not that he do not tell lies and cheat—counsel him thus and the blood mantling to his cheeks will declare how cruelly you have wounded his honour—but that he see well that he is able to distinguish between truth and falsehood, between honesty and cheating. He will not probably be false if he know it, but is he sure that he knows and appreciates a falsehood when he meets it? He will neither steal nor swindle willingly, but will he always recognise the dishonesty of a theft when the circumstances are patent to him?

Do we recognise the dishonesty of our tradesmen with their advertisements, their pretended credit, their adulterations, and fake cheapness? Do not such of us as are tradesmen ourselves fall into the same courses, without the slightest conscience stricken sense of dishonesty? Have we the slightest feeling of a sin against truth or honesty when we hear some learned lawyer use all his wit to protect a criminal by legal chicanery? Do we feel our sense of honesty in any way offended when a Right Honourable gentleman in opposition attacks with frightful acerbity those very measures which he in power would be the foremost to promote?

It is not of swindlers and liars that we need live in fear, but of the fact that swindling and lying are gradually becoming not abhorrent to our minds. These vile offences are allowed to assume pseudonyms under which their ugliness is hidden; and thus they show their faces to the world unabashed, and are even proud of their position. Could the career of that wretched man who has lately perished have been possible, had falsehood, dishonesty, pretences, and subterfuges been odious in the eyes of those who came daily in contact with his doings?[3]

It cannot be but that we shall soon awake to see these things as they are. Our eyes are open to the doings of all the world, our hearts are anxious to be dutiful, we have a true desire to be great and good. It cannot be but that we shall learn to call dishonesty and want of truth by their proper names, and to know them when we meet them.

Let us learn to do that, and we shall then do whatever in us lies to postpone the coming of the New Zealander. It is, however, by individual effort that this must be done.

It's gude to be honest and true.

Let every man learn this in his heart of hearts and it will be well with us yet for many an untold century.

---

[3] John Sadleir, banker, politician, and swindler; he committed suicide 16 Feb. 1856. See Introduction, p. xxxviii.

APPENDIX I

Cancelled words and passages

N o t included in the following are mere repetitions of the same word, substitutions of one synonym for another, and simple changes in phrasing. Rather, only Trollope's more significant deletions are here listed (in angular brackets).

Page

3 to bear the enormous cost of ⟨the present⟩ war

3 England ⟨may so fight⟩ has so fought, and she alone

6 Has not virtue produced energy, and energy ⟨talent⟩ knowledge, ⟨talent⟩ knowledge civilization

6 desiring other men's goods ⟨, content to labour truly in that state to which we are called⟩?

8 the very motto is proof of dishonesty. ⟨Let us think well of it and we shall find that the most incompetent General that ever bore a staff may win a battle; and that the ablest soldier that ever led an army may lose one. But we are now less willing than ever to acknowledge such a truth.⟩

16 preferable to Lord ⟨Rochester⟩ and the Marquis of ⟨Hertford⟩.

17 the evil is utterly cured. ⟨It is probable that no evil [is] ever utterly cured.⟩

18 so treated by us? ⟨What best man will consent to rule even a great nation during the [reign?] of a nameless newspaper writer.⟩

31 The most ⟨important⟩ interesting question of the present

31 Success is always ambitious. ⟨No thinking man will be content to have the question thus answered.⟩

36 and at last unendurable. ⟨Before however it reaches this length, it too often crushes the back that bears it.⟩

36 responsible only to its purchasers ⟨; that is, within some wide limits which affect in no way its political bearing. To its purchasers only, is a newspaper responsible.⟩.

48 the discreeter way that we now have of ⟨d———— a fellow's eyes⟩ uttering an oath in our anger.

53 and may therefore hope for ⟨absolution, hope always⟩ improvement.

57 So at least says eloquent Mr. ⟨Allewinde⟩ Allwinde.

77 keen as ⟨we all are now for war⟩ we have all been for war

81 we have done; ⟨What we can do we are doing.⟩ whatever can be done by naval force.

87 no sane man will probably deny. ⟨Jacob Omnium, Hereford-shire incumbents, and those other friendly correspondents by whom public opinion is so powerfully aided may or may not be right in their propositions.⟩[1]

88 the Church of Christ is in truth composed. ⟨It was for such that his sacrifice was made.⟩

89 certainly ⟨quite⟩ true.

91 that ⟨friend⟩ fiend of Satan with his mysteries

91 nor their manservants nor maidservants ⟨, nor their cattle, nor the stranger within their gates⟩.

93 have never yet succeeded in living. ⟨By which Christ has never called upon men to attempt to live.⟩

94 the huge evil of ⟨insincerity⟩ unreality.

95 enter just now the foundry gates ⟨as that fair girl tripped to the chapel door⟩.

96 be built East and West ⟨if it appears good so to the builders⟩.

97 There are ⟨, alas,⟩ many shades of religion among us

97 ⟨"I will sing praises unto the Lord," says David, "because it is so comfortable."⟩ David found comfort in singing

98 having within them the love of the Lord. ⟨But to what now has fallen that truth and love?⟩

110 are held too heinous for pardon ⟨at any distant time⟩

123 represented to the House as being important. ⟨We all remember the committee on Mr. Roebuck's motion regarding the conduct of the War.⟩[2]

131 in the eyes of the nation ⟨, many intelligent people do not even know of the existence of any law on the subject,⟩.

136 pleading that it is ⟨better⟩ somewhat better than our theory

[1] 'Jacob Omnium' was a pseudonym of Matthew James Higgins, a re-nowned and skilful newspaper correspondent. Some of his letters to *The Times* on military reform were reprinted: *A Letter on Army Reform* (London, [1855]), and *Three Letters on Military Education* (London, 1856). Trollope later wrote of Higgins as 'a man I greatly regarded', and 'the most forcible newspaper writer of my days ...', *Autobiography*, pp. 153 and 199.

[2] John Arthur Roebuck's motion of 26 January 1855 was carried on 29 January; Aberdeen's government resigned, and Lord Palmerston became Premier on 6 February.

138 to assist his aged brethren. ⟨He has been made a peer only for his life without the right of inheritance to his heirs male, if he should have any.⟩

141 absurd conditions. ⟨John Doe and Richard Roe still live.⟩ And there is we believe

155 that other old song ⟨much older than the glee of the wagging beards⟩?

157 the change in this respect has been ⟨much⟩ for the worse.

172 addressed by Horace to Augustus.

⟨Praesens divus habebitur
Augustus, adjectis Britannis
Imperio [gravibusque Persis.]

Vos Caesarem altum, militia simul
Fessas cohortes addidit oppodis
Finire quaerentem labores
Pierio recreatis antro.⟩[3]

183 has become a large trade ⟨, and the circulating libraries are suffering much from this new rivalry⟩.

184 comfortable but expensive appendages ⟨which made books too costly for the multitude⟩.

187 aspirations after liberty. ⟨Praxiteles and Phidias were contemporaries of the tyrant Pericles.⟩

187 obliterated fresco, ⟨or the virtue ⟨meaning⟩ of the foliage upon a capital,⟩ would not probably

189 Art no doubt is a ⟨great⟩ luxury

189 into sloth or mock dilettante energy ⟨, rather than to repudiate it as dangerous,⟩.

191 are presumed to be the lowest depth. ⟨Our most peculiar vileness is supposed to be shown in our attempts at Grecian style.⟩

191 Longleat and Montacute ⟨⟨, however,⟩ but if they have seen them they never deign to mention them with praise⟩. But Hatfield

198 Dresden, Berlin, ⟨Innsbruck,⟩ Paris

198 beyond the reach of strangers ⟨because strangers are ignorant of their existence—at least of their whereabouts, & of the manner of approaching them⟩.

---

[3] *Odes*, III. v. 2-4 and iv. 37-40. 'Augustus will be considered a deity at hand when the Britons have been added to the Empire [and the troublesome Persians]. You in the Pierian grotto refresh high Caesar, seeking to finish his labours, as soon as the troops have hidden the weary cohorts in the towns.'

199 on the whole, the collection is ⟨very⟩ good.

200 ⟨nearly two⟩ more than one thousand frames

202 which would empower ⟨, nay compel,⟩ these trustees to make better use

205 It shall ⟨perhaps⟩ be admitted that the fustian

206 such good results as may be ⟨by all due attention to our poorer bret[hren]⟩ procured thereby.

APPENDIX II

Marginal notes

TROLLOPE'S marginal notes are here juxtaposed with the lines or paragraphs which they attend.

Page

105 ~~Dublin May 1856~~	First paragraph, Chapter VII, 'The House of Commons'.
109 Three Clerks	Paragraph beginning 'There is a sport prevalent among the downs of Hampshire ...' This and the following five paragraphs (through 'applaud the craft of the winner.' p. 111) are crossed through once.[1]
116 Three Clerks	Paragraph beginning 'This feeling is like the religion of Imperial Rome.' and the following paragraph are crossed through.
123 Three Clerks	Paragraph beginning 'Let us suppose that a committee ...' and the following 20 (through 'in the inner world the matter is fully understood.' p. 129) are crossed through.[2]
187 Derry March 2 1856	First paragraph, Chapter XII, 'Art'.
187 ~~?~~	Deleted line: ⟨'Praxitiles and Phidias were contemporaries of the tyrant Pericles.'⟩
187 ?	'Velasquez and Murillo were servants of the Philips of Spain.'
188 How long been done	'by our opera house which alone among our theatres can get themselves filled ...'
189 Drogheda 6 March 1856	Paragraph beginning, 'Of the four fine arts three are decidedly ...'
192 Drogheda 7 March 56	Paragraph beginning 'In London we have no Ludwig Strasse ...'
195 Drogheda 8 March 1856	Paragraph beginning 'And yet we can not but be proud ...'
197 Drogheda March 9, 1856	Middle of paragraph beginning 'We have more pictures of worth in England ...'

[1] See *The Three Clerks*, 3 vols. (Bentley, London, 1858), II, 50-1.
[2] Ibid., p. 55 ff.

200 What is the number? <u>1027</u>	'There are we believe more than one thousand ...'
201 See Virgil	Est in secessu longe locus
201 ?	'As Aeneas, carrying in his hand ...'
201 (?)	'Armed with a ticket to be acquired at a certain shop in Pall Mall ...'
202 not a "large portion" I think	'a large proportion of the pictures ...'
205 ? open 5-4 days	'on Sunday, and ⟨one⟩ two other days it is closed ...'

APPENDIX III
Editorial emendations

CHANGES other than those of spelling, capitalization, and punctuation (see Introduction, pp. xliii-xlv) are here given in brackets.

Page

3 Have the glories ... began [begun] to pale?

5 has neither past experience or [nor] future probability

9 and all but lies for his fee to same [save] some rascal

13 The evil of such mistakes as these take [takes] years

14 the joy of angels, to Adam who could not hope to taste of them [it] again

19 but by no means true [that] power is dangerous.

23 the one shall be regarded as [as] undesirable in itself as

40 it is on that [that] he trades to the incredible amount

40 Let us have [public *deleted*] opinion put daily before us in good readable articles, and it shall be public.

44 tone in which it is now the fashion for great people to speak [of *deleted*] on most subjects.

57 prove from [the] baptismal register

63 As well might [it] be argued that justice

69 a recent innovation on [in] medicine.

78 no, nor with Austria, or [nor] Prussia, or [nor] even France.

80 friend ... have [has] never failed to find

85 Every evil ... were [was] magnified

87 that [the] government is anxious

89 That wanting it, they would know that they wanted [it] sorely

91 nor their manservants, or [nor] maidservants

95 prayers be it [they] never so gracefully intoned

100 And the authorized men [man] was there, and the Christian would put its [his] foolish neck beneath the foot of a priest.

104 be its errors what it [they] may

112 a padlock, of which [he] himself must keep the key

114 on any abstract principle if [of] right or wrong.

117 neither public vice or [nor] public virtue

118 On [In] our arena no thumbs are ever withdrawn.

122 ⟨When *deleted*⟩ Were [When] a new House of Commons first meets

123 and hence arises [arise] violent denunciations

123 unless indeed one of [those] few impracticable members

124 with whom ... he thinks [he] may be safe.

127 takes the case in hands [hand]

128 The expenses ... costs [cost] the Crown

146 looks neither to the right or [nor] to the left.

149 a constitutional necessity equal [equally] strong

158 Lady Charlotte De Burgh [Catherine de Bourgh]

158 With the Mansfields [Bertrams] and the Crofts [Crawfords]

163 when men [who *deleted*] behave themselves in this way?

169 Then [This] in the open air would not perhaps be as agreeable in Russell Square

169 the happiness of neither man or [nor] woman.

171 those worse [worst] of [those *deleted*] throned imbeciles

172 the fulsome flatteries addressed by Horace to Augustus. How nauseous would this [these] be now addressed

178 hardly [as] visible as they should be

183 We read books ... We write books ... whether we speak of the efforts of the author or writer [the reader] can be little less than useless.

189 robbed of half of its joy if he [is] debarred

192 to [the] present century

192 how much have [we] to be proud of

197 gapes listlessly out of [the] window

197 But in neither the one or [nor] the other

197 in Tuscany [and] France together

199 But unfortunately that [the hare] and the cook are in different places, and cannot be brought together.

202 not be the first which has [been] set aside

203 no further time should [be] lost in rescuing

204 masters whose name [names] they bear

205 open for the first [two *restored*] days of the week

205 to those who choose [to] pay whatever sum

206 and that the saying that it [is] so

210 it is needful than [that] they do more

Index

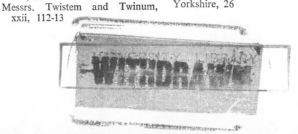